AdvancED Flash Interface Design

Michael Kemper
Guido Rosso
Brian Monnone

friendsof

DESIGNER TO DESIGNER™

an Apress® company

AdvancED Flash Interface Design

ISBN-13 (pbk): 978-1-59059-555-8

ISBN-10 (pbk): 1-59059-555-6

Distributed to the book trade worldwide by Springer-Verlag New York, Inc., 233 Spring Street, 6th Floor, New York, NY 10013. Phone 1-800-SPRINGER, fax 201-348-4505, e-mail orders-ny@springer-sbm.com, or visit www.springeronline.com.

For information on translations, please contact Apress directly at 2560 Ninth Street, Suite 219, Berkeley, CA 94710. Phone 510-549-5930, fax 510-549-5939, e-mail info@apress.com, or visit www.apress.com.

The information in this book is distributed on an "as is" basis, without warranty. Although every precaution has been taken in the preparation of this work, neither the author(s) nor Apress shall have any liability to any person or entity with respect to any loss or damage caused or alleged to be caused directly or indirectly by the information contained in this work.

The source code for this book is freely available to readers at www.friendsofed.com in the Downloads section.

Credits

Lead Editor Chris Mills	**Copy Editors** Ami Knox, Marilyn Smith
Technical Reviewer Sean McSharry	**Assistant Production Director** Kari Brooks-Copony
Editorial Board Steve Anglin Ewan Buckingham Gary Cornell Jason Gilmore Jonathan Gennick Jonathan Hassell James Huddleston Chris Mills Matthew Moodie Dominic Shakeshaft Jim Sumser Kier Thomas Matt Wade	**Production Editor** Kelly Winquist **Compositor and Artist** Kinetic Publishing Services, LLC **Proofreaders** Kim Burton, Elizabeth Berry **Indexer** Toma Mulligan **Cover Image Designer** Bruce Tang
Project Manager Elizabeth Seymour	**Interior and Cover Designer** Kurt Krames
Copy Edit Manager Nicole LeClerc	**Manufacturing Director** Tom Debolski

I am encouraged to take on endeavors like this book in great part due to my family's pride in me; for that I am forever grateful.
—Michael Kemper

Family and friends are all we really have. To my wife, Julie, and two daughters, Madison and Lauren, and to my parents, Joe, Gabrielle, David, Cheryl, and Robert: I am honored to call you all my family and dedicate this book to you all.
—Brian Monnone

CONTENTS AT A GLANCE

CONTENTS

Chapter 3 **Interface Designers' Guide to Color** **33**

Chapter 4 **Planning Your Interface Design** **61**

Chapter 10   Moving from Photoshop to Flash and Effective PNGs   235

Chapter 11   Creating Animated Effects   255

ABOUT THE AUTHORS

Michael Kemper has managed and deployed interactive, video, and animation projects in every industry vertical for some of the world's largest companies. He has been recognized by *eDesign* magazine and has received numerous Addy Awards and Art Directors Club awards for interactive design and animation. Michael owns a creative consultancy (www.feedyourimage.com) in San Francisco, California, where he focuses on motion graphics and experience design for digital media. When he isn't working on client engagements, he spends much of his free time reading graphic novels and practicing digital photography.

A computer enthusiast his whole life, **Guido Rosso** started designing professionally at the height of the dot-com boom. Surviving the crash unscathed, he and his twin brother (Luigi Rosso) opened RealitySlip Srl (www.realityslip.com), a design and development company based in Rome, Italy. They have since broadened their portfolio to include award-winning web design, application development, and video game projects for companies around the world. Guido's work has been featured in *PC Gamer*, American Design Awards, The FWA: Favourite Website Awards, and numerous other publications, and awarded finalist for Macromedia MAX.

Brian Monnone is more than simply a Flash artist. He is a technologist with a love for great design, motion graphics, and music. Currently, he is a Senior Interactive Designer at nFusion Group in Austin, Texas. His role with nFusion includes creating dynamic Flash demos, videos, and sound design.

His future plans include filmmaking. Becoming a filmmaker has been a lifelong passion for Brian, and until that day comes he'll continue to create unique multimedia. Visit his website: www.monnone.com.

ABOUT THE TECHNICAL REVIEWER

Sean McSharry is a Flash developer of seven years who firmly believes that Flash developers should be as comfortable with design as they are with coding, and he practices what he preaches. "Flash is about bringing everything together into one platform and using the best coding practices, the best design practices, the best video production techniques, etc., to do it." He has worked on projects for some of the world's most influential companies. Sean has a passion for digital video and has been combining this with his Flash skills over the last couple of years to create much Flash video work, recently doing work in the emerging Flash/IPTV broadcasting market. When he's not Flashing, he can be found pursuing his other passions: golf; snowboarding; Pilates; herpetology; and, of course, his wife, Mary, and their two sons, Aston and Jack.

ABOUT THE COVER IMAGE DESIGNER

Bruce Tang is a freelance web designer, visual programmer, and author from Hong Kong. His main creative interest is generating stunning visual effects using Flash or Processing.

Bruce has been an avid Flash user since Flash 4, when he began using Flash to create games, websites, and other multimedia content. After several years of ActionScripting, he found himself increasingly drawn toward visual programming and computational art. He likes to integrate math and physics into his work, simulating 3D and other real-life experiences onscreen. His first Flash book was published in October 2005. Bruce's folio, featuring Flash and Processing pieces, can be found at www.betaruce.com, and his blog at www.betaruce.com/blog.

The cover image uses a high-resolution Henon phase diagram generated by Bruce with Processing, which he feels is an ideal tool for such experiments. Henon is a strange attractor created by iterating through some equations to calculate the coordinates of millions of points. The points are then plotted with an assigned color.

$$x_{n+1} = x_n \cos(a) - (y_n - x_n^p) \sin(a)$$

$$y_{n+1} = x_n \sin(a) + (y_n - x_n^p) \cos(a)$$

ACKNOWLEDGMENTS

Coming together is a beginning. Keeping together is progress. Working together is success.
—Henry Ford

I have accomplished and learned so much from teams staffed with extremely creative, talented, and smart people. This book is a tribute to their lasting impressions on me. Many years ago I joined a team of profoundly creative free-thinkers: Tim Roessler and Anne Alden gave me that opportunity, and thanks to Hugh Graham, Daniel Weinshenker, Jeff Berting, Jeff Ingram, Todd Straka, Jen Thomas, Tara Kelley, Brad Johnson, Amy Morawa, and several others, I got a taste of what my days would be filled with for many years to come. On another team, Michael Stevens gave me the freedom to express myself as a lead designer and Creative Director; Kam Rope, "The Doctor" Andrew Jones, Suzanne Keen, Julie Jagger, Shum Pratts, Nick Hill, and Tom Flanagan are still some of my most enduring friends from that experience and also among the most talented and creative people I know. Currently I have the honor of working with the Metaliq, San Francisco, team comprised of Beau Ambur, Danny Riddell, Mike Lucaccini, Eric Anderson, the Rosso brothers, as well as the Grant Skinner group. Every day with this team is an adventure, and I am honored to be involved in their groundbreaking interactive endeavors. Although we weren't on any team to speak of, Ali Mills and Amanda Thomason offered advice and recommendations during my writing process that was encouraging and valuable.

Of course, I owe a special thanks to Guido Rosso for involving me in this project and to Chris Mills along with the friends of Ed team for their hard work and advice.

—Michael Kemper

Thank you, Luigi, for writing the "ActionScript animation techniques" section in Chapter 11! Thank you, Michael, for stepping into this project. It's largely thanks to your efforts and dedication that we managed to finish this book.

—Guido Rosso

The most important things to me are my wife, Julie, and my two daughters, Madison and Lauren: to you, I want to give very special thanks for always being by my side. I must be the luckiest person alive to have the most beautiful and caring family. I'm especially thankful to Julie for all the countless hours she has had to put up with me sitting in front of the computer working. She has been nothing less than extremely supportive of my endeavors, and I thank her for that. She is the best wife a guy can have.

I would also like to thank my parents, Joe, Gabrielle, David, Cheryl, and Robert, for really believing in me and being proud to call me Son. It means the world to me.

Beyond that, my work is second most important. New media is fun, exciting, and different. I'm in this business because of that. Do I have a mission statement? Sure I do: "To create more smiles and laugh way too often." Secondly, "I'm just a guy that wants to make some cool stuff."

—Brian Monnone

INTRODUCTION

Flash began primarily as an animation tool for designers. Most marketing people shunned the technology because of low plug-in adoption rates. Clients disapproved because of their narrow perspective on usability. Flash wasn't even an afterthought to most developers. And everyone else considered Flash to be the next-level GIF animation—if they had heard of it at all. Things have certainly changed in the industry and with Flash itself. Designers can achieve advanced motion graphics and interface design treatments akin to what is seen in movies and on television. Flash has a 98% install base. More clients recognize the potential success of doing something innovative and different using Flash. Developers can use Flash to create robust on-demand applications that rival any other application platform. And everyone else utilizes Flash to enjoy everything from websites, chat, music, and video across a wide range of connection speeds and platforms.

For a while, emphasis has been placed on getting application developers to migrate over to the Flash platform and use it to create their applications. During that transition, the perception of Flash has morphed, and we designers have been turning into "creative developers" as we picked up these new programming skills. This latest version of Flash has reactivated its base: designers. Those designers who stuck in there and believed in the Flash platform have earned front-row seats for the next evolution of the Internet—and this time it is very much influenced by Flash-based design and technologies. Newer users who have the skills and talent for creating unique digital experiences will multiply and fuel the flames of innovation in this field. Adobe's purchase of Macromedia is but one indication as to how integrated Flash will become not only to the general Internet audience, but also to the products and workflow of professional designers and developers everywhere. Now Flash is becoming the all-in-one creation tool designers and developers alike have wanted for years.

This book is for design educators, students, and industry professionals who have experience with Flash and want to elevate their work to be more meaningful and memorable. It is for designers who want to jumpstart their knowledge of the program and get inspired for their own Flash projects. And it's for developers who are searching for reference material on creating attractive interfaces for their applications. Within the following pages you will be exposed to fresh ideas for interactivity and interface design, learn tried-and-true workflow techniques for maximum efficiency, and gain insight into the new and powerful design features of the latest release. For the more advanced users, it will be a primer for important new features of the application, as well as offer professional insight on how to best implement them. And for every level of designer, it will break down sought-after visual effects for multimedia interface design into comprehensive, easy-to-follow steps.

—**Michael Kemper**

Layout conventions

To keep this book as clear and easy to follow as possible, the following text conventions are used throughout:

Code and URLs are presented in fixed-width font.

User interface elements (menu names, dialog box options, palette names, etc.) appear in this screen text font.

Menu commands are written in the form Menu ➤ Submenu ➤ Submenu.

Where we want to draw your attention to something, we've highlighted it like this:

> *Ahem, don't say we didn't warn you.*

Sometimes code won't fit on a single line in a book. Where this happens, we use an arrow like this: ➡.

```
This is a very, very long section of code that should be written all on the same ➡
line without a break.
```

Chapter 1

FLASH OVERVIEW

by Guido Rosso and Michael Kemper

Believe it or not, many people still harbor serious concerns about integrating Flash into their web strategy. Countless implementations of poorly created Flash intros, confusing Flash interfaces, and long download times have taught far too many users, and prospective clients, to fear the Flash experience. Despite this misconception, Flash is perhaps the most flexible technology for creating interactive experiences. This flexibility can be a Flash designer's greatest asset and also his worse liability.

Flash is the only tool that gives designers total control over audio, video, animation, and lightweight graphics for the Web—which means the possibilities of a designed experience are endless. Flash has groundbreaking new features that enable designers to not only craft tasteful motion design sequences, but also integrate animation that supports the content in an inspiring and meaningful way. Flash is now a widely accepted application development tool, which means usability standards have been developed and adapted for the Flash experience. Plus, when optimized correctly, Flash sites cache and load much faster (up to 5 or 10 times faster) than an equal-sized HTML site.

And that's where this book comes in. On the pages that follow are innumerable techniques from experienced interactive designers for creating professional Flash sites that look fantastic and work like a charm. With this new volume in your Flash knowledge arsenal, you'll help the haters embrace Flash for what it is today, instead of what it has often been in the past.

Why Flash?

Flash is a tool for those who want to expand the idea of a website into a web experience. HTML does offer some options that are better alternatives to that of Flash for certain target audiences. For instance, it is often going to be a good idea to use an HTML display option for a text-heavy site or in the case where accessibility for users with visual impairments is a concern. But exceptions to this rule and many other conventional standards are always emerging. Go to linkdup.com or thefwa.com on any day and see for yourself that the ingenuity and creativity of the Flash community are constantly pushing the boundaries and solving the problems of Flash experiences.

From the user perspective

As much as Flash can hinder usability, it can also enhance it. With the right combination of Flash component sets, object-oriented programming, and design production, and understanding on the part of the designer, any Flash project can be far more intuitive than its HTML-based counterparts.

We can all remember at least one time we visited a Flash site and thought, "Wow." But we might be hard pressed to reflect on the same feeling with regard to a non-Flash site. This is because tasteful Flash sites are more meaningful to the user when compared to other sites of the same caliber. The "sit-back" viewing experience is just as valuable as the "lean-forward" clicking experience, and Flash makes them both happen simultaneously.

Nobody likes to wait. Regardless of whether it's in a line at the post office (what's that?) or in the comfort of your home office, all of us, and the users we design for, would rather be doing anything else. Once again, Flash saves the day. Not only do vector-based graphics in Flash download quicker than conventional bitmap graphics on HTML-based sites, but it is also easy to send and receive data and content in a Flash interface without page refreshes in the browser window. Combine these factors with the way Flash has revolutionized the delivery of rich media content, and you get less waiting regardless of the type of online experience.

Gone are the days of hasty plug-in downloads and installs. FlashPlayer has an auto-update feature, which means it is painless and happens instantly. FlashPlayer is also ubiquitous across all measurable platforms. It has the highest adoption rate of any software platform to date. This ensures that your users see your site just as you intended it.

From the creator perspective

New tools in Flash make it extremely easy to perform complicated tasks. For non-ActionScript users, the Script Assistant is back to help with programming. Filters and blend modes mean less time optimizing bitmaps to work in Flash and more time to tweak the visual styling of your designs.

Drawing is much easier in this version, as well. The tools in Flash are becoming more like the tools designers are trained to use, like those found in Illustrator and Photoshop (see Figure 1-1). It is now possible to create photo-realistic illustrations and UI elements in Flash without importing any additional assets. More now than ever, drawing in Flash is much more rewarding, and designers can achieve higher-quality animated effects as well. Designers familiar with animation created in applications like After Effects are eager to create similar effects with the new filters and blend modes in Flash. In addition, CPU strain is less of a burden for motion sequences due to the new Bitmap Caching feature in the Property inspector.

Figure 1-1. This image was completely created from scratch with only the vector tools available in Flash. It looks as sharp as any bitmap counterpart, yet its file size is only 8 kilobytes as a result of its mathematical creation.

Using Flash as a vehicle to distribute rich media content like MP3s and video has also gotten extremely simple. Designers no longer have to toil over using third-party compression tools or creating and scripting UI buttons for control over media. Flash provides everything necessary to get you up and running with little upfront knowledge.

All of this and more is discussed in the following pages. Flash has given you the tool to enhance your design and development work, and now we will add to your know-how by sharing tips and tricks on new Flash features as well as tried-and-true methods for creating your best work ever.

Ease of use

This book will focus on using vector- and raster-based tools like those in Adobe Illustrator and Adobe Photoshop as well as in Flash to create interface designs. It is much easier to edit vector graphics than to modify raster images in Flash mainly because Flash is a vector-oriented application. Since vector art is essentially mathematically created, it is very easy to manipulate and gets crisp results when used correctly. Raster art, on the other hand, is pixel based and more limited in Flash with regard to its post-creation edit options. There is an overwhelming number of benefits to designing your Flash interfaces mostly in vector. One of the greatest of these is the vast array of editing options you have once you work with the design in Flash. Here is a brief list of Flash vector advantages:

- Vector art requires less CPU power to view than comparable raster images.
- The file size of vector images will always be smaller than comparable raster images.
- Since Flash is vector based, it is easy to modify your vector graphics right in Flash without hassling with external editing and reimporting.
- You can apply nondestructive filters and blend modes to vector art in Flash to attain bitmap quality dithering and gradations without the bitmap file size.
- Vector art can be scaled infinitely up in size without losing detail or quality.
- Even if you use an external application like Illustrator to generate your graphics, the importing process is seamless.

One of the most exclusive features of Flash vector graphics is the ability to navigate through them by clicking fills or strokes. With this ability, it becomes second nature to surf through massive groups of many different vector shapes to select the portion you want to edit. By double-clicking a stroke, you can select all adjoining strokes of the same style. To further add to the intuitive interface, Flash allows you to then click anywhere on a stroke or fill edge and drag it into a Bezier curve. This allows for very quick-and-smooth tracking of curves when creating base shapes for complex objects. By using the Pen tool and clicking a rough angular shape of the intended object, you can then quickly drag each edge into curves to create anything from simple shapes to complex masks.

By its very nature, the idea of having dynamic fills and strokes on all of the vector objects is a brilliantly quick and easy one to take advantage of. Never is the appearance of any vector object beyond your ability to change drastically with a simple click or two of the mouse. This is incredibly handy when performing fast color or style changes to a portion or the whole of a sites' interface.

Gradients in Flash are simple to use, as well. They do add more CPU strain for the viewer, but vector-based gradients are still far easier to process than comparable PNGs or JPGs. Flash gradients are also editable at any time after initial creation right in the Flash environment, all with a simple drag or click. In complex situations, it is effortless to change the angles of a multitude of different gradients to alter a lighting scheme in a design.

Another great little Flash drawing feature is the ability to subtract shapes from one another. By dropping a circle into the middle of a square of a different fill style, it is easy to remove the circle or delete it and leave a square with a hole in it. This is admittedly a rudimentary example, but it becomes important when using Flash as a drawing tool. Flash is also fine-tuned for having exact pixel-shaped objects and placement if you know how to go about it the right way. When used correctly, it is simple to set a series of meticulous proportions and dimensions throughout your vector artwork, thus rendering them very smooth and defined.

Animation

The most evident and prominent of Flash's great number of benefits is, of course, its ability to create the simplest or the most complex types of animation you can imagine. We won't bother to argue points for why animation is a better solution than static imagery, because it is plain to see. It is relevant, however, to note the different types of animation Flash offers and what can be accomplished with each. There are four completely different ways to animate objects in Flash, motion tweening, shape tweening, cell animation, and ActionScript animation, and each option has its own set of rules that govern what can be done with it.

Motion tweening is the easiest way to animate things in Flash. Any object, whether it's a movie clip, graphic, or button, can be animated with a motion tween. Motion tweening simply moves an object from point A to point B while allowing for a variety of property changes along the way. Flash is great in that it will automatically calculate these changes and employ them on your object for you. Everything from height and width to color and location can be changed automatically with the click of a button. This provides for extremely precise command over objects in your timeline. Later in the book, we will demonstrate motion theory and high-end motion tween effects, and you will learn how to create them yourself.

Unlike motion tweening, with *shape tweening* you cannot animate movie clips, graphics, or buttons. Instead, you have complete control over the shape and fill style of a raw vector object from point A to point B. This type of animation is well known and very useful in transforming one vector shape into another, but it also has a variety of other important uses. For instance, shape tweens are helpful in creating pulsating light effects or changes in gradient backgrounds. You cannot apply filter effects or blend modes to shape tweens unless they are nested in a movie clip. In the later chapters of this book, we will show you how to do amazing things you probably never thought you could do with a shape tween.

Cell animation is the most traditional type of animation, historically speaking. Flash designers seldom use it. For the purposes of interface design, using timeline and ActionScript tweening is far more practical because it requires less production work and takes less time. But there are instances where creating something frame by frame is beneficial in order to achieve a unique effect for a transition or button rollover. Flash does have a handy onion-skinning feature, which improves the designer's workflow for creating frame-by-frame animations. And, of course, it is still the foundation for cartooning in Flash, as well. Flash does very well when animating things frame by frame and actually can perform as good or better with these types of animations than with either form of tweening. It seems to affect the CPU much less when you use cell animation instead of tweens for large shapes and images. In fact, some of the more complex and stunning effects we will show you later in the book are done by this method.

ActionScript animation is very different from using the other timeline-based methods. It requires more planning and foresight. A timeline-based animation can be scrubbed in the editing environment for a quick-and-easy preview. Using ActionScript to animate differs because you need to anticipate properties such as position and scale beforehand. Although extremely beautiful and complex animations can be achieved using ActionScript, it is more common to use this method for animating interactive elements of interfaces and page transitions rather than true motion design sequences. It has become increasingly easier to animate using ActionScript thanks to talented developers like Keith Peters and Robert Penner sharing their work with the rest of the community. Although it is also possible to use the tween and easing class files that ship with Flash, originally intended for component animation, to animate movie clips on the stage. Using ActionScript to animate generally lowers file size and strains the viewer's CPU less than timeline-based animation, so it's beneficial to use it whenever possible.

Video integration

This is a very important time for online video and Flash. There is no other way to have video brought into a website and made to look a part of the interface and/or design without using Flash to do it. Flash has a great number of ways to seamlessly integrate video into interactive experiences. Designers have many new options for Flash/video integration, and users have the ability to view that video content now more than ever before. It has become simple to integrate video into buttons and transitions, and use it as a main content focus in Flash. Thanks to the VP6 Flash compression tool shipped with Flash 8 and the built-in Flash Video Import Wizard, video is going to become a fundamental content platform for Flash experiences and the Internet as a whole. This, of course, is something we all want to participate in, and with this book you can get started or enhance your existing knowledge base. We will show you everything you need to know to begin creating and deploying video online using Flash.

Browser autonomy

One of the great things about using Flash is that it's supported by all the most popular browsers these days, and it looks exactly the same on each one. This makes Flash an ideal tool for applications or websites that require complex functionality. It might be possible to create this complex functionality in one specific browser with complex DHTML, JavaScript, and specific components or extensions, but it will require at least a lot of additional coding to get such functionality to work with all browsers on all platforms, and you might end up discovering that it just can't be done. Therefore, using Flash means that you don't have to spend countless hours tweaking HTML and CSS code, creating hacks, coding browser-specific functions, and finding workarounds to make your site look and behave the same on every browser and platform. With the exception of a few JavaScript integration issues (which we'll cover later in the book), you have a guarantee that anything you create will most likely work flawlessly on all browsers.

Does this mean you need only create and test the site on your computer? No! You should always test your site on all major browsers and platforms. Furthermore, you should test your site with older and newer computers in multiple platforms.

Your site may look great on your computer at 120 frames per second with tons of PNGs flying around, but we guarantee that those with an older computer will not appreciate the massive slowdown they'll be experiencing. Don't worry if you don't work in an office with multiple workstations and dedicated testing machines. Ask friends, relatives, neighbors, instant messenger contacts, and anyone else you can think of to check out your site. Ideally you'll want to see it in person while it's running on their computer. That's not always going to be possible, obviously, so have a few questions ready to ask your testers. Try to ask specific questions like "Does the sound appear to be synchronized with the animations?" and ask your testers for specific details. Sending your testers to another site you've tested before or that you know works well on all platforms is a good idea, as you can have them compare the fluidity of motion and audio synchronization. Be sure to check out Chapter 14 for more details and suggestions on different testing phases.

Note: Older-generation Macs struggle a lot more with rendering Flash movies than older-generation PCs. The old iMac had trouble playing back even the simplest of interfaces, so don't despair if your site runs really slowly. You have to accept the fact that even though Flash makes your interface look exactly the same on each platform, it will not be able to play back at the same speed simply because it's primarily CPU driven. This is something we've always hoped Macromedia would address. With today's video card rendering technology, and dedicated graphics processors, it just doesn't make sense to have the entire load on the CPU. Older machines could always fall back to CPU rendering; however, most computers nowadays (even older ones) have at least some form of graphics processing. This has been improved significantly in Flash 8. According to Adobe, there is some form of hardware acceleration now. However, the performance is still a far cry from OpenGL hardware acceleration. For now, the important thing is that the site be usable and that even Mac users on older machines can still access the information on the site.

Browser embedding

So how do you get Flash to work in your website? After creating your work in Flash, you need to export it into a SWF file. This is a proprietary file format that Flash uses to efficiently store your movie. Newer versions of Flash also compress the file data with the zlib compression library (essentially the same compression as gzip and Zip files), which helps minimize file size and bandwidth usage even further.

You should never link your site directly to a SWF file. To correctly display a Flash movie in a browser, you need to create an HTML file that contains the tags that tell your browser to load the Flash player. To do this, you need to add <OBJECT> and <EMBED> codes to your HTML code. The <OBJECT> tag displays your Flash file in Internet Explorer (IE) on Windows, while the <EMBED> tag displays your Flash file in Netscape, Mozilla, Firefox, Safari, and IE Mac.

Following is an example of the HTML code required to include Flash in an HTML file. Change myMovie.swf to the relative location of your SWF file. Remember to also customize the height and width parameters to match your movie.

```
<OBJECT classid="clsid:D27CDB6E-AE6D-11cf-96B8-444553540000"
codebase="http://download.macromedia.com/pub/shockwave/cabs/
flash/swflash.cab#version=6,0,40,0"
WIDTH="100" HEIGHT="100" id="myMovie.swf">
    <PARAM NAME=movie VALUE=" myMovie.swf ">
    <PARAM NAME=quality VALUE=high>
    <PARAM NAME=bgcolor VALUE=#FFFFFF>
    <EMBED src="/support/flash/ts/documents/myFlashMovie.swf"
 quality=high bgcolor=#FFFFFF WIDTH="100" HEIGHT="100"
NAME="myMovieName" ALIGN="" TYPE="application/x-shockwave-flash"
PLUGINSPAGE="http://www.macromedia.com/go/getflashplayer" />
</OBJECT>
```

You can customize or add several properties to this code. All required attributes are included in the preceding code; however, you can add additional parameters and attributes to customize the context (right-click) menu of your movie, to make the background of your movie transparent, and to pass variables to Flash. We'll cover these and other attributes in later chapters, but the important thing to understand now is that these need to be included in both the <OBJECT> and <EMBED> tags, as the tags are mutually exclusive. If the <OBJECT> tag fails, the browser refers to the <EMBED> tag, therefore any attributes that were specified in the <OBJECT> tag (using <PARAM>) are no longer valid and need to be specified as an attribute of the <EMBED> tag.

> Tip: You don't have to type out the <OBJECT> and <EMBED> tags every time you want to add Flash to an HTML file. You can use the Publish feature to automatically generate an HTML file, and you can customize the parameters and attributes of the code before it is published under File ➤ Publish Settings.

Benefits of vector graphics over raster graphics

In today's computer design world, artists can create graphics using raster (defined by pixels) or vector (defined by point-to-point math). In this part of the chapter, we'll cover the differences between the two and their respective advantages and disadvantages.

Raster graphics are what we generally associate with traditional computer design using Photoshop and bitmap images. A bitmap is made up of a grid of pixels, as you can see in Figure 1-2. Each one of these individual pixels can be one color.

The problem with raster graphics is that they become jagged as you scale them. The larger you make them, the more jagged they appear. Flash compensates for this by *anti-aliasing*, which is a technique used to make edges appear smoother. Anti-aliasing applies subtle transitions to pictures around their edges. This is not ideal for Flash, especially if you're doing a lot of scaling effects, unless you're specifically going for that particular look. If you're going for a smooth look, then vector is the way to go.

Vector graphics are created using math, particularly geometry. Let's say we wanted to create a blue circle on a white background. The creation of this circle in either the raster or vector art method is pretty much the same. You use the Circle tool to click your center point and then drag to get the desired size and shape. The underlying difference between vector and raster is in how the objects are actually rendered by your computer. Instead of recording the color data for each pixel as in raster images, vector uses math to simply dictate the center point and the radius of the circle. The computer then calculates the shape of the circle using just these few bits of information. As we have seen, raster images need to record data for each individual pixel, which will give you vast file sizes in many cases. In the case of a raster blue circle, the file size will increase as the physical size of the object increases. In the vector example, the object can be scaled to oblivion, and it will still retain the same tiny file size, as it only needs the geometric data to render it.

We will go in depth into the various pros and cons of the two formats later on in this book. For now, it is important that you have a basic understanding of their differences so that you appreciate the unique power Flash has with its tools. Knowing the strengths of vector will most definitely empower you to create richer and more practical website designs as you grow as a designer.

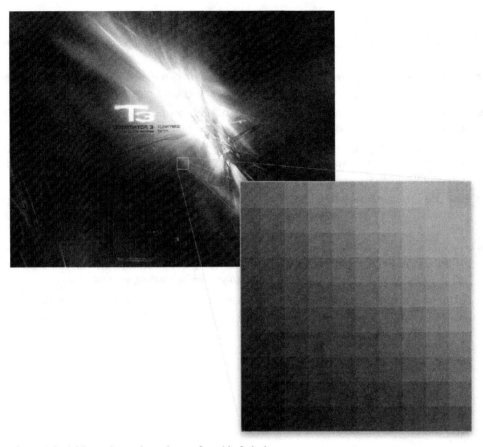

Figure 1-2. A bitmap image is made up of a grid of pixels.

Summary

Flash is easily the most impressive and important rich media tool available for the Web today. Understanding all its strengths and weaknesses will vastly increase your ability to sell its use to your potential clients, and as a result increase your confidence as a designer. Let's imagine a future board-room meeting with a prospective client.

After you hear the question "Why Flash?" disperse into the heavily vented boardroom air, you'll watch as its asker leans back in defiance, palpably waiting for your response. This is where you will feel free to paraphrase from this chapter. The principles discussed in the upcoming text should arm you with more than enough information to turn the question around on its head. Flash isn't good for every-thing. But in the high-impact, low-cost, fast-paced, modern business world, it is the champion of the present and the near future of web design.

Following is a list of lessons you've learned in this chapter:

- Flash is an easy-to-use program that has so many benefits, it takes this whole book just to mention a few of them.

- Increased ease of object manipulation with the tools in Flash makes it very good not just for animating and interaction, but also for conception and graphic creation.

- Animation is the number one sales point of Flash. No other program on earth is as vast in its ability to grant seamless animation and dynamic content into your website.

- Flash can easily integrate video to create large but practical multimedia experiences for your clients. It is important to know the right times and the wrong times to use video, as it does add considerable file size.

- Flash is a plug-in, and as a result it will display exactly the same across different browser types, unlike HTML. There are a few exceptions to this rule, but they are minor and we will touch on them later.

- Knowing the difference between vector and raster is as important to a Flash designer as knowing the difference between up and down. Vector can greatly decrease file size and exponentially increase the animation options available to you while creating your site.

- Vector art is mathematically based and will remain just as sharp even if scaled to 1 million times the size of its original. Just don't expect to find a monitor big enough to display that size yet.

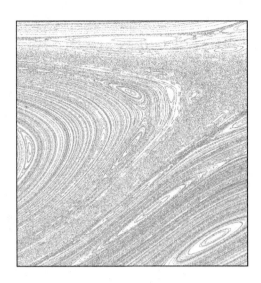

Chapter 2

CREATING USABLE AND
INNOVATIVE EXPERIENCES

by Michael Kemper

Designing interactive experiences in Flash is such a fast-paced profession that it is subject to an abundance of superfluous visual trends, which usually look dated shortly after they are published online (if not before). Another challenge to designing Flash interfaces is creating something that is intuitive enough for the user to learn and navigate. This is demanding because we have so many options that making the appropriate choices often means practicing self-restraint.

In this chapter, you will learn concepts and theories to help you find successful design solutions for Flash. You can depend on this chapter for that next inspiration to help you create something appropriate and innovative. It will also give you some verbiage to assist you in selling your Flash-based ideas to your clients.

Creative direction

First, let's characterize some ingredients of a successful interface design. Just about every project comes about by using the basic research, plan, design, develop, and deploy process. It doesn't really matter if you are a mechanic, a chef, or a web designer. Chances are, if you are a seasoned professional, you are familiar with and use some variety of this process on each of your projects. The part of the interface designer, especially when designing for a Flash solution, is an integral role during each of these phases.

Design layers

Think of the structure of your creation as a delicious cake, as illustrated in Figure 2-1. Each element is represented by another layer in the cake. The icing and decoration might look fantastic on the surface, but without all of the good stuff inside, it would be hollow—and no one wants to eat a hollow cake!

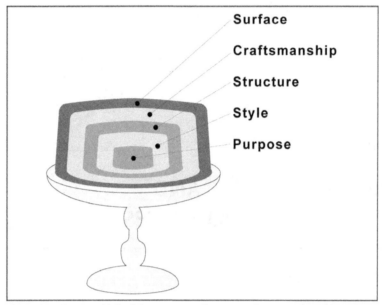

Figure 2-1. You can think of the structure of your creation as a cake, with each element represented by a layer in the cake.

Now let's look at each of these layers in your design, starting with the innermost one.

Purpose

As advanced designers, we want our designs to be part of the solution, not simply decoration for content and functionality. The first step in this process starts by understanding the project's purpose. What will the content be? What are the business or nonbusiness objectives? Who will be using it? What is the desired path or action a user should take? Understanding a project's purpose will help you come up with the best solutions for your interface when time is a commodity in short supply.

Compiling all of this information into a *creative/design brief* is a good exercise for understanding the project's purpose. Creating a creative/design brief will also provide the nondesigner members of your team with a deliverable that helps them understand the creative decisions you will make during the project. The following is an example of what you might include in a creative/design brief:

- **Audience:** Consider to whom the design is supposed to appeal. Use age, sex, ethnicity, income, hobbies, or anything else that is relevant.

- **Technical considerations:** Determine which plug-ins will be needed. Are there special considerations for style sheets? How much content is anticipated and in what format?

- **Objectives:** State the specific goals of the project—it will achieve *x, y, z*, and so on.

- **Positioning:** Clearly state in one sentence the message the users of the project will get. Describe how the design will support this message.
- **Tone:** List keywords that express the atmosphere of the interface. For example, clean, natural, modern, classy, and so on.
- **Imagery:** Describe the types of images, photos, illustrations, typography, and colors you propose to use on the project. Describe how this imagery supports your tone.
- **Desired actions:** Decide which actions the user needs to take while visiting the interface to complete the objectives.

Flushing out all of these ideas and putting them on paper will help you point to something later on during the project to help you justify your design decisions should they come under scrutiny. It also serves as a basic road map to use when trying to come up with ideas during your design phase.

Using a creative/design brief gives everyone an opportunity to put in their two cents about what they expect the project to include. This gives you a good idea about how to design for the project and makes it easier for everyone else on the team to support your creative decisions, since they can see their input being implemented in the design.

The foundation of your soon-to-be-successful project is its purpose. So do a little research and know your subject.

Style

In how many other jobs do you get to be an integral part of a music label one week, a blockbuster movie promotion the next, and a modern furniture company the week after that? Truly one of the things to absolutely love about being a creative professional is that the job is also a vehicle to learn about so many subject matters. The job of the designer is to place those subject matters in their proper context. We communicate messages by using the visual vocabulary of our project's genre. We determine if a design is exciting, relaxing, fun, sad, scary, and so on.

For example, for a ski resort client, one of your assignments might be to create a Flash site that appeals to families looking for winter vacations, and another assignment might be to create something that encourages college students to apply for part-time jobs as ski instructors or lift operators. Aside from the related subject matter of winter activities, these are very different audiences that would require very different styles.

Designers understand how to appeal to an audience of BMX enthusiasts, as well as to consumers of high-fashion apparel. In other words, the style must make sense for the subject matter.

Structure

By nature, most interface designers are multimedia mavericks. We bend, twist, and combine text, animation, video, and sound into interactive experiences. And what better medium for all of these different media types to converge than in Flash?

When thinking about the structure of any interactive project, the designer must consider the content first and foremost. Select the technologies and production techniques that best support the content. You must also select the technologies that will best support the user's experience. Is it all Flash? Should you use HTML/CSS? Does the project require a database or an XML feed? There are a myriad of different ways to integrate search functionality with Flash interfaces, and all of those decisions impact design and animation.

Consider designing a map-based search that shows ski lifts and lodging accommodations vs. a drop-down menu interface that sorts available job schedules. The impact is obvious to an interface designer. Always remember that the best interfaces are intuitive *and* look good at the same time.

To the advanced interface designer, there are very few limits to what technology or interaction we can design on any given project. It is the appropriate use of these tools that challenges us.

Craftsmanship

It takes a natural problem solver to take on a complicated medium like the Web and tame it enough to craft a quality experience. Many tools are available for interface designers, but it is the practical knowledge designers bring to the table that carries the key ideas and goals through to fruition.

Ironically, sometimes the best test of craftsmanship is whether or not the user noticed it. The most polished and intuitive interfaces are transparent to the point that the user doesn't even think about whether anything is misplaced or accidental. Through testing, failure, and determination, the advanced designer practices a heightened level of craftsmanship that allows everything else to shine as bright as it can. This aspect of interface design is probably the most frustrating because of all of the options we have for constructing a project. Fine-tuning how those options fit together isn't always the same on a per-project basis, which makes each solution unique.

For example, when I designed the streaming media showcase for VitalStream, shown in Figure 2-2, the assignment was to seamlessly integrate video controls and video sorting/preview options into a branded interface. The challenge of designing these types of elements and interactions is that they need to be intuitive enough for most users to notice and understand but cannot overpower the content itself.

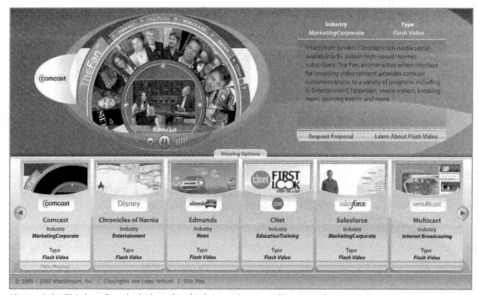

Figure 2-2. This interface is designed to be interactive as well as autoplay.

The craftsmanship of a project is apparent in all of the tiny details. High-quality design and craftsmanship cannot carry an interactive experience alone, but they can most certainly single-handedly destroy its effectiveness.

Surface

The surface of your design is the first superficial exposure a user has to the work, and it is where everything comes together or falls apart. To the trained eye, the surface of a project shows the production value and the effort that went into the project.

If the designer didn't take the time and effort to explore all of the necessary building blocks leading up to the surface, it will be obvious, and the whole experience will most likely lack the consistency and continuity that are expected from advanced designers. If all of the fundamentals were given proper consideration, the typical user won't notice at all. Ironically, this is the reaction you want. It shows that you have created an intuitive design solution—one that doesn't require any second guessing. It's a somewhat thankless job, but you still get the satisfaction of knowing that what you've accomplished provides the perfect solution for the client, and hopefully you enjoyed creating it as well.

From the surface perspective, all of the elements that create the experience should be present in the design. Consistency and attention to detail will prevail over corner-cutting production techniques on the surface of any interface design.

Critiques

Generally, an interface design is deconstructed in team critiques during the design and development process. This is a good exercise for getting professional feedback from people who understand the project. It is important for those participating in a critique to constantly approach the design from what they perceive the perspective of the target audience to be. Critiques can provide a valuable opportunity to deconstruct the user from many different perspectives, and this usually improves your design.

Anyone who has experienced the critique can tell you that it can be the best or worst thing to happen to a design. At worst, it can be a design-by-committee session, where your design will get ripped apart and put back together inappropriately. At best, it is a pleasant gathering where everyone on your team congratulates you for finding the perfect solution and gives you meaningful feedback on how to improve the concept.

In most cases, the work generally speaks for itself, and an impartial jury of your peers is the best place for it to succeed or fail. But critiques don't exist to simply showcase the work; they are supposed to make it better. The level of purpose, style, structure, craftsmanship, and surface should be analyzed in these sessions. Here are some general guidelines for critiquing an interface:

- Does the design make a clear statement that supports the content and goals of the project? (This addresses the purpose layer.)
- Does the style make sense for the subject matter? (Obviously, this is about the style layer.)
- Is the important content easy to get to and is the design intuitive? (This relates to the structure layer.)
- Is there anything that looks out of place or seems like a mistake? (This deals with the craftsmanship layer.)
- Does it look like a professional design and is it memorable? (This addresses the surface layer.)

Many designers succeed by seeking criticism more than praise. If you are stuck on a design for whatever reason, show it to someone on your team who knows the project and get her critique. If you don't have that luxury, show it to anyone who will give you his opinion. Generally, if you get an "I think it's perfect" type of reaction, disregard it and move on to the next person. Get a consensus. Working through criticisms will most likely guide you to a better solution.

The experience

Interface designers generally must consider many aspects of a project beyond simply the way it looks. They also need to create how the interface feels. Using metaphors, visual/animated narratives, and consistent interactions can also add to the "feeling" of your interface design.

The goal of every interface should be to extend the user identity to include the experience you created. This means that the interface should completely absorb the users, as if they were playing a game or driving a car. A successful interactive experience usually happens in four steps:

- **Departure:** The user is sent to a website, uses a kiosk, or is given a CD-ROM. The first impression is made from the surface of your design.

- **Discovery:** The user is exposed to the surface of the experience and interacts with it. At this point, all of the elements of your interface design will intrigue the user into digging deeper into the experience. He can identify with the style, and the structure *is intuitive.*

- **Point of no return:** The user is hooked. He has found something of interest in the content and is actively interacting with your interface to learn more. At this point, your surface design is secondary to the content, but the structure of the navigation and content is what is keeping your user engaged. The craftsmanship of your work is imperative to maintaining this successful experience.

- **Realization:** The user has made a personal connection with the material. He has found meaning in the content and hopefully accomplished the task at hand. Later, when thinking about the material, the user will most likely first visualize the interface as a point of reference.

Flash is the best tool for creating these types of immersive interactive experiences because it gives designers a fundamental tool for making broadband-type interactions accessible to broad audiences. As interface designers, we can create animation- and video-based experiences for kiosks and CD-ROMs, as well as for a majority of websites. Flash interface designers have the freedom to choose the context of content based on how it will be the most meaningful. This flexibility makes interactive experiences in general more meaningful for everyone.

Metaphors

The vernacular of Interface design largely consists of metaphors designers have taken from real-life objects. Using metaphors can be a risky business, as they can easily be overimplemented or too cute to be effective. Perhaps in the future, metaphors will be less relevant and the use of them will be more sentimental. But for the foreseeable future, metaphors are a practical tool for solving design problems.

Three main types of metaphors are used successfully in interface design:

- **Tangible:** These types of metaphors are usually seen on interactive elements in the form of textures, bevels, drop shadows, and so on, but they can also include using real-world bitmap textures throughout an interface.

- **Conceptual:** These are very common in navigation as icons, such as a printer to indicate printable content or a clock to indicate a block of time. Using conceptual metaphors is extremely helpful when you don't have room on a button label to fully explain the button's purpose.

- **Physical:** These metaphors imply a sense of place, such as a map or a house as the structure of the experience. Physical metaphors are most common in game interfaces, but more and more Flash interface designers are using them successfully for all types of experiences.

Let's take a closer look at each of these types of metaphors.

Tangible metaphors

Most browser or operating system scrollbars emulate something tangible. They look like something you can literally grab onto and move inside a track. Designers have harnessed bevels, gradients, drop shadows, textures, and so on to indicate interactive elements so that they are more intuitive for a broader audience. This phenomenon may be due to the fact that using a screen to accomplish tasks is still relatively new when you compare it to something like a typewriter or printed materials. Users seem to intuitively comprehend these types of tangible cues more than flat shapes. As a result, the use of this metaphorical technique has become a convention of interface design. The book you hold in your hands is chock-full of helpful lessons for pulling off similar techniques.

You can find inspiration from many types of tangible objects you interact with all the time: car dashboards, kitchen appliances, stereo receivers, cameras . . . you name it. If you look around, you will find that your world is packed with toggles, switches, push buttons, scroll wheels, knobs, levers, and other objects for you to emulate in your interfaces.

Figure 2-3 shows an example of an interface I created for prospective patients to take a virtual tour of a private hospital facility. I used textures from photos I took while taking a real tour of the facility to serve as background textures in the interface. You can see how I used the woodwork and wallpaper textures throughout the interface to help convey the atmosphere of the place.

Figure 2-3. An interface that uses a tangible metaphor

Conceptual metaphors

The best interface designers make it a point to immerse themselves in as many different types of media and entertainment forms as possible—movies, magazines, video games, theater, architecture, and so on. You will never have to create something in a vacuum if you take advantage of these resources.

Many Flash designers use visual techniques that have been adapted from these other types of media. This is especially true with transitions between content and navigation sets. You may have seen plenty of "Flashturbation" in the form of website transitions. But if they are done graciously, transitions can assist in extending the user-based identity to your interface.

A plethora of styles and effects implemented in film and television also work well in Flash. In fact, some broadcast designers use Flash as an animation tool to generate basic animations for segments in network television. Taking animation and type concepts from other forms of media and combining them with your own ideas is a great technique for creating transitions in Flash. It is this type of innovation that has made Flash what it is today.

Figure 2-4 shows an example of an interface I created for a DVD release of a movie about backroom

Figure 2-4. An interface that uses a conceptual metaphor

gamblers in Las Vegas. The transitions between screens are video footage I edited and cropped using the footage I received from the studio that made the film. Every time the user moves into a new section, she gets a preview of a scene from the movie with a transparent overlay of cards being shuffled and dealt. In this way, the interface itself becomes a trailer as the user navigates through it, and the transitions maintain continuity with the content of the site. I used conceptual metaphors throughout the experience, formatting pictures in the photo gallery as playing cards, animating them as if they were being dealt, and playing a card flip sound as they loaded.

Other conceptual metaphors include icons and pictograms, where you visually encapsulate a complete idea into something as small as 20 × 20 pixels, as illustrated in Figure 2-5. These are especially appropriate in designing data visualizations.

Figure 2-5. Icons of real-life objects also serve as conceptual metaphors.

Thanks to the innovations with ActionScript, Flash is now one of the most robust development tools for creating Rich Internet Applications (RIA). This has created a market for reporting dashboards of all types that include many different kinds of charts and graphs. Thoughtfully designed icons and pictograms enhance these dashboards greatly.

The reporting dashboard can be the most challenging type of project to design because of the many factors to consider. Not only are you charged with creating a consistent virtual identity and visual language that are easy to understand, but your designs must also have continuity with the data being presented. This requires a solid understanding of what is being reported, as well as how the data is being used. Sometimes, the simplest of sites require this type of design as well. Using a clock icon to indicate time or a television screen icon to indicate video are common applications for this type of metaphor.

Physical metaphors

Another common interface design strategy is the implication of a physical place. Your interface design could be a house with many rooms for the user to navigate through, a map with interactive regions containing the content, a book in which the user actually turns pages to view content, a card table for a poker game, and so on.

It is helpful to use physical metaphors when designing games. As an example, the interface I designed for a Flash Texas Hold'em game, shown in Figure 2-6, has a tabletop, cards, chips, and even other players present. This enhances the play experience much more than just having card graphics and buttons.

When using this tactic, you can have a lot of fun creating the ambiance and considering the architecture of a place. But physical metaphors can be difficult to execute successfully for a few fundamental reasons. When creating a virtual "model" of a real or imaginary place, there seems to be no end to how far you can carry the metaphor. This can be a huge task to design, especially if you are modeling a real place. At some point, you will have to decide when the metaphor ceases to be effective and integrate other intuitive Interface elements for navigation and content.

Designing an interface based on physical metaphors is especially challenging if the navigation structure needs to be fluid or dynamic. Many projects need to allow for growth in the future. This is a huge challenge for most Flash interface designers. Oftentimes, when designing an interface based on a defined space, making navigational changes after the implementation can get overly complicated. So know your content and plan for change.

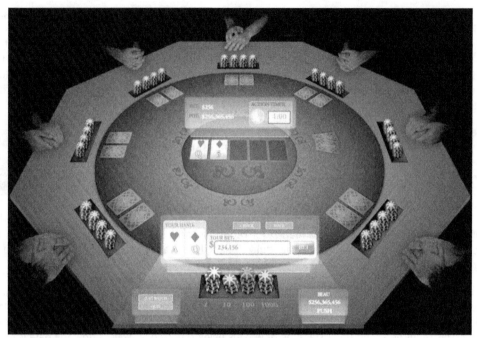

Figure 2-6. An interface that uses a physical metaphor

If metaphors are implemented tastefully, using them in your interface designs can greatly enhance the user's experience by making the interface easier to use and learn, and generally making the experience more memorable.

Narrative in Flash

There are many reasons for distilling ideas into graphic and animated form in Flash. Most of them involve engaging the user on an instinctual level and using the powerful multimedia features in Flash to create a memorable interface.

In most Flash interfaces, it's much better to use multimedia rather than long spans of body copy because it's usually a real pain to read text on the screen. Most people who read content from online sources print it out because it's easier on the eyes.

One issue designers are constantly running into is the scrolling problem. Many times, you need to create a scrolling text box inside your Flash site to accommodate long blocks of copy. Unfortunately, your entire interface is most likely inside a browser window that, if resized, will also contain a scrollbar. Double scrollbars are widely accepted as unusable, not to mention a huge eyesore.

A good reason for using animation or video in Flash instead of long blocks of copy is because they can be universal, and text can't. Using visual language can transcend any language barrier.

The Flash medium has many better ways to convey a message than spelling it out in hundreds or thousands of words. So, choose your technology wisely based on the content of your project. If you are creating an interface that requires a ton of body copy, your best option might be to use Flash sparingly and build the foundation of your site based on another more text-appropriate technology. But for those instances where your content is a prime candidate for creating a multimedia experience complete with animation, sound, and video, there really is no other choice than Flash.

As an example of multimedia use, Figure 2-7 shows a series of micro sites I created for the Colorado Ballet. I filmed and edited backstage interviews with the dancers, coaches, and production staff to promote each production for the season. Viewing online documentaries for each ballet was a lot more interesting than just reading an HTML page about them. I shot the digital video on a Canon GL1 and edited everything in Final Cut Pro and After Effects. The video was compressed using Squeeze. The interface is all Flash and streams FLV (Flash Video file) content. This project had a real impact on ticket sales for the season and generated interest in a previously unattainable younger audience.

Figure 2-7. This interface uses multimedia rather than a lot of body copy.

Interactive animation

High-quality, expressive animation in interface design is a rare and sought-after commodity. We all know the saying, "A picture is worth a thousand words." If that's true, then an animated image must be worth a million. Combine the animation with a few select words for clarification, and that experience becomes priceless. There is just no comparison to how much you can express in a short amount of time using consistent and basic animation principles when featuring content, creating an interaction, or planning page transitions. Finding a balance with images, motion, and text is an art in itself and can help a project accomplish a lot of its communication goals from the client perspective as well as the user point of view.

Benefits of animation

Animation can add volumes of meaning to interactive experiences when it ties into how the interface functions. Unfortunately, it is often overused in instances that don't improve the experience for the user. But animation is still yet another meaningful tool that can contribute to creating a meaningful and intuitive interface. Animation can fill in the gaps of technical restraints, contribute to the learnability of an interface, and add to a design's ease of use.

The most valuable interactive animations fill in the gaps of technical restraints. Not only can animation be the vehicle for simplifying an interactive experience in this way, but it can also shave valuable hours off your work on a project.

For example, if you want the user to "zoom" into a map from a bitmap version that shows geography (like mountains and bodies of water) to a vector version that shows specific roads and highways, you could choose for the bitmap to fade its alpha channel and reveal the vector map. This would fill in the gap of not technically being able to convert the dithers and gradients of the bitmap to the clean, crisp lines of the vector version. Consistency and continuity are imperative when attempting to bridge this gap. In the map example, if the zoom-out animation is not consistent with the zoom-in animation, the user might get confused about what the map is doing. The flow of that interaction would be lost, and the experience would not seem like a coherent whole. It would be best to handle the zoom in just like the zoom out but in reverse, so that the functionality of that interaction is clear to the user.

Ease of use is yet another facet of interface design that animation can improve. Indicating rollover states for interactive regions of your designs help users understand what parts are available for interactions. It is helpful to always include rollover and rollout animations on all of the interactive elements of a Flash interface. Generally, the length of these types of animations is dictated by the size of the area you are moving, balanced by the fluidity with which the rollover and rollout states create during the quickest of mouse movements. Of course, your movie's frame rate has a lot to do with this equation, too.

Animation can also contribute to an interface's learnability. This is particularly challenging when designing for Flash because of the wide variety of interaction choices designers have for creating their design, not to mention the client's or team's expectations for designers to design something innovative with Flash technology.

Components for interaction

In Flash, designers can create drag-and-drop, sliding, zooming, and many more types of interactions to guide a user through an interface. Sometimes, it is valuable to take a step back from a project and remember that people come to an interface to accomplish a task. It is the job of the designer to make sure users can accomplish those tasks in a quick and efficient manner.

Our mission is to create normalcy out of chaos and make it feel and look good at the same time. There are plenty of predetermined interaction standards that most users have learned as the result of their exposure to technology as a whole, and those are cherished staples of interface design that we can all use to solve design problems on the fly.

For elements like drop-down menus, tab navigation, form buttons, list boxes, and so on, I use Flash almost exclusively, because I enjoy the freedom it gives me to iterate on some of these basic interactions and design new combinations that add more meaning to the experience I am creating.

Figure 2-8 shows some mCOM components created by Metaliq, Inc., which exemplify how common interactions are translated into Flash components. Counterclockwise, the figure shows the following components:

- The TabBox contains CheckBoxes and RadioButtons.
- The ComboBox (or Drop-Down) contains a scrolling ListBox.
- The Accordion menu expands and contracts to show content or menu options.
- The ScrollBar can slide specified content vertically and horizontally.
- The Button is a standard form button.

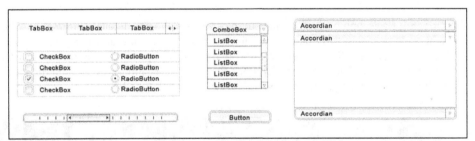

Figure 2-8. Some mCOM components created by Metaliq, Inc. exemplify how common interactions are translated into Flash components.

Emerging interactions

Over the years, I have coined and learned some advanced interactions that I incorporate into my work or see in other designs on a regular basis. Here's a rundown of types of interactions you might incorporate in your interface designs:

- **Buffet:** An advanced interface that allows a user to compile many different types of content/functionality into a "holder" and save them for later. This is useful for storing the user's path (like a breadcrumb trail) or compiling information to send in an e-mail message, for example. Figure 2-9 shows an interface where I used a buffet-style navigation system for the users' saved searches. Users can pick and choose options for each word they have saved without needing to select it and load a new page with those options. This makes users more mobile in the experience by organizing more options higher up in the site flow.

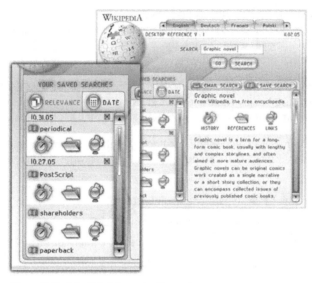

Figure 2-9. A buffet-style navigation system

- **Origami:** Navigation or content that "unfolds" to reveal more detailed information. This content could be menus that open to show links to more pages, for example. Figure 2-10 shows an example of a Flash MP3 player I created that uses an origami-type interaction to transition through music selections. It opens up once the user selects a music genre, and the inside navigation scrolls, expands, and collapses to reveal artists and song titles.

Figure 2-10. An origami-type interaction to transition through music selections

- **Toolbox:** Used to navigate through options of an experience or modify the content of an interface. This is a useful interaction for attaching preferences to a content area. Figure 2-11 shows an example of a toolbox for a content page that needed additional navigation other than the global and secondary navigation sets. The toolbox navigation is specific to the content on that page, and it does not apply to the overall structure of the site.

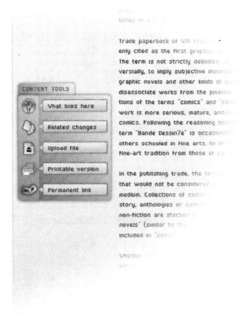

Figure 2-11. A toolbox for a content page

- **Tray:** A "micro" interface that is revealed based on user interaction. You typically see these sliding out from under other interface elements. Figure 2-12 shows a Flash Video Player that I designed, which has its controls in a tray that slides out from the bottom of the player when the user rolls over the interface.

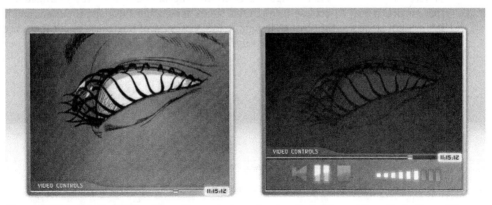

Figure 2-12. In this Flash Video Player, the controls are in a tray that slides out from the bottom of the player when the user rolls over the interface.

- **Pod:** A draggable, expandable, collapsible content area, sometimes containing navigation unique to it. The defining characteristic of a pod is that it is clearly its own entity, separate from other elements of an interface. Figure 2-13 shows an example of a panel (described next) consisting of many pods. The header of each pod appears when the user rolls the mouse over the pod, showing additional options for the displayed data. The user can reorganize the pods by clicking and dragging them to a new location in the panel.

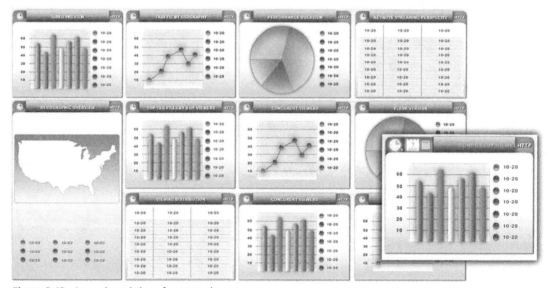

Figure 2-13. A panel consisting of many pods

- **Panel:** Contains content and navigation and or content in a defined space, as shown in the example in Figure 2-13. Typically, a panel contains special preferences that apply only to that space, but that doesn't need to be the case. You could put pods or trays inside a panel, but not the other way around.

- **Carousel:** An interface that slides to reveal additional options. Generally, these are horizontal or vertical navigation systems. Figure 2-14 shows an example of a carousel navigation system that enables a user to browse through this list of application tutorials. The user can click the left or right arrows to sift through the entire list. A preview of how many applications are available in the entire list is available in the upper-right corner to help orient the user.

Figure 2-14. A carousel navigation system

- **Genie:** A navigation system that gravitates toward mouse movement. Figure 2-15 shows an example of a genie menu in which the globes react to the user's mouse. They grow towards the mouse's x-coordinate and show a tooltip with the language that corresponds to the flag on the globe.

Figure 2-15. A genie menu

Many types of advanced interactions are out there, some of which you may have created yourself. When designing unique interactions into interfaces, you may find that taking proven intuitive experiences and combining them with your desired interaction gives you a successful intuitive result.

Summary

One of the most fantastic aspects of designing Interfaces in Flash is the freedom you have from the restraints that are common in other interactive technologies. As a tool, Flash empowers interface designers to push the creative limits of interactive work. As an experience, Flash provides more meaningful interactions for users. Designing for these experiences requires an understanding of more than just Interface design techniques, but also knowledge of the types of interactions that make Flash interfaces unique. Visual trends come and go, but the foundations outlined in this chapter can remain in your idea arsenal throughout your career. They can grow with you, as you become a more advanced interface designer.

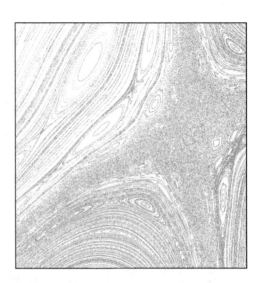

Chapter 3

INTERFACE DESIGNERS' GUIDE TO COLOR

By Michael Kemper

One of the most challenging aspects of interface design is utilizing colors to their fullest potential. As interface designers, we seem to have limitless color options at our disposal during our design process, unlike with print design, where the amount of color a designer uses directly impacts the cost of a project. So why is it still so challenging? It could be that each color you infuse into your interface has meaning and sends a message to the user. Perhaps having so many options makes it a struggle to pick the best possible combinations. Then again, the main issue could be matching a color scheme established by print advertising or a direct mail piece. Before even selecting color, designers must understand how to use the many color systems and tools available for digital design. And to complicate things even more, onscreen color presentation is not an even playing field across computer platforms or monitor types. It's difficult to be certain you are making the right color decision for the broadest audience with all of these factors to consider.

I believe that rules and guidelines in any endeavor encourage people to be more creative with their solutions. And color is no exception. When interface designers understand the tools, rules, and guidelines of digital color, it is easier for them to make the perfect color scheme selections with confidence and please their audience, too. This chapter will touch upon the foundations of color theory and apply them to digital design, then demystify the implications of technology on digital color for interface design. It will offer suggestions for communicating using color and wrap up with practical techniques for applying color in Flash.

Basic color theory

Figure 3-1. The three primary colors of additive color synthesis: red/green/blue (*A full-color version of this figure is available in the color insert.*)

Most of us already know that there are two main ideologies to color theory: subtractive and additive. *Subtractive color synthesis* uses pigments to create color by absorbing some wavelengths of cyan, magenta, and yellow light. The varied reflected wavelengths of light create the colors we see. Black is formed when all of these subtractive primary colors are combined equally, and white is the absence of subtractive primaries. This is color as it's applied to tangible objects and, yes, print design.

Additive color theory is the model of color that mostly concerns us since it's the method by which color is displayed onscreen. Now let's take a closer look at how additive color works in the world of the interface designer.

Additive color synthesis creates color by combining red, green, and blue wavelengths of light to create additive primary colors. The additive primary colors are red, blue, and green (see Figure 3-1).

Combining two equal parts of primary colors creates a secondary color:

- 1 red + 1 blue = magenta
- 1 blue + 1 green = cyan
- 1 green + 1 red = yellow

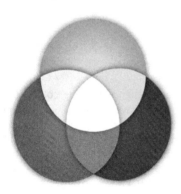

Figure 3-2. Additive secondary combinations (*A full-color version of this figure is available in the color insert.*)

The absence of additive primaries produces black. Combining equal portions of all three secondary colors produces white, as shown in Figure 3-2.

One way to understand the primary colors and their relationships is to see them organized into a color wheel, as shown in Figure 3-3.

Mixing one equal part of primary with secondary color creates a tertiary color, as shown in Figure 3-4.

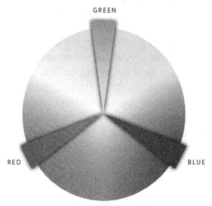

Figure 3-3. Additive colors inside a color wheel (*A full-color version of this figure is available in the color insert.*)

Figure 3-4. Additive tertiary combinations (*A full-color version of this figure is available in the color insert.*)

Selecting color

Colors have properties that can be modified to provide variety in a design without using additional colors. An important benefit of these properties for interface designers is that we can vary a color's property many times in a single layout to create hierarchy in information without using a new color for every level of content. This keeps layouts organized without looking too busy. Color properties are

Hue: A hue is a pure color with no black or white added. This is what makes a color unique. Figure 3-5 shows how the primary hues appear in Flash Color Mixer.

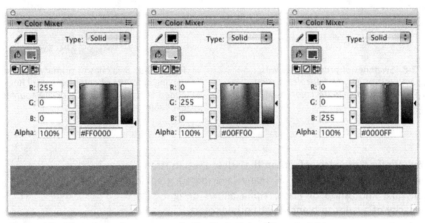

Figure 3-5. The primary hues as seen in the Flash Color Mixer. Red, blue, green—each set to 255 or 100%.

Intensity: Also called saturation, this describes the amount of hue in a color. For example, a blue with RGB (0,0,255) is considered intense or completely saturated (100%). A gray, however, has no identifiable hue, and is termed achromatic with 0% saturation.

Shade: A shade is a hue with varying amounts of black added (see Figure 3-6).

Tint: A tint is a hue with varying amounts of white added, as shown in Figure 3-7.

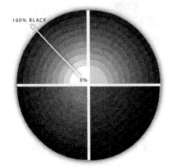

Figure 3-6. Multiple shades of the primary hues (*A full-color version of this figure is available in the color insert.*)

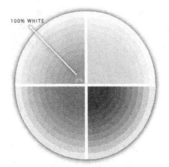

Figure 3-7. Multiple tints of the primary hues (*A full-color version of this figure is available in the color insert.*)

Tone: A tone is a primary hue with gray added making it more neutral as shown in Figure 3-8; it's also a tertiary hue with some strength of its complementary color added as shown in Figure 3-9.

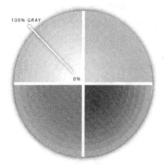

Figure 3-8. Swatches of primary hues with varying amounts of gray (*A full-color version of this figure is available in the color insert.*)

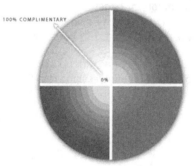

Figure 3-9. Swatches of primary hues with varying amounts of complementary hues added (*A full-color version of this figure is available in the color insert.*)

Alpha: Yet another property of color that describes its transparency as shown in Figure 3-10. In many layer-based graphic applications like Photoshop or Flash, alpha allows designers to vary the opacity of a color to blend it with other colors.

Vibrate: This is an effect created by placing two primary colors of equal or similar intensity right next to each other as shown in Figure 3-11. The viewer's eyes can't fully adjust to where the colors meet, so the result is a "bounce" or vibrate of the two colors.

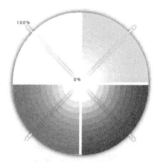

Figure 3-10. Demonstrating color alpha with the primary hues (*A full-color version of this figure is available in the color insert.*)

Figure 3-11. Example of vibrating color (*A full-color version of this figure is available in the color insert.*)

The color wheel is organized into color schemes. Designers use these schemes to create color harmony. I'll introduce you to these schemes next.

Monochromatic

A monochromatic color scheme utilizes a single color divided into different swatches of varying saturation/tint/shade (see Figure 3-12). Using this type of harmony is a simple technique for setting a distinct mood.

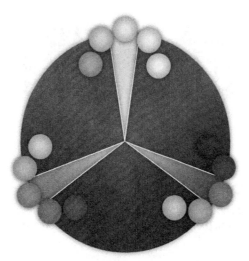

Figure 3-12. Monochromatic scheme (*A full-color version of this figure is available in the color insert.*)

Analogous

The analogous color scheme combines hues that are next to each other on the color wheel (see Figure 3-13). This mixture creates a soothing color harmony.

Figure 3-13. Analogous scheme (*A full-color version of this figure is available in the color insert.*)

Complementary

A complementary scheme consists of hues on opposite sides of the color wheel from each other (see Figure 3-14). Two sets of complementary colors is called a *double complementary*. A *split complementary* is a hue and two colors adjacent to its complementary. Complementary harmony creates contrast and has a tendency to grab the viewer's attention.

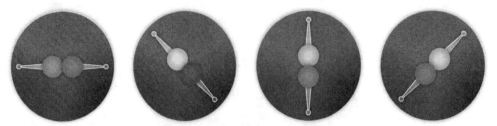

Figure 3-14. Complementary scheme *(A full-color version of this figure is available in the color insert.)*

Split complement

A split complementary is a hue and two colors adjacent to its complementary. This is one of the more flexible ways to mix color, but tougher to create harmony than some of the simpler schemes (see Figure 3-15).

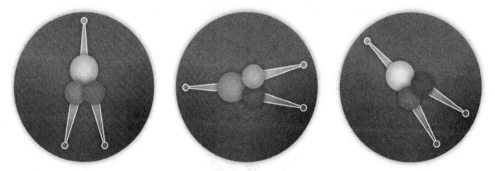

Figure 3-15. Split complement scheme *(A full-color version of this figure is available in the color insert.)*

Triadic

Combining three colors that are 120 degrees from each other on the color wheel creates a triadic color scheme (see Figure 3-16). This is one of the more complex schemes and creates contrasting harmony that is also balanced.

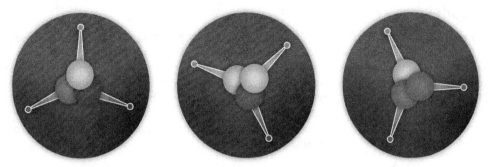

Figure 3-16. Triadic scheme (*A full-color version of this figure is available in the color insert.*)

Tetrad

The tetrad scheme is a four-color scheme selected from the points of a square within a color wheel (see Figure 3-17). Like alternate complements, this is a flexible method, but it requires a trained eye to create harmony with this scheme.

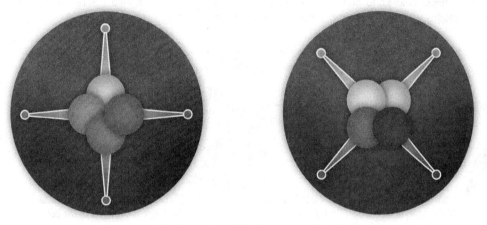

Figure 3-17. Tetrad scheme (*A full-color version of this figure is available in the color insert.*)

Color on the computer

As technology becomes increasingly advanced, so too does your ability to display true color in digital environments. Even though a majority of your audience can view true color design work, the systems and tools currently available for color are a legacy from the beginnings of interface design. And these systems aren't dead yet: many people rely on limited color systems designed to use interfaces on cell phones and PDAs that don't have the processors or screen technology to display true color. And as you may know, this is an immerging market for Flash designers and developers alike. So how does this technology affect a modern interface designer's color decisions? The answer starts with understanding a little bit of digital design history.

Color modes

When web design was in its infancy, designers were limited to designing for users with 8-bit video cards. This was the result of low video memory on older monitors that only supported color depth of 256 colors. To accommodate these machines, the three primary colors had to be assigned an even number (because computers process in terms of evens and not odds) that, when multiplied together, would not exceed 256. The magic number was 6. So 6 bits for red × 6 bits for blue × 6 bits for green = 216 possible combinations of additive colors. The remaining 40 bits of colors available were reserved for both Mac and PC operating systems to use as they wished. And of course, they both selected different palettes for their remaining 40 empty slots.

Today, most modern video cards support 24-bit color depth and process each primary color in a range of 0 to 256, which means computers can create exactly 16,777,216 colors (256 × 256 × 256 = 16,777,216). This is also known as "millions of colors," which you might recognize from when you calibrate your own computer monitor, or "true color," because scientists believe humans can see just over 16 million colors. 24 bits means each additive primary color gets 8 bits to work with, and some video cards that support 32-bit color have the extra 8 bits of processing to enhance render speed. 16-bit cards are considered "high color" and provide "thousands of colors" (65,536 to be exact), a palette that has far fewer colors and isn't entirely parallel to the true color palette. Figure 3-18 illustrates how the color modes vary onscreen, and Table 3-1 details the differences.

Figure 3-18. Comparing 8-, 16- and 24-bit color (*A full-color version of this figure is available in the color insert.*)

Table 3-1. Color Modes

Maximum colors	Bits per pixel	Description
256	8 bit	216 web-safe colors
65,536	16 bit	High color
16,777,216	24 bit	True color
16,777,216	32 bit	True color

Gamma

Although almost all video cards currently process millions of colors, the way monitors and operating systems display that color data isn't equal. The main difference between color display across platforms and monitors is gamma. *Gamma* is a formula that describes the relationship between the voltage input and the brightness of the image on a computer monitor. When generating additive color, gamma expresses the amount of light that will be emitted from each phosphor on a monitor's screen in terms of voltage. Conventional logic would say that if 100% of all colors creates white, and 0% of all colors creates black, then 50% of all colors produces a 50% gray. But this isn't so. The result is actually darker than a linear 50%. And there lies the difference with color display between Macs and PCs. Most PCs do not correct for this gamma inconsistency unless they have upgraded hardware, but all Macs try to. Gamma measurements will range from 1.0 to 3.0. A typical Mac gamma correction is 1.8, while PCs maintain a darker default of 2.5. Generally speaking, if you're on a PC and want to emulate a Mac's gamma, you should adjust your gamma correction to emulate the default Mac of 1.8. And if you're on a Mac and want to emulate a PC, you would adjust your gamma correction to about 2.5.

Nuts and bolts

Not only are the ways in which computers process color information different, but today interface designers also use several different types of displays. Interface designers need to plan for multiple viewing options not just for different gamma settings, but also for CRT, LCD, and projection display.

Most computer users are familiar with CRT monitors: the large tube-based monitors that resemble televisions. CRT stands for cathode ray tube. As shown in Figure 3-19, a CRT has a heated cathode and grids in the neck of the tube, making up a "gun." Electrons are accelerated from the gun toward the surface of the screen, producing a beam. The surface on the back of the screen is coated with phosphors and aluminum that light up when struck by the beam. 70% of all desktop computer users use CRTs, so most onscreen design is created for CRT viewing. But that's changing. Personally, I haven't owned a CRT monitor in years. In fact, I gave my last one away once I discovered LCD displays.

LCDs, or liquid crystal displays, use layers of electronically charged optical glass and liquid crystals to bend and reflect light to display contour and color, as you see in Figure 3-20. The result is that each pixel is divided into three parts called *subpixels*—one part for red, one for blue, and one for green. This allows LCD monitors to display millions of colors similar to a CRT (in fact they even use the same phosphor technology), except that LCDs are extremely thin and light by comparison. The entire laptop population is looking at interface design using LCDs, and eventually CRT

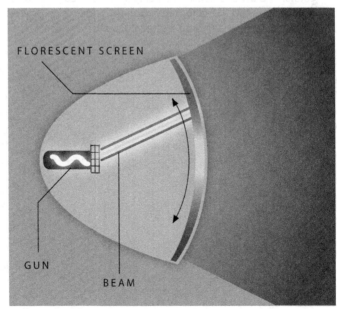

FLORESCENT SCREEN

GUN

BEAM

Figure 3-19. Diagram of how a CRT monitor works

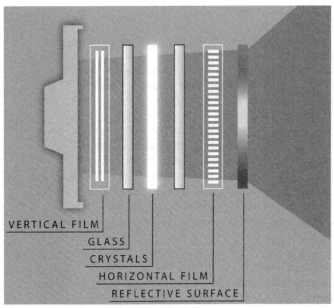

Figure 3-20. Exploded view of an LCD display

VERTICAL FILM
GLASS
CRYSTALS
HORIZONTAL FILM
REFLECTIVE SURFACE

monitors will be rendered obsolete for most desktop users as well. So how do you design for this next generation of displays? Although most manufacturers promote LCDs as being every bit as accurate as CRTs, an experienced designer knows better. LCDs produce mixed results when viewed in different lighting scenarios and at different angles. They produce brighter results; if you need to plan for LCD viewers, it's a good idea to incorporate higher levels of contrast in your color scheme. Keep in mind that near-white colors such as cream, beige, or silver can appear indistinguishable from white.

Most offices are equipped with a digital projector for displaying presentations in a conference room. And of course, most designers are more than likely going to have to justify color and design decisions while presenting their work using these same projectors. DLPs, or digital light projectors, use a semiconductor chip with tiny mirrors mounted on it to project light. Each mirror represents 1 pixel, so the resolution of your projection is directly related to the complexity of the mirrors on the chip. The chip, also known as a digital micromirror device (DMD), is divided into four sectors, as shown in Figure 3-21: one for each additive primary color and one for additional brightness. The projector lamp is positioned before the DMD and shoots light through the chip as it spins to reflect the appropriate colors. The DMD is constantly being synchronized to display the red, then blue, then green parts of each image—just like color separation for print design. The result is a "full color" image going through the projector lens and onto a screen or wall.

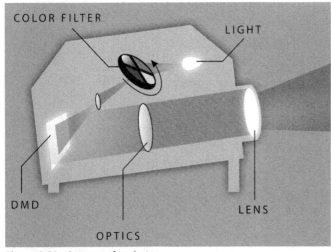

COLOR FILTER
LIGHT
DMD
LENS
OPTICS

Figure 3-21. Cutaway of projector

Since this is a time-based process dependent on the speed the DMD is being synchronized, you can think of DLPs in terms of frame rate. Most DMDs repeat the color patterns twice per frame, a total of six revolutions per frame. All of these factors impact color representation in a major way. Although projecting interfaces is a good solution for accommodating a large audience, it isn't so good for showing complex interface designs. Projectors are generally a little bit fuzzy due to the DMD being in constant motion. Contrast is lost due to the additional "brightness" sector of the DMD, and designs are also at the mercy of whoever decided to focus the lens, not to mention additional light from nearby windows. In some instances, the target audience will be mostly projector viewers, but generally this isn't the case. In those instances when you need to plan for an audience of projector viewers, you should remember that tiny type or very small/detailed icons will not be represented properly. And like the brighter LCD screens, certain light colors will be hard to differentiate from white, and many very dark colors will gravitate towards black.

Color systems

Now that you've seen how color is created with light and how it's displayed using different methods, it's important for you as an interface designer to understand the way color is organized for you in this digital environment. Older color systems were limited because of hardware ability, so those web-based palettes can be considered two-dimensional. Today, in the world of true digital color, our systems are three dimensional, or cubes.

Hexadecimal color

As technology advanced, 12-, 16-, and 24-bit capabilities extended interface designers' standard web palette. But the system that was developed through that evolutionary process is still with us in the era of "true color" on computers: hexadecimal color (see Figure 3-22). The Internet Explorer and Netscape teams developed this system due to hardware limitations. It was made popular for designers by Lynda Weinman back in 1996 in her first book, *Designing Web Graphics*. The Hexadecimal Color System converts RGB values into a hexadecimal triplet that can be used programmatically to apply color to the background and text in web browsers. The hex triplet is a six-digit, 3-byte hexadecimal number. Each primary color gets 1 byte (two digits): byte 1: red; byte 2: green; byte 3: blue. Hence the Color Look-Up Table (CLUT) was developed for designers to easily find browser-appropriate colors to use in their design work (see Table 3-2).

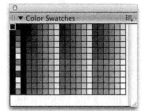

Figure 3-22. Web-safe color in the Flash Color Mixer palette (*A full-color version of this figure is available in the color insert.*)

Table 3-2. How Hex Color Is Determined

Digit	Hexadecimal	Decimal (shades)
0	00	0
3	33	51
6	66	102
9	99	153
C	55	204
F	FF	255

The system was developed to arbitrarily divide each color six times evenly across all 255 of its possible shades to get the greatest range. 51 is 1/5 of 255, which gives six evenly spaced points along each shade axis (0 being the 256th color, or black). The results for the color shades are the values 0, 51, 102, 153, 204, and 255. Corresponding digits can go up to 9 since each color only gets two digits; C and F take the place of 12 and 15 but maintain their value. The previous palette was created using this system and includes each color's corresponding hex values.

Other web palettes

Earlier in this chapter, you learned the limitations of 8-bit monitors and how that brought about a "web-safe palette" of only 216 out of a possible 256 colors. Inadequacies of lower-bit video cards meant that browsers and operating systems compensated for colors outside of the safe palette by using an algorithm to blend two of the closest possible colors out of the available 216 in a pattern to attempt a match. These patterns are known as *dither patterns* and are still used today to blend colors in GIF images.

Life would have been easier if there had only been one color palette to end all color palettes, but of course everyone had to use color as a tool to differentiate their products. I touched upon both Apple and Microsoft selecting unique colors for each of their operating systems for the remaining 40 open slots in the 256-color palette. Netscape also came up with slightly different palettes than Microsoft did for Internet Explorer. And to further complicate matters for designers, Unix based operating systems on color shade values of 0, 64, 128, 191, and 255. So the challenge for designers who were striving to appease the broadest audience possible became creating CLUTS that would display colors across systems without dithering. During the 1990s, when I was designing web interfaces, I would get requests from clients and managers that you think would seem absurd in today's design climate, but the ubiquity of portable devices such as phones and PDAs are making some those requests relevant again today. Ironically, I've found myself getting nostalgic while designing color palettes for Flash interfaces intended for smart phones and PDAs—I guess the occasional challenge of finding the perfect nondithering color scheme still intrigues me after spending the early years of my career waiting for universal true color to become a reality.

HSL color

The Hue, Saturation, Lightness (HSL) color system, also known as the Hue, Saturation, Intensity (HSI) color system, is based on a three-dimensional model that forms a hexcone (like a mirrored pyramid, as you see in Figure 3-23). The two apexes of this hexcone

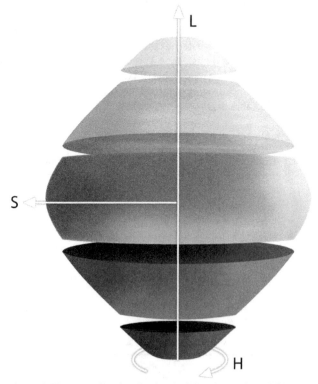

Figure 3-23. HSL color visualization (*A full-color version of this figure is available in the color insert.*)

correspond to black and white. The angular parameter corresponds to hue, distance from the axis corresponds to saturation, and distance along the black-white axis corresponds to lightness. The Saturation axis in HSL allows designers to select color from fully saturated color to the equivalent gray. This is the model used in the Microsoft Windows System Color Picker and is the preferred true color model of the W3C.

HSB color

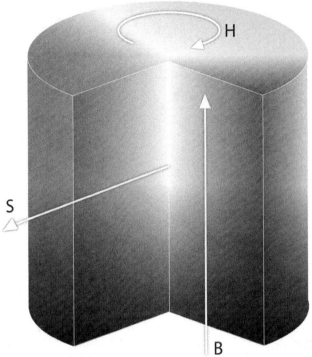

Figure 3-24. HSB color visualization (*A full-color version of this figure is available in the color insert.*)

The Hue, Saturation, Brightness (HSB) color system, also known as the Hue, Value, Saturation (HVS) color system, is the default option in Flash for the Color Mixer palette, and it's also used in Photoshop. The hue, or color type, ranges from 0 to 360, but in most applications, like Flash, it's normalized to 100%. Saturation in this system can be lowered to create colors like grayness. This three-dimensional system is similar to HLS, as you see in Figure 3-24, with the exception that when brightness is at 100%, it moves from a saturated color to pure white (HLS moves to a gray equivalent).

LAB color

CIE L*a*b* (CIELAB) was developed by the International Commission on Illumination (Commission Internationale d'Eclairage, or CIE). The three parameters in the model, shown in Figure 3-25, represent the luminance of the color (L), its position between red and green (A), and its position between yellow and blue (B). LAB is used by Adobe in their Adobe RGB color space to accurately express printed color ranges onscreen. The result of this conversion is generally seen as a wider flexibility with shades of greens and cyan on monitors. Any onscreen interpretation of this system is merely a close reference at best to the actual product on paper—almost completely dependent on the calibration of the monitor displaying the colors. This system is mainly accessible in Adobe applications. Since what you see is what you get in a true color digital world, LAB can be used for interface design, but it's intended for use by print designers on a computer.

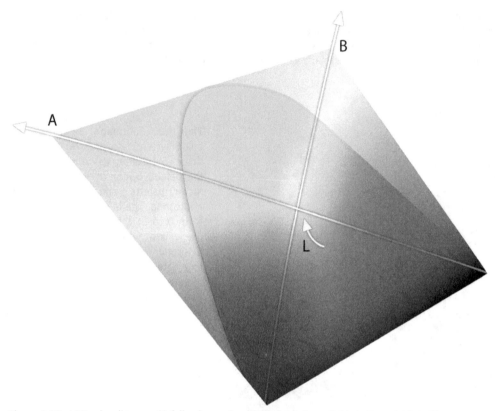

Figure 3-25. LAB color diagrams (*A full-color version of this figure is available in the color insert.*)

Communicating with color

> *I found I could say things with color and shapes that I couldn't say in any other way—things I had no words for.*
>
> Georgia O'Keeffe

Color is considered one of the most significant design tools for communicating to an audience. On a biological level, colors appeal to our survival instincts. Humans recognize food colors like green or orange, and "danger" color combinations like black and yellow. These colors have deep primal significance, which can be used to a designer's advantage. Colors also carry psychological significance. Certain ranges of the color wheel evoke emotions from people that couldn't be solicited in any other fashion. Yet another layer of significance that color contributes to is that of spirituality. From the dawn of civilization through the ages, colors have been ingrained into our belief systems. Colors carry meaning beyond what can be verbally expressed, and as designers, we create, mix, and bend them to communicate more effectively. As interface designers, we have a greater challenge: to harness the power of color not only to enhance our work's visual appeal, but also to make interfaces easier for our audience to use.

Color symbolism

The symbolism of colors varies from culture to culture. The meanings can often be traced to traditional spiritual beliefs. For example, Navajo Indians in Colorado (where I am from) believe that their Creator placed them on the land between four mountains representing the four cardinal directions. Generations of Navajo mythology based on this core belief assigned spiritual significance to blue beads, turquoise feathers, white shells, shiny rainbow abalone shell, and charcoal-black jet stones. As a result, the Navajo national flag was designed to include all of these important symbolic colors. Unless you have Navajo blood in you or have been exposed to Navajo culture, the vernacular of Navajo color is meaningless to you.

This is the case with every other culture on the planet. Learning as much about color significance in different cultures is a good exercise, and a fun hobby for designers. This knowledge will also most likely prove beneficial on a future project. Researching possible symbolic connections that a project has to the culture in which it will be experienced may also offer inspiration for selecting a color palette. A relatively global symbolic representation of colors can be found in the signs of the zodiac, shown in Figure 3-26. The zodiac is steeped in mythology, science, and tradition, so it's a perfect example of symbolic meaning through cultural significance. Each astrological sign is associated with a unique animal, but also has color relationships that give each month of the year additional meaning. Perhaps the color associated with each month is the result of its signs corresponding metal or gem—or it could be the other way around.

Figure 3-26. Color-coded zodiac with corresponding gems and metals (*A full-color version of this figure is available in the color insert.*)

Color psychology

Humans have intuitive reactions to colors. This knowledge is woven into our subconscious survival skills. For instance, fight or flight survival senses might take control if we are exposed to a large quantity of bright red blood (especially if it's our own!). We're also conditioned to respond certain ways to colors in our environment. Take traffic signals, for example: colors tell us when to go, slow down, or stop; they warn us of danger and inform us about road conditions. As globalization progresses and cultures blend, our perceptions of color meaning will unify. All of these factors and more play a role in how color affects people psychologically. It's generally accepted that the color wheel can be divided into sections that reflect our general sensibilities toward colors.

Cool colors like blue, green, and white, shown in the color wheel in Figure 3-27, tend to have a calming effect. They are perceived as professional and impersonal. We associate the blue range of cool colors with water and the sky. The green ranges of cool colors represent greed, envy, and inexperience. Not so surprisingly given these social associations in congruence with human perseverance, they mean growth and renewal. Greens are also abundant in nature, and for this reason it's a color that signifies plants and the environment. White, of course, has contrary associations and meaning. White is worn at weddings and is the presence of light. It's thought of as the color of purity, peace, and cleanliness.

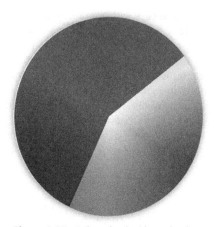

Figure 3-27. Color wheel with cool colors highlighted (*A full-color version of this figure is available in the color insert.*)

Warm colors like red, yellow, and orange, as you see in Figure 3-28, are energetic. These colors express a wide range of emotions from anger, to optimism and excitement. They are also colors we associate with food. Red is the color of the devil, love, and war. It signifies both extreme anger and passion. Yellow is associated with the sun, flowers, and traffic signs. It's perceived as being the color of happiness and joyfulness, as well as hazard and caution. Orange is found in citrus fruits, fire, and a wide range of natural occurrences like sunsets and changing fall leaves. It's a stimulating color that carries the combined associations of both red and yellow.

Neutral colors such as black, white, brown, silver/metallic, and gray can walk the line between the warm and cool colors of the wheel (see Figure 3-29). They generally serve to unify color palettes of stronger warm and cool shades of color. Black is worn at funerals and is the absence of light. It's often associated with mourning, rebellion, and evil. Brown colors are earth tones. Brown shares much of the associations that green does, since it appears in natural often. It's perceived as a color of stability (this is no doubt an association with the ground), endurance, and reliability. Silver and metallic colors relate directly to manufactured items like jewelry, cars,

Figure 3-28. Color wheel with warm colors highlighted (*A full-color version of this figure is available in the color insert.*)

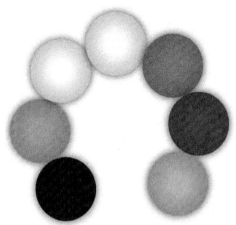

Figure 3-29. Color swatches of neutral colors (*A full-color version of this figure is available in the color insert.*)

furniture, etc. For this reason, we think of this range of cool colors as modern, refined, sophisticated, and wealthy. Gray ranges are both warm and cool. Gray shares characteristics of every other color range because it basically spans the entire color wheel.

Color strategy

Many interface designers are required to work within the confines of existing color standards as dictated by a corporate guideline manual. These manuals can come in handy for interface designers and save lots of time when it comes to color selection. They also help designers keep their work consistent with the other types of marketing materials a company offers to its audience. The best manuals come complete with breakdowns for color in a variety of systems like CMYK, RGB, and hex for easy reference. Even though all of the colors for a particular client might be specified in a manual, it doesn't necessarily mean you can't try to introduce a new hue as an accent to highlight certain content or increase usability. Experimenting with colors complementary or analogous to those within the corporate scheme guarantees creating an eye-pleasing variation to the existing scheme.

Another technique for increasing usability is to assign roles to your colors. I see this a lot with Cascading Style Sheets (CSS) for HTML-based pages. The idea is to use colors to keep the hierarchy of content consistent in each screen layout and throughout the overall experience. Assigning roles to colors also maintains consistent navigation structures by reserving certain hues or tones for button text or hyperlinks.

The following is a Cascading Style Sheet example that demonstrates assigning roles to colors in an interface design (the results of which appear in Figure 3-30):

```
.body
{
    FONT-SIZE: 9px;
    COLOR: #000000;
    FONT-FAMILY: Verdana, Arial, Helvetica, sans-serif;
    TEXT-DECORATION: none
}
.bodylink
{
    FONT-SIZE: 9px;
    COLOR: #666666;
    FONT-FAMILY: Verdana, Arial, Helvetica, sans-serif;
    TEXT-DECORATION: none}
A.bodylink:hover
{
    COLOR: #000000
}
.pagetitle
```

This is a Page Title

This is a Headline

Body Text with a link here for you to click on.

Figure 3-30. The preceding styles applied to text in an HTML page

```
{
    FONT-WEIGHT: bold;
    FONT-SIZE: 16px;
    COLOR: #003366;
    FONT-FAMILY: Verdana, Arial, Helvetica, sans-serif;
    TEXT-DECORATION: none
}
.headline
{
    FONT-SIZE: 14px;
    COLOR: #003366;
    FONT-FAMILY: Verdana, Arial, Helvetica, sans-serif
}
A:hover
{
    TEXT-DECORATION: underline
}
```

> *The file for this CSS example (*exampleStyle.css*) is available in the code download at* www.friendsofed.com.

Interface designers are also often presented with the issue of redesigning an existing experience that has no current recognizable brand. This is a great opportunity to practice some of the color theory discussed in this chapter without the restraints of being confined to the hues dictated by a manual. In an instance like that, the best advice I can offer is that oftentimes less is more when creating color schemes for interactive experiences. There are of course exceptions to that rule, but they are few and far between. A good exercise to run through when creating color schemes is to grab color swatches from digital photos in Photoshop. I keep a folder of photographs on my hard drive just for this reason.

Design tools and techniques

Several options exist in Flash for applying color to design work. Designers can use the assortment of palettes to select color from hex, default and custom swatches, or RGB values, or grab color from existing images. Programmers can assign color to movie clips using ActionScript.

Using Flash color palettes

The Color Mixer palette is the main utility for creating, selecting, and saving color swatches. The functionality that designers use to color strokes and shapes are replicated in the Tools palette and Property inspector, as well (see Figure 3-31).

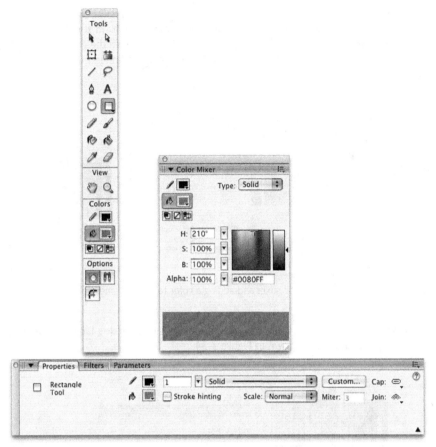

Figure 3-31. Color Mixer, Tools, and Property inspector

Users have the flexibility of switching the color model between RGB and HSB (see Figure 3-32). In RGB mode, you can use the sliders to modify hue, while in HSB mode you can tweak a hue's saturation and brightness. In both modes, users can tweak the alpha of the color they are modifying.

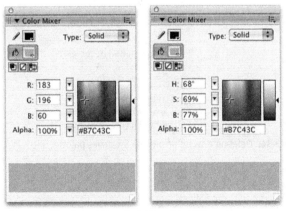

Figure 3-32. Color Mixer in RGB and in HSB modes

Creating custom swatches using the Color Mixer palette is easy. Create a color by either clicking a hue on the color preview pane or modify an existing swatch by selecting it from the Swatch palette and scrubbing the slider preferences in the Color Mixer palette. Once you have the color you wish to save, just select Add Swatch from the Color Mixer's options menu, as shown in Figure 3-33, and it will add the new color to your Swatch palette.

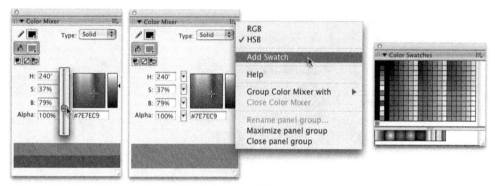

Figure 3-33. Modifying a hue in the Color Mixer and adding a color to the Swatches palette

Once a swatch is saved in the Swatches palette, you can delete it by selecting Delete Swatch from the Swatches palette's options menu, as shown in Figure 3-34.

Figure 3-34. Deleting a swatch from the Swatches palette

To save color schemes, start by creating as many swatches as you like using the Color Mixer. Then, select Save Colors from the Swatches palette's option menu and save the scheme to your hard drive.

You can load a custom color scheme that was previously saved by selecting Add Colors in the Swatches palette's option menu, as shown in Figure 3-35, then opening a color scheme from your computer.

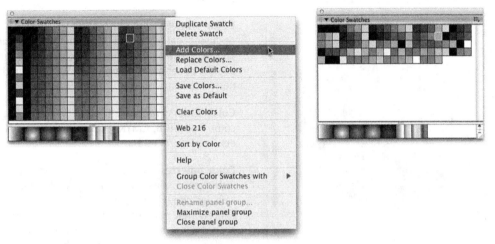

Figure 3-35. Loading color schemes into the Swatches palette

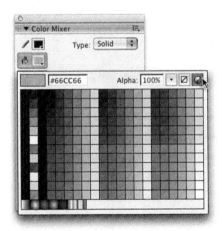

Figure 3-36. Accessing the Colors Preferences window from the Color Mixer

Many different color systems are at your disposal in Flash, and they are all accessible from the Tools and Color Mixer palettes and the Property inspector. To access these systems, click either the fill or stroke preview, and then hold and roll over to the tiny color wheel icon on the far right, as shown in Figure 3-36, and release your mouse button.

A Colors Preferences window will open, as you see in Figure 3-37. As you select hues in this window, a preview swatch appears right below the window header. You can click and drag this swatch to the grid along the bottom of the window to temporarily save swatches during your selection process. Once you close Flash, this grid will reset itself the next time you open the application. Another helpful feature of this preferences window (especially when selecting from the color wheel) is the magnifying glass beside the color preview. When the magnifying glass is selected, it offers an additional zoomed view of

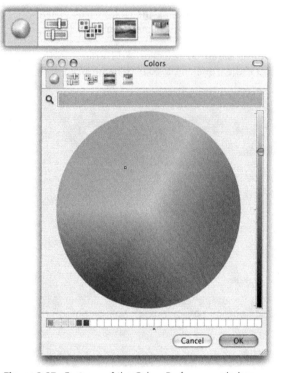

Figure 3-37. Features of the Colors Preferences window

each color system. Keep in mind that the color preview in the Color Mixer will display the temporary swatch that was last selected once you click OK.

From here you can select from many different systems:

Color wheel: This is the additive color wheel discussed earlier in this chapter. You can click and drag within the wheel to select a hue, and use the slider along the right to vary the brightness (see Figure 3-38).

Color sliders: You have the option of creating a color from RGB, CMYK, HSB, and grayscale sliders (see Figure 3-39).

Color palettes: Here you will find a list of preselected color palettes including Apple and Web Safe, as shown in Figure 3-40. You can create entirely new palettes by selecting New from the drop-down menu. If you have temporary swatches in the grid along the bottom, simply drag the ones you want to save into the list box

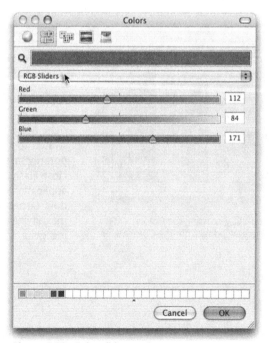

Figure 3-38. Color wheel option

Figure 3-39. Color sliders option

Figure 3-40. Color palettes option

of colors for the new palette. Unless you delete the individual colors or the entire palette, they will be saved to your copy of Flash forever.

Image palette: This is perhaps the coolest feature of this window, because it allows you to load an external bitmap image and grab a hue from it using your mouse picker. To load an external image, just select New From File from the drop-down menu underneath the color preview, and then select an image from your hard disk. The new image will load into the preview, as you see in Figure 3-41, and you then click and drag your mouse to select hues from the image.

Crayons: This is the most the most novel system for picking colors. It's a box of crayons with colors like Lemon and Sky. Who doesn't remember how to use this one?

A cool feature of the Color Mixer in Flash is the ability to fill vector shapes with bitmaps. To make a bitmap available for a fill, select the drop-down menu along the top right of the Color Mixer and choose Bitmap. This puts the Color Mixer into Bitmap mode, as shown in Figure 3-42.

Figure 3-41. Image palette option

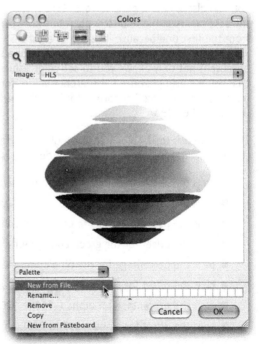

Figure 3-42. Color Mixer with the Bitmap option selected

Next, click the Import button, and then find a bitmap on your hard disk. A tiny thumbnail preview of the bitmap is created along the bottom of the Color Mixer inside the preview window. Simply select the shapes you want to fill with the image and click the preview icon in the Color Mixer (while in Bitmap mode) to apply the bitmap.

Applying color using ActionScript

ActionScript offers a few of different techniques for dynamically setting the color of movie clips. The most basic way to set an object's color value is to use the setRGB method. This technique "tints" objects to a solid color based on a hex value. The format for how this technique applies color settings is 0xRRGGBB. RR, GG, and BB each consist of two hexadecimal digits that specify the offset of each color component. The 0x tells the ActionScript compiler that the number is a hexadecimal value. The following statement creates an instance of the Color object, in this case called mkColor, and targets the movie clip instance item, which resides on the main (_root) timeline along with the script:

```
//create a color object and apply it to a target
var mk_color:Color = new Color(item);
```

The next line sets the RGB value of mkColor to a hexadecimal value of 663399, which is an orange color. setRGB is a method of the Color object created in the previous line.

```
// use setRGB to apply a hex value to the color object
mk_color.setRGB(0xFF8000);
```

The result of the preceding code on a movie clip instance is that it will color the target a solid color, as shown in Figure 3-43.

You can also create a generic colorTransformObject parameter and use the setTransform method to apply it to movie clips. This technique differs from the first one because it uses a straight RGB system instead of a hex value. It also gives you a lot more flexibility for applying color dynamically because it not only allows you to set color values for each primary color channel, but also provides transparency values for each channel as well as for the overall setting. The format for how this technique applies color settings is 0xRRGGBBAA.

Figure 3-43. Published result from using the setRGB method

The parameters for a color transform object correspond to the settings in the Advanced Effect dialog box and are defined as follows:

- ra is the percentage for the red component (–100 to 100).
- rb is the offset for the red component (–255 to 255).
- ga is the percentage for the green component (–100 to 100).
- gb is the offset for the green component (–255 to 255).
- ba is the percentage for the blue component (–100 to 100).
- bb is the offset for the blue component (–255 to 255).
- aa is the percentage for alpha (–100 to 100).
- ab is the offset for alpha (–255 to 255).

The next code block sets the RGB value of mkColor to the same hexadecimal value of 663399 as earlier, except it uses pure RGB values. The following also sets each hue's alpha channel to 50%, allowing the viewer to still see the design work within the target being colored:

```
// set color variables
ra = 50;
rb = 255;
ga = 50;
gb = 128;
ba = 50;
bb = 0;
aa = 50;
ab = 50;
//
```

Now a function is created that contains a new color object applied to the target item. A transform object constructor is used to create the color transform object, mkColorTransform, that sets the appropriate properties from the variables created in the preceding code block.

```
// apply color variables
function colorStuff() {
 // create a color object called my_color for the target
 var mk_color:Color = new Color(item);
 // create a color transform object called mkColorTransform
 using Set the values for mkColorTransform
 // created with the new object constructor
 var mkColorTransform:Object = {ra:ra, rb:rb, ga:ga, gb:gb, ba:ba,
bb:bb, aa:aa, ab:ab};
 // associate the color transform object with the color object
 mk_color.setTransform(mkColorTransform);
}
//
```

The function is called and sent the values created in the first block of code.

```
// send colorStuff variables
colorStuff(ra, rb, ga, gb, ba, bb, aa, ab);
```

The result of the preceding code on a movie clip instance is that it will color the target a 50% tint of the specified RGB values, as you see in Figure 3-44.

Figure 3-44. Published result from using the color transform object method

Summary

Color is an extremely valuable tool for solving interface design problems such as communicating a feeling or idea and improving usability. It's also an important factor when creating an identity across digital and printed mediums. With a better understanding of how color is created, organized, and displayed in the digital medium, designers can select color schemes and apply them to interfaces with confidence.

With this chapter behind you, you've learned the following lessons:

- Additive color theory is the model of color theory for onscreen designs. Additive color is based on the ranges of hues in light. It consists of the three primary colors: red, green, and blue. Blending the hues of light creates all of the colors in our viewable range.

- Additive color is organized into the color wheel by hue. The color wheel displays relationships between the primary hues of color and how they blend to create secondary and tertiary colors.

- Colors have properties—hue, intensity, shade, tint, tone, and alpha—that can be modified to provide variety in a design without using additional colors.

- Designers use schemes such as monochromatic, analogous, complementary, triadic, alternate complement, and tetrad to create color harmony.

- Color on a computer is displayed based on bit depth. Today, most modern video cards support 24-bit color depth and process each primary color in a range of 0 to 256, which means computers can create exactly 16,777,216 colors.

- Gamma is a formula that describes the relationship between the voltage input and the brightness of the image on a computer monitor. When generating additive color, gamma expresses the amount of light that will be emitted from each phosphor on a monitor's screen in terms of voltage. Gamma varies based on operating system and monitor type.

- CRT, LCD, and projected displays use different technology to display color. As a result, color representation varies from system to system.

- Color is organized in many different systems for designers such as hexadecimal, HLS, HSB, and LAB color. These systems are accessible across design applications, programming languages, and media types.

- You can use instilled symbolic and psychological human perception of color to set moods, communicate more effectively, and improve usability.

- Flash has a wide variety of design production tools to create, mix, and save colors.

- Designers can set color schemes dynamically in Flash using ActionScript.

Chapter 4

PLANNING YOUR INTERFACE DESIGN

by Guido Rosso

Starting a web design project can be overwhelming if it's not planned out carefully. Yet many designers and studios still jump right into drawing concepts and preparing demo interfaces with very little or no planning (often due to unrealistic turnaround times from clients). Regardless of whether you're working on a personal project within an in-house team of designers and developers, or directly for a client, it simply isn't enough to have a general idea of where the project is headed and what the final outcome should be. There needs to be some kind of preplanned workflow that both you and your client have agreed to undertake together.

In this chapter, I'll cover the process of using whatever initial information you have to plan out and prepare your site's interface, site structure planning, wireframing, how to use your space efficiently, and layout do's and don'ts. I'll start with a brief explanation of general practices when planning any site, whether it's a Flash site, a hybrid site, or an HTML/CSS-only site. However, the majority of the chapter will focus on the process from an interface designer's point of view.

Initial information

Information gathering should be the first step of any web design project. I'll cover this topic briefly, as it's not the purpose of this book to give you a detailed walk-through of how to plan every aspect of a project; I'll focus mainly on what is relevant to the planning of the interface of the site.

Depending on what kind of relationship you have with your client, or whoever you're developing the site for, information gathering can happen in a number of ways. If you can meet in person, it's generally best to do so, at least for the first meeting. If the client is over-seas, then be sure to give them a sense of security and reliability by replying to e-mails quickly. At your first meeting you should get a general feel for the project and listen to what the client has to say. Chances are they haven't planned things out as much as they should yet, which is why it's important to have a checklist of general questions with you (bring some blank sheets of paper for notes and sketches). Remember that at this point you're trying to collect all the information you'll need at a later stage to clearly define the project, create a sitemap, and wireframe your interface. Make sure to ask design-related questions as well, such as how they want their company to be perceived (cutting edge, fun, professional, etc.) and to make a list of sites they find graphically appealing.

Following is a list of information you may want to gather from your client. Keep in mind that all proj-ects are unique; you'll most likely have to add other items to the list on a project-by-project basis.

- General client information, company structure, company history, and contact information for all departments you may have to get in touch with.
- Detailed understanding of the client's products and services.
- Who are your client's competitors and what are the addresses of their websites?
- What does the client specifically hope to achieve with the new site (or redesign)? This should include both short-term and long-term goals.
- What kind of budget does the client have in mind? Always try to get some kind of reply to this, even if it's just a general range. This will make it easier to judge whether specific features will be feasible.
- Profiles of your client's customers to help you understand the site's audience and their techni-cal capabilities. (Always keep in mind that you should be designing the site for your client's audience; remind the client of this if you have to!)
- Domain information, where the server will be located (shared or dedicated?), and FTP information.
- Find out if the client has any content already available, or whether someone else is developing it for them and when it will be ready. Discuss this in detail. You should have enough informa-tion to create a sitemap.
- Technical information, including whether the site will display dynamic content, whether it will require a search engine, whether e-commerce capabilities should be included, etc.
- How will the site be tested and how much of the budget is the client willing to invest in Quality Assurance (QA)?
- Understand how much development time will be available. Ideally, you would be able to deter-mine this yourself. Many times, however, the client already has a specific deadline in place to coincide with an already existing marketing plan, a PR event, a corporate meeting, etc. Gather as much information that could affect time in development as possible.
- Understand the client's brand and what kind of image they want the site to portray. Discuss colors, look, and feel.
- Ask about maintenance. Who will be updating the site? Will they require a content manage-ment system?

Once you've gathered as much information as possible from your client, don't stop there. Analyze your client's business, their competitors, their audience, their website, and any offline materials (posters, books, brochures, products, etc.). Make sure you identify your client's audience's technical compatibilities and abilities (what platforms do they use, bandwidth limitations, what technical actions do users need to perform to be able access content on the site, etc.). You'll use what you've discovered to prepare a proposal for a project that will achieve your client's goals and surpass or improve upon what their competitors are already doing.

Structure planning

When you feel that you've gathered as much information as you need, it's time to start preparing the content structure. The easiest way to do this is by creating a sitemap, which is also the first step in visualizing the site.

A sitemap, such as the one shown in Figure 4-1, should visually represent every section and every page of your site. If the site will be integrated with a back-end, it's a good idea to represent which pages will communicate with the database or require complex functionality. However, keep in mind that this doesn't need to be incredibly detailed as it's not the purpose of the sitemap to represent the entire functionality of the site. It should be detailed enough so that designers and developers can view the structure of the site as a whole.

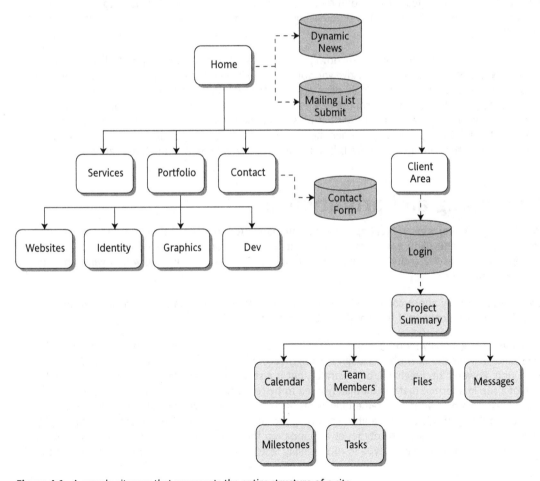

Figure 4-1. A sample sitemap that represents the entire structure of a site

Your initial sitemap will probably be sketched on paper, but at some point you're going to have to use a program to create a cleaner and easier-to-update schematic. Several programs are available online specifically for creating sitemaps. The most-used program tends to be Visio; however, the fastest and most intuitive I've used so far is OmniGraffle. Unfortunately, it's Mac only, but it's compatible with Visio. You should have a Mac for testing purposes anyway, even if you are primarily PC based.

Creating a sitemap should be as much your client's job as your own. Be sure to specify that the sitemap is indicative of the size of the site, therefore it's in their best interest to be as accurate as possible when supplying information; otherwise, any cost estimates and budget plans will most likely be off (it's a good idea to get the sitemap approved and signed).

When planning the structure of a site, keep in mind that you're trying to create something that's very easy to navigate. You won't necessarily be showing the sitemap to the site's visitors; however, they should be able to mentally trace a path to any specific information they are looking for in your site.

Make sure you identify any Flash-specific functionality at this stage as well. Will any of the interface elements appear or be modified dynamically? Will there be a need to integrate your interface with a database? Should the back button of the browser behave in Flash as it would in HTML? Which sections of the site should load from a different SWF? These are all features that need to be identified immediately; otherwise, you might end up having to significantly modify the entire structure of your Flash files.

Once you've got the structure of the site down, it's time to start writing your proposal. This book won't cover how to write a proposal, but I'll give you some advice: Remember to keep it as easy to follow and personalized as possible; avoid using 50-page proposal templates with only one paragraph relevant to your client's project. The proposal should be entirely about their company and their project. Let them know just how well you understand their business and their needs. Include a schedule for delivery of the content (text, images, and any other media) that will fill the pages described in the sitemap. Remember that the content of the site is just as much a design element as the layout graphics.

Wireframing and prototyping

Wireframing is the process of creating a skeletal foundation for your site. It should include where content will appear, entry and exit points, and all primary and secondary navigation, as you see in the examples in Figures 4-2 and 4-3. Ideally, you should represent your entire site with a wireframe for every possible page.

You shouldn't worry about colors and graphics when creating a wireframe. Use square buttons and boxes to represent content if text has yet to be established.

Wireframing is generally more common with HTML sites, as it may not be feasible to create an entire wireframe of your site in Flash (although I strongly recommend it). It's possible to create wireframes with Visio, PowerPoint, Freehand, or Illustrator, but it just doesn't seem right to develop the foundation of a site in a format that will ultimately need to be redesigned in Flash or HTML anyway. It makes more sense to create your wireframe in Flash as you can later build your final interface over it. The only exception to this is DENIM, a little-known application that can help you create prototypes very quickly. You can't use these prototypes as a foundation for your actual interface, but you can save a lot of time and still have a prototype to run usability tests on and find shortcomings in your structure.

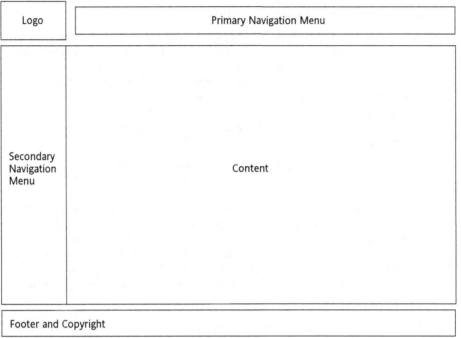

Figure 4-2. A very simple wireframe of the main interface of a site where content has not yet been established

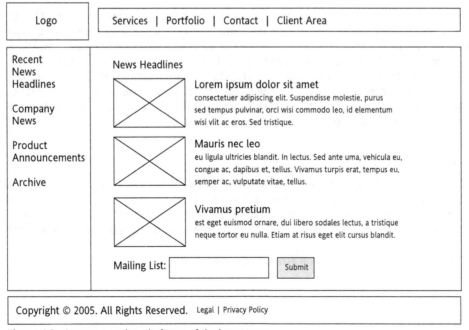

Figure 4-3. A more complex wireframe of the home page

Using DENIM as a wireframing and prototyping tool

DENIM is a Java-based application created by the Group for User Interface Research at the University of California, Berkeley. It's pen based and allows you to sketch wireframes of your pages much like you would on paper. You can create relationships between the pages simply by drawing a line from a link to another page. The final prototype can be exported to HTML, which makes it great for testing with your entire team. It's an easy-to-use program, and it allows you to create prototypes very quickly. For this reason alone, I recommend using it for Flash projects, if it's absolutely not feasible for you to prototype directly in Flash.

DENIM can be downloaded at http://dub.washington.edu/denim/.

When constructing wireframes, keep in mind the different screen resolutions that site audiences will be using and try to place all primary content in the 800✕600 screen size. Ask yourself what is the first thing a user should do or see when they open this page (or refer to your proposal, which should already have a detailed explanation). If it's the home page, then you're probably going to want to have some kind of information that updates often, such as news, features, or promotions. Site visitors shouldn't have to scroll to view this information; it should be one of the first things they see.

Tip: Even though statistics show that more and more computers are using a screen resolution of 1024✕768 (53% global share), you should always design for a minimum 800✕600 screen resolution (29% global share). Designing specifically for 1024✕768 and higher resolutions can create usability problems for 800✕600 users.[1]

A wireframe should take into consideration positioning of navigation menus. Most sites tend to have a primary and secondary navigation. As with the primary content, a visitor should not have to scroll to view the primary navigation immediately after loading the page. The position of your navigation menu will depend on your design; however, try to keep in mind that a good design doesn't necessarily have to revolutionize the way visitors have become accustomed to navigating a site. A good design takes the functionality that visitors are used to seeing and interacting with everyday, and improves upon it slightly without redefining the way they're used to doing things. In other words, be creative but don't reinvent the wheel (or the scrollbar).

What is prototyping?

There are different interpretations in the web design industry as to what a prototype is. Some designers define a prototype as a functional skeleton, where you can click any navigation item to link one wireframe to another wireframe. This makes it possible to conduct usability tests even in the very early stages of development. Other designers define a prototype as an actual demo or concept of what the

---

1. W3 Schools, "Browser Statistics," www.w3schools.com/browsers/browsers_stats.asp

final interface might look like. This tends to be more common in large agencies that can afford to spend a good deal of time preparing one or multiple concepts for a pitch. Depending on the agency and the project, these can be simple static images to heavily developed concepts with detailed presentations, animations, sounds, and video. These generally tend to be pitches for projects with very large budgets, which will ultimately justify a large commitment of time and resources to craft the concept. Use your best judgment to determine how much you should develop your concept (this is one of the reasons why it's important to have a general idea of your client's budget). The better the concept you present, the higher your chances are of winning the contract. However, you will also be risking a lot of time and resources on something that your client might not like at all. This is why the initial information-gathering phase is so important. If you've done your research correctly, the chances that your client won't like your concept are rare!

Using your space efficiently

Keeping interface elements positioned where users expect them to be is a key point of good design, not to mention good usability. For example, a primary navigation menu generally appears on the top of the interface, and a secondary navigation menu generally appears on the left or right. Using this as a standard will increase the usability of your sites. If your site is very big, you may want to use a local navigation menu on the left or right side of your interface. The local navigation menu displays subcategories and related pages based on the global section (top menu) you're currently visiting.

Aside from positioning, it's a good idea to also take into consideration spacing of elements. Proper spacing can be one of the most powerful ways to keeping your site looking clean, clutter free, and highly usable. Spacing should be used to make text easy to read, to associate similar content, to distinguish separate interface elements, and to guide the user's eye from one point to another.

Text spacing

Increasing the default text line spacing (or *leading*, from the strips of lead that printers used to insert between lines of type to increase space) in Flash will immediately make your site easier to read and will improve its appearance at the same time. If your lines are very long, you should increase line spacing even more. As a general rule, however, try to keep your line lengths to 70–80 characters per line. This is ideal for legibility.

Take a look at Figure 4-4. The text has a line length of approximately 100 characters, which isn't too bad and does seem to be pretty clean. However, when compared to Figure 4-5, which shows a text length of approximately 80 characters, it becomes evident that a shorter character count per line is more legible. By using the space more efficiently, I've made the content easier to read and more the central focus of the interface. It still isn't perfect though. Legibility could be further improved by increasing line spacing and padding.

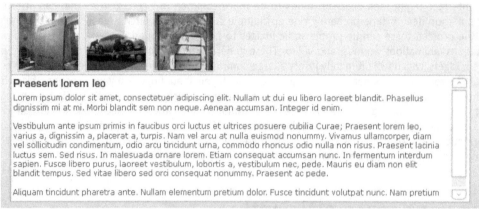

Figure 4-4. An example of a badly spaced interface with poor text spacing

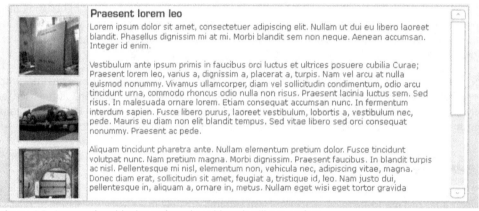

Figure 4-5. Improved positioning and spacing, although still not perfect

Interface padding

For the same reasons, legibility and appearance, padding is just as important as line spacing. An element's padding is the space between its border and the content of the element (almost like internal margins). In general, an unstyled but well-padded content area looks more appealing than a very well-designed area with no padding.

This applies to logos, navigation menus, and any other element of a site interface. Take a look at Figure 4-6 and notice how much the legibility and the appearance of the interface has improved. In comparison, the legibility and appearance of Figures 4-4 and Figure 4-5 suffer greatly.

There's a lot of personal judgment and "designer's eye" involved with choosing just how much padding and spacing to apply to different elements. You need to find the proper balance without overdoing it; you don't want to waste valuable space. Once you have chosen a specific spacing, you need to keep it consistent throughout your site.

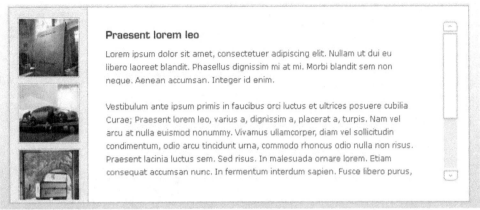

Praesent lorem leo

Lorem ipsum dolor sit amet, consectetuer adipiscing elit. Nullam ut dui eu libero laoreet blandit. Phasellus dignissim mi at mi. Morbi blandit sem non neque. Aenean accumsan. Integer id enim.

Vestibulum ante ipsum primis in faucibus orci luctus et ultrices posuere cubilia Curae; Praesent lorem leo, varius a, dignissim a, placerat a, turpis. Nam vel arcu at nulla euismod nonummy. Vivamus ullamcorper, diam vel sollicitudin condimentum, odio arcu tincidunt urna, commodo rhoncus odio nulla non risus. Praesent lacinia luctus sem. Sed risus. In malesuada ornare lorem. Etiam consequat accumsan nunc. In fermentum interdum sapien. Fusce libero purus,

Figure 4-6. Increased line spacing and padding drastically improve the overall appearance of this interface. This content has approximately 70 characters per line.

Uniformity

Now that you've developed your site prototype, you need to enforce consistency and uniformity. If your navigation menu appears on the left side of the interface, don't move it to the right side on another page! Header styles, text sizes, buttons, pull-down menus, check boxes, and other elements should look the same on each page. It's very important that users have a sense of familiarity when viewing subpages of your site; otherwise, they'll feel lost and they won't be able to intuitively navigate the site.

Be consistent with language too. If you have a "search" function on the top of your home page, don't change it to "find" on another page. If you use "submit" on a form button, don't change it to "send data now" on another form button. The same goes for sounds and animations. Use the same "loading" animation for your entire site and use the same "loading complete" sound effect. This can greatly aid usability by helping the user associate features and functions to graphics and sounds. It's also more professional and creates a unique identity for your site that your users will be able to easily recognize.

Summary

This chapter covered how to plan an interface design from the initial meeting with the client to presenting your concept. I didn't go into details regarding how to actually design and build your concept because that will be the focus of most of the remainder of the book. However, you should now have a good idea of what needs to be done outside of the design realm before hazardously jumping into the concept creation process without a plan.

By now, you also have enough information to prepare your own client survey, which you should always have with you when first meeting a client. The guidelines included in this chapter should generally be sufficient for most web design projects. However, do try to customize them as much as possible to fit your client. You don't want to give them the feeling that you're just using a bunch of template material. Ultimately, you want to make the client feel like you're the safe choice, so demonstrate that you really understand their company and their customers.

You should apply the same line of thought to your concept presentation. Don't show your client a bunch of generic templates! You need to customize your designs as much as possible to fit the research you've done and to really let them know that with you they will get the job done and achieve their goals. Also keep in mind that it's better to present one excellent, carefully planned out concept than ten random templates with no relevance to their company.

Chapter 5

VECTOR DRAWING AND EFFECTS IN FLASH AND ILLUSTRATOR

by Michael Kemper

When I began designing for the web, it was common for clients to make a request like "We are looking for that flat, clean, bold web style like you see in a Flash site . . .". Many didn't know it, but they were talking about vector-based graphics. Back then, I used to shudder at the appearance of poorly applied gradients, dithers, drop shadows, and bevels in any type of design. I still do. I suppose that most of the time it seems to me those are a visual "trick" instead of a solution to a design problem. Popular interface design has evolved, for better or for worse, into something very different over the years; and I've learned a thing or two as well. Now, it's common for interactive elements of an interface to appear raised and candy-like. I believe we really owe this to tasteful video game and broadcast television design and its heavy influence on interface design. And don't forget companies like Apple, well known for their advertising graphics and the design of OS X. Users have learned that this styling indicates on-screen interactive elements, and clients associate it with higher production quality, just like the interfaces for games people buy or the fancy OS on the new computer sitting in their home office. In this section, you'll learn vector-drawing techniques to improve your workflow and help you translate the next big thing from your head to the screen. Along the way you'll pick up some ideas on how to achieve a candy-like styling in preparation for a more in-depth Flash-based deconstruction on this technique in Chapter 7.

Pros and cons: Illustrator and Flash

The ability to utilize vector images is the primary reason for using Flash in an online environment. Vector graphics have many obvious advantages in Flash over bitmap graphics. First of all, vector graphics minimize your users' download time so that they can experience the design efficiently without having to wait for a large download. You can pack more graphics into your design by using vector images instead of bitmap images as well as minimize the user's download time. Also, using vector graphics will enhance your animation quality because it's less processor intensive for a computer to process tweening mathematically placed points of a vector shape (or anchor points) compared to thousands, and possibly hundreds of thousands, of pixels in a bitmap image. There are, of course, still many instances where you would consider using a bitmap to accomplish certain visual effects. But these key arguments for using vector images over bitmap images should be taken into consideration during the design phase.

Many designers prefer to design their interfaces outside of Flash and then import the graphics for several valid reasons, the predominant being because Flash simply isn't as good of a drawing tool as some of the alternatives, namely Adobe Illustrator. Can you achieve the same effects in Flash as in Illustrator? The answer is "yes." But it's my experience that Flash is a much more "clunky" application to draw in than Illustrator. And, of course, like many other designers with formal design education, I too learned how to draw in applications like Illustrator and Photoshop. So, naturally, those are more natural environments for me to design in.

Another good reason for designing graphics in these traditional programs and porting them over to Flash is retaining the ability to transfer the design, or elements of that design, to other media like video or print. This is something that is complicated when your original graphic assets are built in Flash. In today's business climate, it's more and more common for a company's identity to evolve from their web presence. Chances are if you design an interface for a company, your client will more than likely want to take the header or button styling, maybe even the way you treated the company's logo, and use it in print advertising or a video presentation. Having those assets as an EPS or AI format will save time for you when a client requests those assets in a usable format. It might even give you the opportunity to absorb part of the budget for that extended project since your client won't need its advertising agency to re-create it at an expensive hourly rate. So now that old saying about working smarter and not harder also applies to this instance of your client/designer relationship—assuming, of course, that you follow some of the technique tips in this chapter. Having your interface design in a more widely accepted format suitable for video and print could come in handy for your own self-promotion with formatted screenshots for a printed portfolio, online demo reel, or large-format award show ceremony presentation.

On the other hand, there are several good reasons to adapt certain aspects of your design workflow for Flash, especially with some of the new features that have been introduced in the latest version, Flash 8. For a few versions of Flash, designers have had the ability to use transparencies in gradients. This is easily replicated in Photoshop, but very difficult to represent accurately in Illustrator. Gradients with varying opacity can be invaluable to a designer if they're used tastefully. Now, you can even apply gradients to line strokes in Flash, whereas in Illustrator you would need to outline your stroke and then apply a gradient fill. This is a great way to achieve the finest line that fades to full transparency or transitions into another color entirely. Other effects such as nondestructive drop shadows and bevels are also available in this latest version of Flash, using the newly available filters. These effects are attainable in Illustrator, but I actually find that I get better results for them in Flash.

Still, when designing a vector-based design I find that Illustrator is the better design tool to begin with because of its ease of use. I typically use Flash as a production tool when preparing a design for development.

The main consideration for a designer when creating an interface should be to select an application and workflow that will best represent the final product and enhance his or her skill set the most. And every designer is different. So, to accommodate different preferences, I'll deconstruct examples in both Flash and Illustrator. Then I'll cover importing Illustrator graphics into Flash along with additional design production techniques unique to Flash. Also, for reference, you should know that the examples in this chapter are for real web projects, and the final designs can be viewed online at www.feedyourimage.com/AdvancedInterfaceDesign. You'll need to have basic knowledge of Flash and Adobe Illustrator to understand the step-by-step instructions for each example.

Making it pop

Thanks to nondestructive filters and the following workflow tips, giving elements of your interface design a sense of depth has become easier when using vector-based drawing tools. I achieve these effects by using a variety of drawing and coloring techniques, but the real "magic" starts with the application of gradients.

In Figure 5-1, I show the button style that will be established for many of the interactive elements of the example site. On the left you can see the vector lines and nodes that construct the graphic. To the right you can see the filled, final version.

Figure 5-1. Button style for interactive elements of the site, with the vector lines and nodes that construct the graphic on the left and the filled, final version on the right

Creating button graphics using Illustrator

First, we want to create the base shape of the button. For this design, we want the corners of the button to be rounded. Begin by selecting the Rectangle tool from the Tools palette. Click and hold your mouse on the tool. As you see in Figure 5-2, the tool expands to a secondary palette containing many alternative options for the Rectangle tool. The first option on the far left is the Standard Rectangle tool. You would use this for a common sharp-cornered rectangular shape. We want the second tool in this palette set: the Rounded Rectangle tool. Roll your mouse over the Rounded Rectangle tool and release to select it. As illustrated in Figure 5-2, other items of the Tools palette we'll be using in this section include the Selection

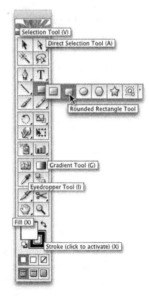

Figure 5-2. The Adobe Illustrator Tools palette with the Rectangle tool selected and its palette expanded, and the Rounded Rectangle Tool option highlighted

and Direct Selection arrow tools along the top of the window; the Gradient, Pen, and Eyedropper tools; and the fill and stroke options along the bottom. Notice in Illustrator that when you hover your mouse over each tool in this window, a tooltip appears for an instant to give you a hint at what you're about to select with its corresponding keyboard shortcut. Also, if you roll your mouse all the way over to the left of the expanded palette, you can select the Tear Off option for this tool and leave this palette permanently exposed.

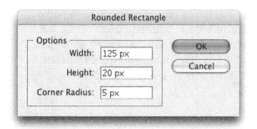

Figure 5-3. The Rounded Rectangle Options window allows you to enter exact measurements for the width, height, and corner circumference of a rectangle.

By clicking the canvas once, you'll be prompted by the Options window for the Rounded Rectangle tool, as shown in Figure 5-3. Here you can specify the width, height, and corner radius of the button shape. In this example, we want the width to be 125 pixels (125 px), the height to be 20 pixels, and the corner radius to be 5 pixels. Click OK to draw the shape. An alternative way to draw a rectangle with or without a corner radius is to simply click and drag to draw the shape directly onto the canvas—but you won't get the flexibility of defining the radius of the corners unless you activate the Options window as described. For future reference: until you change these options for this specific tool, the default corner radius will remain the last measurement you entered into this Options window.

Next, we want to fill and specify the stroke for the button shape. Open the Gradient palette, shown on the left in Figure 5-4, by selecting Window ➤ Gradients (or press F9 on your keyboard). Also open the Color palette, shown on the right in Figure 5-4, by selecting Window ➤ Color (or press F6 on your keyboard). Select the button shape using the Filled Arrow tool located along the top of the Tools palette in the far-left corner (refer back to Figure 5-2). In the Gradient window, click your mouse along the bottom of the gradient preview to create more pointers of fill color. In my example I only use three pointers, which you can see in the bottom of Figure 5-4. Select Linear from the Type drop-down menu in the Gradient window. You should notice that your shape is now filled with the gradient you specify; and the fill of your color window also displays the gradient in the foreground color preview. The applied stroke color appears in the background color preview.

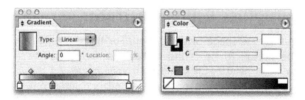

Figure 5-4. The Gradients palette and the Color palette

The default for a linear-type gradient on any object in Illustrator is a horizontal gradation fill. To modify your gradient to be vertical, start by selecting the object you want to change using your Selection tool and then select the Gradient tool from the Tools palette (refer back to Figure 5-2). Next, click and drag the Gradient tool vertically over the shape. As you can see in Figure 5-5, the gradient supplies a fill inside your object along the path of your drag.

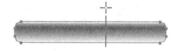

Figure 5-5. The Gradient tool being applied vertically to our button shape from bottom to top

Now you need to specify the colors of your gradient fill. Simply select the pointers along the bottom of the gradient preview inside the Gradients palette (refer back to Figure 5-4). Notice in Figure 5-6 that the fill preview inside the Color palette displays the selected color of the gradient arrow. I am showing the center color of the gradient for the current example as being Red: 102, Green: 102; Blue: 102. You can see that the end colors of my gradient are white, or Red: 255, Green: 255, Blue: 255, respectively.

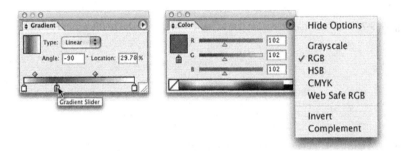

Figure 5-6. The Color palette in Illustrator allows you to view your colors in many different ways.

You can view your colors in many different ways through Illustrator's Color palette. For example, if I were to view the currently selected color as a plain grayscale, it would be K: 60%. I typically use the HSB option to explore variations of a color once I have my design's overall color selections locked down.

Next we want to create a shape along the top of our button to emulate a glossy shine. First we want to reveal three new palettes: select Window ➤ Transparency (or press Shift+F10 on your keyboard); select Window ➤ Pathfinder (or press Shift+F9 on your keyboard); again, select Window ➤ Align (or press Shift+F7 on your keyboard). You should see the following three Illustrator palette windows, shown in Figure 5-7 from left to right, adorning your screen:

- **Transparency**: Lets you manipulate the opacity of one shape over another as well as apply layer filters similar to Photoshop layer effects
- **Pathfinder**: Allows you to subtract and combine overlapping shapes in every way possible
- **Align**: Gives you the ability to exactly and quickly align multiple shapes

Next, select the Ellipse tool located to the right of the Rounded Rectangle tool and draw an oval over the button shape. Leave the oval selected and give it a 60% opacity by selecting the Opacity field in the Transparency palette and typing 60; then click the oval to apply this setting, as shown in Figure 5-8. If you would like a real time preview of the oval becoming incrementally transparent as you vary the Opacity setting, you could alternatively click the arrow next to the Opacity field in the Transparency palette and slide the pointer until the Opacity field says 60% to achieve the same result (see Figure 5-7).

Figure 5-7. Illustrator palettes from left to right: Transparency, Pathfinder, and Align

Figure 5-8. A selected oval with 60% opacity overlapping a button shape

Our next step is to subtract the usable portion of the oval shape from the rest of the oval. To do this, we must start by duplicating the button shape. Grab the Selection tool from the Tools palette and then use it to select the button shape. Hold down the Option key on your keyboard, then click and drag the selected shape to a new position to the right of your existing button shape on your canvas. Release your mouse and then release the Option key. Now you'll see a duplication of the button shape without the overlapping oval. Select the two original shapes by holding down the Shift key and clicking each shape once. In the Pathfinder palette, select Divide—this is the far-left option in the bottom row of the Pathfinder palette (refer back to Figure 5-7). You should notice a slight shift in the contour of your selected shapes indicating they are now broken apart into multiple pieces. Illustrator automatically groups items after a Pathfinder palette option has been applied to them. Ungroup the selected shapes by pressing Ctrl+Shift+G (Cmd+Shift+G on a Mac, where Cmd refers to the Command key, or the key with an symbol), or by selecting Object ➤ Ungroup. Click the background of your canvas to deselect everything. Now select the overlapping "highlight" shape of the oval you just applied the Pathfinder option to and, while holding down the Shift key on your keyboard, click the original button shape to the right. In the Align menu select the Vertical Align Top and then Horizontal Align Center options, the latter of which you can see in Figure 5-9. Use the arrow keys on your keyboard to bump the newly aligned shapes free and clear of your Pathfinder leftovers. Delete the leftovers.

Figure 5-9. Horizontally aligning the center of the selected overlapping highlight shape with the button shape using the Align palette

Now it's time to add the drop shadow. Note that you might want to wait to add this after importing the button into Flash; creating one at this point is strictly to demonstrate the shadow for design purposes. Start by selecting both the button shape and the reflection shape by clicking them while holding down the Shift key on your keyboard (you can also click and drag over both shapes, then release your mouse to select them both). Group the shapes together so that the drop shadow will be applied to them as a group instead of each shape individually by selecting Object ➤ Group (or pressing Ctrl+G, or Cmd+G on a Mac). Then choose Effect ➤ Stylize ➤ Drop Shadow and the Drop Shadow window, shown in Figure 5-10, will appear. I prefer subtle drop shadows so the setting for this button will have an opacity of 20% and a blur of 1 pixel (1 px). The Preview check box is deselected by default, so if you want to see your drop shadow applied in real time, you need to check this box before fiddling with the options.

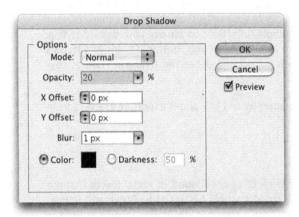

Figure 5-10. The Drop Shadow Effect window allows you to customize every aspect of a drop shadow.

You can tweak the drop shadow after applying it by selecting Window ➤ Appearance (or pressing Shift+F9 on your keyboard) to view the Appearance palette. Simply select the shape you wish to modify and then double-click the Drop Shadow button in the Appearance palette, shown in Figure 5-11, to relaunch the Drop Shadow Effects window. Before porting all of my graphics over to Flash, I usually strip drop-shadow effects from all of my shapes in Illustrator because the nondestructive nature of this effect doesn't translate nicely through the exporting/importing process. Flash usually imports complex Illustrator shapes like drop shadows as bitmaps. This complicates the workflow because then you have to redraw the shape in Flash and delete the bitmap. No big deal if it's just one item. But this can be a timely mistake if you have multiple items with drop shadows applied to them from Illustrator. You can eliminate drop shadows by selecting the objects that contain them and then dragging the effect to the garbage icon in the Appearance palette.

Figure 5-11. The Appearance palette shows you all the nondestructive effects applied to shapes.

The last graphical touch you can make to the button shape in Illustrator is applying a color stroke to its contour. Illustrator applies a default black stroke to freshly drawn shapes. Select Window ➤ Stroke (or press F10 on your keyboard) and the Stroke palette will appear on your screen, as you see in Figure 5-12. Select the Direct Selection tool from your Tools palette (refer back to Figure 5-2) so you can select the button shape without selecting the reflection shape (since they are now grouped). Click the button shape to select it and in the Stroke palette type .25 in the Weight field and click your shape to apply the stroke. (Other options in this palette include rounding ends and corners as well as defining dashed lines.) You can vary the color of your stroke by either double-clicking the stroke preview along the bottom of the Tools palette or selecting the stroke preview in the Color palette and using the sliders along the right to manipulate colors, as shown in Figure 5-13. Note that I am using a black RGB stroke on my button example.

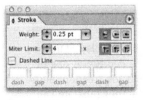

Figure 5-12. You can vary the line weight for a selected stroke using the Stroke palette.

Figure 5-13. It's easy to manipulate colors for strokes on shapes using the Color palette—it's just like manipulating colors for shape fills.

Now add your label text by using the Character and Paragraph palettes, which you display by selecting Window ➤ Type ➤ Character (or pressing Ctrl+T, or Cmd+T on a Mac) and Window ➤ Type ➤ Paragraph (or pressing Shift+Ctrl+T, or Shift+Cmd+T on a Mac). Type the label, and you're finished with your glossy vector button! Keep in mind that you can vary this styling dramatically by manipulating the fill using the Gradient and Color palettes. Make it lit from above or below, tweak the opacity of your reflection, change the shape of your reflection, or add multiple reflections to achieve your desired styling. You might even want to build all of your button designs and layouts in Illustrator and then import and tweak the styling in Flash as covered in Chapter 7.

Save your button so that you can use it later in this chapter when I talk about exporting graphics from Illustrator and importing them into Flash.

Creating inlays using Illustrator

When some of you hear the word "inlay," you might think of colored wood or metal pieces that are inserted into the veneer in furniture. The art of inlay could possibly be traced to Greek and Roman mosaics or earlier. Beginning in the 16th century, inlays were a common decorative technique used in fine furniture and woodwork. Furniture is still made with veneer and inlays to this day. And it seems that once again new combinations of old ideas are bridging the gap between the physical and digital world with this type of styling. There are as many variations for digital inlays as there are real life influences to draw from—needless to say it far too many to count. Figure 5-14 shows an example inlay for a design I did for Find Furniture's website; the contour of the entire homepage was offset 4 pixels to create a framing effect and add depth to the design. Vector inlays can add form and function to your design work when a simple line or color variation isn't enough. Next you'll see techniques for creating this effect in Illustrator.

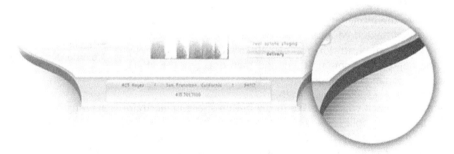

Figure 5-14. A slightly raised inlay for the Find Furniture website

To create an inlay in illustrator, we first want to define a shape for the contour of our inlay. Start by selecting the Pen tool from the Tools palette. as I demonstrate in Figure 5-15. The Pen tool is one of the most important tools in any vector drawing program, as it provides you with the freedom and structure needed to translate your ideas to the digital canvas. Illustrator gives you four separate Pen tools. Let's take closer look at these tools before we actually create the inlay contour. Going from left to right in the Pen Tool palette:

- The basic Pen tool is for general drawing purposes. Use this tool to plot anchor points that create lines.

- The Add Anchor Point tool lets you add additional individual anchor points to vector lines.

- The Delete Anchor Point tool allows you to eliminate anchors from a line without breaking the line's path.

- The Convert Anchor Point tool lets you reset the nodes of an anchor point (those little blue pixels attached by a line that intersects the anchor point) so the curvature of the line can easily be redefined without having to redraw the shape.

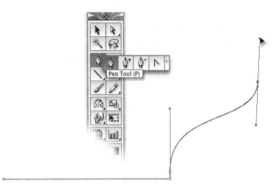

Figure 5-15. Using the Pen tool to draw the frame of our site

The Pen tools in Illustrator are far more flexible to use than the Pen tool in Flash, but you can achieve similar results from either. When you use the Pen tool in Illustrator, you can convert the pen icon on your mouse to a cross-hair by having your Caps Lock feature turned on. This helps you see exactly where you want to click when drawing lines.

Now that you know a bit about the Illustrator Pen tools, draw the contour of the shape you wish to inlay. When drawing with a Pen tool, the most important thing to do is click and drag the tool in the direction you want your line to go. This technique will plot an anchor point and stretch out the nodes in the proper direction. Stay one or two steps ahead of your clicks in your head and plot your anchor points where you anticipate corners or curves.

When you draw your shape, for this example, make sure the ends of your lines are closed so that there are no loose end points, as shown in Figure 5-16. Next, we want to offset the path of the shape. Once you have your shape drawn, select the shape with your Selection tool, and then choose Object ➤ Path ➤ Offset Path. For finer inlays with thin line work (0.25 pt), I would offset the path only -1 or -2 pixels in the Offset field. For this example, you want a pretty large "gutter," so make the offset -4 pixels. Click

OK. Now you can see that your line has been duplicated within itself, as shown in Figure 5-17. You can also make your offset a positive number if you want to create a line outside the contour of your shape. Make sure that your inner shape is on top of the outer shape by selecting it with the Selection tool and choosing Object ➤ Arrange ➤ Bring To Front.

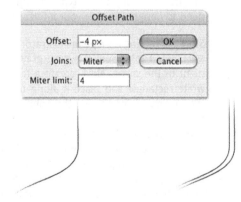

Figure 5-17. On the left, you see an example of a shapes contour before you apply an offset path. On the right, the same shape has an offset path of –4 applied to it.

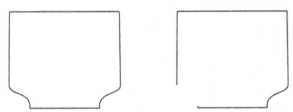

Figure 5-16. On the left is a closed shape. On the right is an open shape.

Next you want to apply some coloring to imply depth, as shown in Figure 5-18. I typically fill the outer shape with a subtle gradient and the inner shape with a solid color or another gradient similar to the first one, but with a slightly different color or direction. I also generally apply a subtle drop shadow to the inner shape to achieve the illusion of more height.

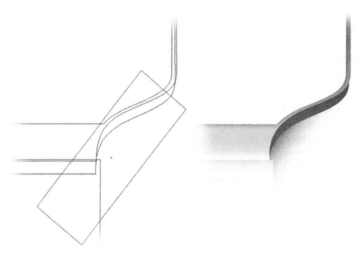

Figure 5-18. The basic vector outlines of my shapes appear on the left with gradient and bevel styling applied to the same shapes on the right.

Creating indents using Illustrator

Another easy way to imply depth in your vector design work is to use indents. This effect resembles the fine bevels along the spine of a CD case or book. They are very subtle variations in the surface of manufactured objects. Expressing these types of surface variations in an interface provides opportunities for text boxes, image placement, or just about any other type of content you need to design a spot in your interface for.

Start by creating a shape in Illustrator using the Rectangle tool. Apply a vertical grayscale gradient to the shape. Next, create a transparent white rectangle and place it along the top of the original shape to give the impression of a fine glossy surface to the shape. In Figure 5-19, you can see how I have created a rectangle on the right and applied the grayscale gradient to it in the Gradients palette. There is also another white rectangle along the top of the base rectangle that has opacity of 20% as you can see by the Transparency.

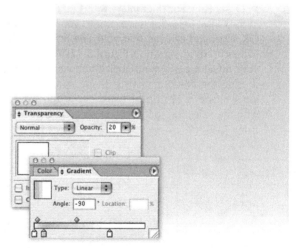

Figure 5-19. Creating a rectangle with applied grayscale gradient and placing a white rectangle along the top of it that has an opacity of 20%

Next, use the Pen tool to create parallel white and gray lines over the rectangles you've just created. For darker lines, use a fine line (0.25 px) and for lighter lines use a standard line (1 px). In Figure 5-20, observe how the indent lines are applied to the rectangles. Tight proximity and line weight make or break this technique. Notice the varying line weights for lighter and darker lines in the detail bubble.

Figure 5-20. Applying indent lines to the rectangles

To further the effect of independent surfaces, we need to imply slightly different surface planes for each panel. To achieve this styling, draw additional rectangles inside each sector of your image. Select those new rectangles and fill them with a black-to-white gradient. In the Transparent palette, vary the opacity of your new rectangles to the styling that best suits your needs, as shown in Figure 5-21. You can see how visually defining different planes on your surface gives an enhanced indented effect. In this example, I use a black-to-white gradient in the transparent rectangles because I am working in grayscale. Their opacity is set to 20%. If you use a different color palette, then you probably want to use a variation of the colors you applied to the main surface. In the detail bubble, you can see that I drew the transparent rectangles to fit flush within the line work of the indent.

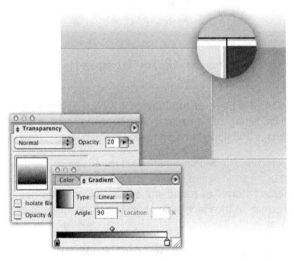

Figure 5-21. Transparency and gradient applied to outer frame and a detail of line work indents

Technical drawing in Illustrator

One of the benefits to using Illustrator for your initial design and production before moving over to Flash is the flexibility you have for drawing complex vector images very quickly. By using a combination of the tools you've encountered so far along with a couple of improvised tricks, you can create very complex vector graphics in Illustrator and then easily import them into Flash.

Photo illustration using Illustrator

It's common for designers to import bitmaps into Flash and utilize the trace bitmap feature to accomplish vector traces of complex images. This technique generally creates additional nodes and more than likely won't give you the clean even lines you'll be able to draw in Illustrator and then import later. The examples in Figure 5-22 demonstrate the problem. On the left appears an illustration imported from an Illustrator file, and on the right appears the trace bitmap version. Clearly there are a lot more nodes resulting from the trace bitmap technique, as well as extreme loss of contour detail. Not only will creating graphics first in Illustrator conserve file size over the trace bitmap feature in Flash because of an optimized node count, but doing so will also give you more flexibility to recolor the illustration in Flash after the import.

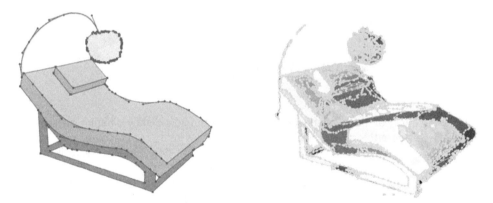

Figure 5-22. On the left you can see an illustration imported from an Illustrator file compared to a trace bitmap version on the right.

In this example, I'll walk you through an illustration of a piece of furniture that I'll use on the Find Furniture website. You can follow along by downloading this image at www.feedyourimage.com/AdvancedInterfaceDesign, or choose your own image and apply similar drawing techniques.

Begin by importing the image into Illustrator by selecting File ➤ Place and select the image you wish to trace for your illustration; in my example, I am using an image of a chair that will appear on a furniture website, which I chose because it's the "perfect storm" of round and angular objects and has perspective. Make sure you enable All Readable Formats in the Place dialog box. Select the image and click OK. You'll see your image placed on the canvas inside illustrator.

Now that you have you photo in Illustrator, you're going to "lock" it so you don't accidentally move the image while you're tracing it. Select Window ➤ Layers from the menu options. Illustrator uses layers in much the same way Flash and Photoshop use them. Simply click the hollow box beside the eye icon in the Layers palette to lock the layer the image was imported on. A small lock icon will appear indicating that you may not move or adjust the layer in any way, as shown in Figure 5-23. Next, create a new layer to draw on by selecting the Create New Layer icon (indicated by a page icon) along the bottom of the Layers palette, again shown in Figure 5-23.

Figure 5-23. The image of the chair I use to create my illustration on a locked layer

Select the Pen tool from the Tools palette and begin tracing the contour of the chair, as shown in Figure 5-24. The best way to do this is to make sure you don't have a fill color specified so that you can "see through" the shape you're drawing. You can also zoom in and out quickly by pressing Cmd++ (plus sign) or Cmd+– (minus sign) on your keyboard. Move about the canvas easily without leaving the Pen tool by pressing the spacebar to get the Grabber tool—then click and drag to move your view of the canvas.

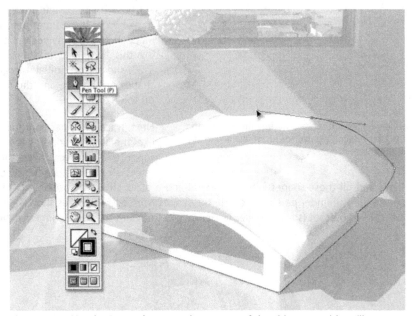

Figure 5-24. Use the Pen tool to trace the contour of the object you wish to illustrate.

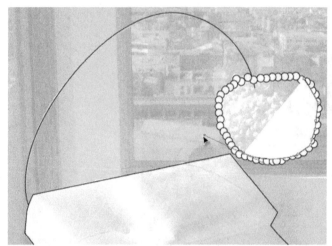

Figure 5-25. The cluster of little circles along the countour of the pillow and a new shape being drawn inside the cluster

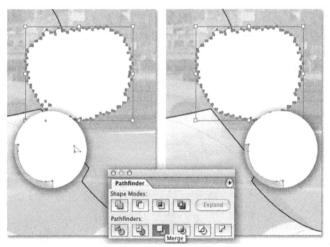

Figure 5-26. The preview on the left is after the first merge, and the preview on the right is after refilling the entire cluster again with all white and merging it once more.

For the long, skinny pole that comes out of the top, use a 1-pt stroke. For the pillow outline on the end of the pole, create one tiny circle using the Ellipse tool. Then, using the Selection tool, hold down the Option key on your keyboard and drag the little circle incrementally around the contour of the floating pillow. It's important that the edge of each little circle slightly overlaps the one before it, since we'll be using the Pathfinder palette to combine them later. Now using the Pen tool again, draw a shape inside your cluster of little circles, as shown in Figure 5-25. Again, it's important that the contour of this new shape overlaps all of the little circles.

Now select Window ➤ Pathfinder to view the Pathfinder palette. Select all of the little circles in your cluster and also select the new shape in the center by clicking your mouse and dragging over the entire area. Be careful to ONLY select the images over the pillow area. Once they are selected, click the Merge icon in the Pathfinder palette to join all of the pillow shapes together. You may need to fill the cluster with color and merge the whole thing two or three times before you eliminate all of the stray vectors created during this technique in the shape. Figure 5-26 shows the initial merging of the shapes on the left, and the final merging on the right.

Next, trace the inner contour of the chair like the hollow space between the leg supports. Once you have those traced, select all of the shapes except the pole and the pillow, and fill those shapes with a white fill and a black stroke by pressing D on your keyboard. Then use the Pathfinder palette to divide the shapes from each other, as shown in Figure 5-27. Use the Direct Selection tool (shown earlier in Figure 5-2) to delete the useless inner shapes.

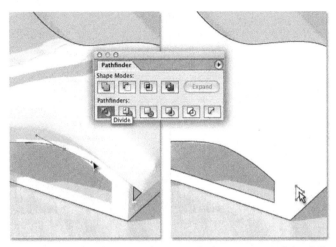

Figure 5-27. Using the Pen tool to trace the inner contour of the chair (left) and filling with a white fill and a black stroke (right)

Now trace the rest of the contours of the image, such as the edges of the cushions. As you draw lines along the image, make sure the ends of your new lines exceed the edges of the original shape, since we'll be using Divide to separate each interior shape into its own graphic for coloring purposes (see Figure 5-28).

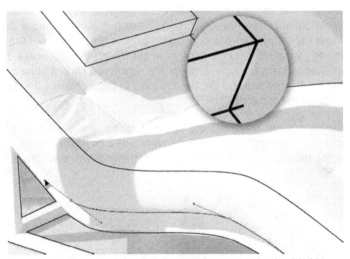

Figure 5-28. The rest of the chair lines getting traced; the detail bubble shows how careful I am to overlap the original shape with my new lines.

Select all of your new lines and the original chair shape, except the pole line and the pillow cluster. Once all of the shapes and lines are selected, choose Divide in the Pathfinder palette. Now, all of the different lines that were drawn over the chair have sliced up the main chair shape, leaving many graphics representing the different planes of the object. Once again, use the Direct Selection tool (shown earlier in Figure 5-2) to delete all of the unnecessary shapes, as shown in Figure 5-29. You might notice some inaccuracies around the illustration, but deleting anchor points with the Delete Anchor Point tool easily eliminates undesirable curves and angles.

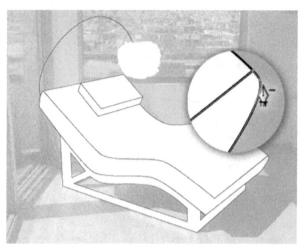

Figure 5-29. The clean vector illustration of the chair. Using the Pen tools like the Delete Anchor Point tool is the best way to eliminate extra anchor points.

And finally, we want to color the illustration using colors from the actual photo. Select the illustration, including the pole and the pillow cluster, using the Selection tool, and move the entire illustration so that you have the original image and the vector drawing in clear sight. You may need to zoom out to see both at the same time. Then, select the Eyedropper tool from the Tools palette (refer back to Figure 5-2), and toggle the tool by pressing Ctrl/Cmd on your keyboard to bring up the Direct Selection tool. While holding down the Ctrl/Cmd key, select a plane from the illustration and then release the Ctrl/Cmd key on your keyboard to toggle back to the Eyedropper tool. Make a selection from the same region you selected on the illustration but from the photo image. Notice the selected graphic on the illustration turns the same color as the region you clicked using the Eyedropper tool. Continue using the Eyedropper tool and the Ctrl/Cmd key to finish coloring the illustration until all of the shapes and lines are the correct color.

Figure 5-30 shows the original image and the new illustration. The illustration matches the photo's proportions exactly. This illustration could even be taken one step further by depicting the dimples in the upholstery or the shadows created by the light from the windows, even the seams at the joints of the exposed frame.

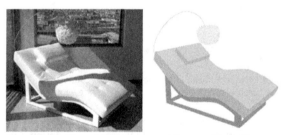

Figure 5-30. The original image, and the new illustration

Now that we have a clean vector illustration of the chair, once we import it into Flash, there are all kinds of cool things we could do with it. For example, imagine allowing the user to instantly change frame and fabric color before ordering the piece without having to load a large bitmap every time.

Interface layout design in Illustrator

Every interface design I create begins in Illustrator not only because it's an easy environment for me to draw in, but also because my interfaces tend to be complex experiences that need to be designed quickly without development implications. As is the nature with most Flash interfaces, they require quickly designing multiple screens, masked bitmap images, transitions, detailed icon work, and multiple navigation sets. Illustrator facilitates all of these requirements. Designers can quickly create, duplicate, and tweak visual solutions in Illustrator without having to plan for implementation, whereas when designing in Flash you can easily run into problems with modifying nested movie clips. Not only are the interfaces complex, but the other stakeholders and their requests are, too. Designers can quickly duplicate an entire interface design and try a variation, all within the same Illustrator file, without destroying the master or having to manage multiple design files. I often only have to keep a single Illustrator file per design phase when working in a client scenario. Plus Illustrator allows me to generate high-quality printouts on the fly for marking up at team meetings or as leave-behinds at client meetings.

Figure 5-31 shows an example of how I used Illustrator to design one screen and duplicate it to serve as a template for other pages on the project, all in the same Illustrator file. This workflow helps me keep continuity across different screens of the same project and allows me to keep all of my designs in a single file. And it's easy to keep track of and back up on my local network server.

Figure 5-31. Designing one screen and duplicating it to use as a template for other pages on the project, all in the same Illustrator file

Moving from Illustrator to Flash

Once you're done with your design in Illustrator, you can export your design from Illustrator in SWF format. This makes it very simple to import your graphics into Flash and begin developing the interface further using animation and ActionScript. This transition from Illustrator to Flash also provides you with a clean vector archive of the design prior to development.

Exporting SWF graphics from Illustrator

In Illustrator, open the file for the button we designed at the beginning of this chapter. Before exporting it, we need to remove the drop shadow we applied. This isn't critical, but if you export a graphic out of Illustrator with nondestructive effects applied to it like drop shadows, that particular graphic will most likely be converted to a bitmap when you import the graphic into Flash. If you need to tweak the colors or modify that graphic later in your development process, having it as a bitmap will make it more difficult than it needs to be.

To begin, select File ➤ Export from the options menu. The Export window, shown in Figure 5-32, will appear. Through this window, you can export your Illustrator graphics as just about any format available, from AutoCad Drawing (DWG) formats to Macromedia Flash (SWF). Name your button and select the Macromedia Flash (swf) format from the drop-down menu. Click Export to continue.

Figure 5-32. The Export dialog window in Illustrator

Next you'll see the formatting options specific to the Flash (SWF) format, as shown in Figure 5-33. You have available a plethora of different combinations for exporting using the SWF format out of Illustrator (see Figure 5-34):

- **AI File to SWF File**: This is the default option and it's the one I always use. With this option, all of your graphics will appear on a single frame on the timeline. I prefer this option because when I export a group of graphics or even an entire interface design from Illustrator, the layout stays intact when I import them to the stage in Flash. My results vary with regard to keeping everything it its place when I use the other options from this drop-down menu.

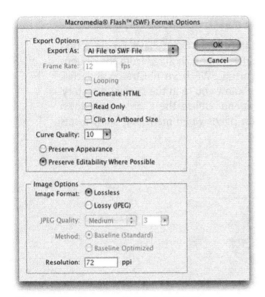

Figure 5-33. Macromedia Flash (SWF) Format Options window in Illustrator

- **AI Layers to SWF Frames:** If you wanted to create a frame-by-frame vector animation in Illustrator, you would create each frame of the animated sequence on an individual layer in Illustrator. In the Macromedia Flash (SWF) Format Options window, you would then select AI Layers to SWF Frames. This would place each AI layer onto an individual frame on the same layer in Flash. I find that the default 12 Frames Per Second (fps) is a good choice for this technique, because I end up tweaking the time in Flash later anyway.

- **AI Layers to SWF Files:** This option gives you the flexibility of separating each of your Illustrator layers into individual SWFs. This might be convenient if you prefer to build a library of individual vector graphics to use as you design in Flash. In Illustrator, to place ungrouped graphics onto individual layers, select Release to Layers in the Layers options menu, shown in Figure 5-35. When using the Release to Layers (Sequence) option, I get duplicate layers, which makes importing graphics into Flash overly complicated. Therefore, I always choose Release to Layers (Build) when using this technique because I get more consistent results with the export/import process.

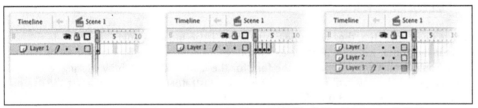

Figure 5-34. The results of choosing the options AI File to SWF File (left), AI Layers to SWF Frames (middle), and AI Layers to SWF Files (right)

For this example, use the default AI File to SWF File option; I tend to rely on this option for instances when I've got a relatively basic graphic and I prefer to animate my design in Flash. You want to export the highest Curve Quality (10) because you can minimize anchor points later in Flash to preserve file size if need be. You also want to make sure the default Preserve Editability Where Possible option is selected, as shown earlier in Figure 5-33; otherwise you'll get a mish-mash of bitmaps and masks when you import the graphics into Flash. Click OK.

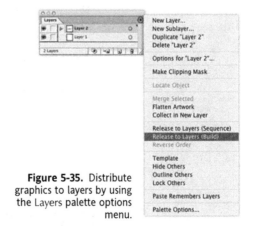

Figure 5-35. Distribute graphics to layers by using the Layers palette options menu.

89

Importing SWF graphics created in Illustrator

Now you have a SWF file on your computer ready to import into Flash. Open Flash, create a new Flash file (Ctrl+N, or Cmd+N on a Mac), and select File ➤ Import ➤ Import To Stage from the options menu (or press Ctrl+R, or Cmd+R on a Mac). Find your exported SWF from Illustrator and click Import, as shown in Figure 5-36. If you can't see the file and you know you're in the correct directory, make sure All Formats is selected in the Enable drop-down menu. Utilize the Enable drop-down menu to sort file formats in the Import dialog window's preview panes when managing many assets in the same directory.

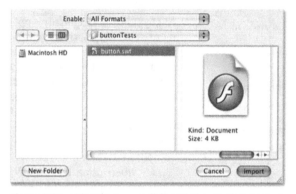

Figure 5-36. Using the Import dialog window in Flash to find Illustrator SWFs and selecting them for import

Once the graphics have been imported, they will appear on a single layer and on a single key frame in Flash just as they were in Illustrator, with one possible exception regarding the font of the button label text (see Figure 5-37). You'll probably have to reset the font for the label text in Flash by clicking to select the label text using the Selection tool (just as you would in Illustrator) and breaking apart the grouped text by pressing Ctrl+B, or Cmd+B on a Mac. Next, in the Property inspector, notice that the classification given to the text object has changed from Group to Static Text and the font name is in parentheses. Select the original font from the Font drop-down menu in the Property inspector.

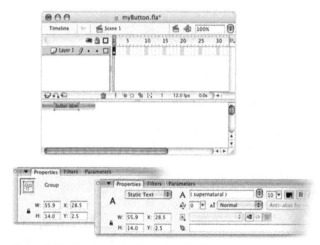

Figure 5-37. Now the graphics created in Illustrator are intact on the stage in Flash.

Look at your Library palette in Flash and notice that there has been a symbol created for you called Symbol 1, as you can see in Figure 5-38. This graphic is the image we created in Illustrator to emulate a glossy shine styling on the button. It was automatically made a library symbol to preserve its coloring and opacity because we selected Preserve Editability Where Possible in the Macromedia Flash (SWF) Format Options (refer back to Figure 5-33) in Illustrator. Notice how the registration mark for our Symbol 1 graphic is top left by default—this is the preferred handling for most graphics by many Flash programmers. You can adjust the coloring and opacity using the Color drop-down menu in the Property inspector. This is the typical result when importing vector graphics from Illustrator that have less than 100% opacity. I always rename these items in my Library palette once everything has been imported into Flash to keep them organized; you can double-click the text area of a library item to rename your symbol. When you import more complex graphics from Illustrator into Flash using this technique, you'll find that items grouped in Illustrator before your export remain grouped in Flash. I don't know if these results are serendipitous or intentional on the part of Adobe or Macromedia prior to their merger, but either way I find them very helpful.

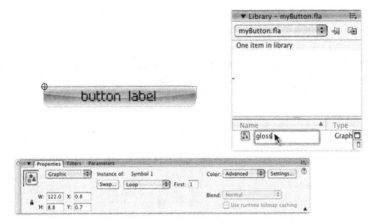

Figure 5-38. A preview of the selected Symbol 1 flanked by the Library palette on the right and the Property inspector below

Next, select all of the graphics on the stage and press F8 on your keyboard to turn them into a symbol—set the type as Movie Clip, and the registration point as top left, as shown in Figure 5-39. Notice that before the graphics are turned into a symbol that the Property inspector recognizes them as a mixed group of graphics, and afterward they are known as a movie clip. Name the symbol glossyButton. From a design perspective, this will allow you to apply nondestructive filters and effects to the entire group. From a development perspective, this allows you to reference the entire group using ActionScript. I make most of my instances movie clips with a registration mark at the top left because it gives me the most flexibility when I begin creating my ActionScript.

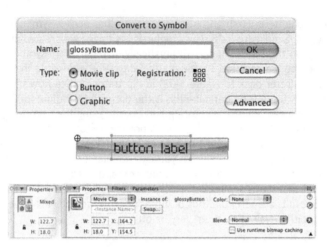

Figure 5-39. Selecting all the button graphics and turning them into a single movie clip instance in Flash

Apply a drop shadow to glossyButton in the Filers tab of the Property Inspector. I generally apply very subtle filters to Flash instances to maintain sophisticated styling, as you see in Figure 5-40. Notice the preview in Flash makes it appear blurry (left), but when it's exported as a SWF, the final product looks very crisp (right).

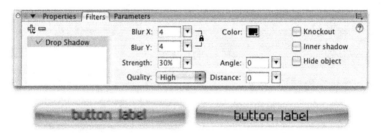

Figure 5-40. Applying a drop shadow filter to the glossyButton instance

Summary

Using the techniques in this chapter, you can expand the breadth of your vector drawing capabilities for interface design to include Adobe Illustrator. We reviewed how combining the power of Illustrator with Flash increases production speed and design flexibility. These techniques include a workflow for creating simple and complex vector graphics and using them in Flash, while reserving the flexibility to keep the original production file in a more widely accepted format. You can even design entire animated sequences and interfaces with the ease of use provided by Illustrator and import them into Flash using the Macromedia Flash (SWF) Format Options dialog window.

Now that you've completed this chapter, you've learned the following lessons:

- Vector graphics have a considerably lower file size than bitmap or raster graphics. Using vector-based graphics in your Flash design work wherever possible instead of bitmap graphics will produce quicker download times when a user is visiting the interface you created. Vector-based graphics will also animate smoother when compared to raster images.

- Flash is a valid drawing tool with many new features to enhance a designer's workflow. Combining those features in Flash with the flexibility and drawing capabilities in Adobe Illustrator increases a designer's productivity along with his or her skill set.

- You can quickly create and duplicate entire interface designs and try variations in Illustrator without having to keep track of multiple files.

- Designers can easily create frame-by-frame storyboards in Illustrator and export them as SWF sequences to use in Flash.

- Exporting SWF graphics from Illustrator into Flash facilitates your design production workflow by automatically creating library items out of complex vector shapes and preserving advanced color treatments like gradients and opacity.

- Flash and Illustrator are both vector-based programs, so many of the tools in Flash and Illustrator are very similar—even to the point of sharing the same keyboard shortcut commands. This maximizes a designer's efficiency when moving between programs.

Chapter 6

UNDERSTANDING THE TIMELINE AND LAYERS

by Brian Monnone

Often while I'm working with Flash, a creative director or account executive looks over my shoulder and says, "How can you tell where anything is? You have so many layers and objects, I don't see how you do it!" There is no secret to my workflow. It really does come down to how I structure my timeline and layers. I just stay organized and use my layers wisely. Now, you will, too.

All too often, layers are not something designers consider an actual tool. Some might believe that while designing in Flash, the timeline and its layers are really not that important and cannot add value to the finished art. You'll soon discover there is nothing further from the truth.

Layers are truly multifaceted. They perform several completely different functions. As well being essential in the design of complicated objects, they are also needed when you're using guides or masks. You can also use layers as a visual reference to find animations while you're developing applications. Flash has the ability to create up to 16,000 layers (although I've never seen a project use anywhere near that many), and it provides a way to organize them in an efficient manner to increase workflow and more important, productivity.

In this chapter, you'll explore all aspects of the often-overlooked subject of the timeline and its layers to see how you can get the most out of them.

Anatomy of the timeline

First and foremost, you need to get familiar with all aspects of the timeline before you can fully realize its potential. The timeline consists of many elements, some of which you will use more often than others.

Figure 6-1 shows a timeline window with many different elements labeled with numbers. Here's the key, along with a description of each item:

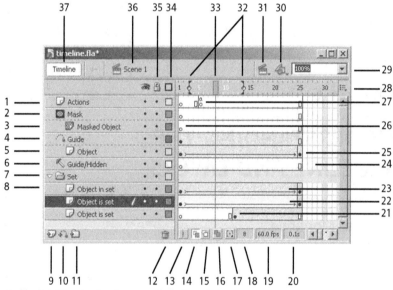

Figure 6-1. The timeline has a vast number of elements.

1. **Standard layer:** It's good practice to place all the ActionScript here in the topmost layer. I name this standard layer Actions. This makes the debugging process manageable. If you are working on the project with other Flash developers, it makes it easy for them to follow and locate your code. To create a new standard layer, click the Insert Layer button (9).

> The absolute best way to manage ActionScript is to create an included .as file. This is a file that includes only the ActionScript, much like a text document. In the .fla you are working with, you will need to link to this .as file with something like #include main.as. Main.as would be the file name for the ActionScript file. This feature is available only in the Pro version of Flash 8.

2. **Mask layer:** This type of layer makes is easy to create a quick mask to reveal only certain portions of the layers below it. Any layers that need to be masked must be linked to the mask (3). To create a mask layer, first create a standard layer, and then right-click (Windows) or Ctrl-click (Mac) and choose Mask.

3. **Masked object layer:** This is a layer linked to the mask layer above it, and it contains the content to be masked. It's easy to tell which layers are linked to the mask above it because the

linked layer will be indented slightly to the right. The mask and linked layer also share a similar icon, indicating they are a set. You can add a new linked layer to the mask by either selecting any linked layer under the mask and then clicking the Insert Layer icon (9) or by simply dragging a layer already created on the timeline under the mask layer.

4. **Motion guide layer:** This type of layer allows you to draw a path for animation between tweened instances. This is useful if you want to animate objects, groups, or text blocks along a custom path that you can create. For example, you can draw a circle and have an object animate along the stroke, making the object move in a circle. The motion guide is created with the Pencil tool or the outside stroke of an object. To create a motion guide layer, either click the Motion Guide icon (10) or create a standard layer and then right-click (Windows) or Ctrl-click (Mac) on that layer and choose Add Motion Guide. In both cases, two layers will be created already linked together. To link a normal layer to a motion guide layer, create a new layer and link it to make a guided layer.

5. **Guided layer:** The guided layer, labeled "Object" in Figure 6-1, is the layer that is linked with the motion guide layer. This layer contains the animation.

6. **Guide/hidden layer:** This layer type is essentially the same thing as a motion guide layer without any guided layers linked to it. If you need to temporarily disable a layer or hide it, this is the best nondestructive way to do it. The nice thing about this layer type is that any of its content will not get exported, which means that the hidden layer will not add any unnecessary file size in the exported SWF. To create a guide layer, insert a new standard layer, and then right-click (Windows) or Ctrl-click (Mac) and choose Guide.

7. **Layer folder:** Layer folders make organizing a snap. A layer folder offers a way to organize layers into a single group that can be collapsed and expanded. Insert a new folder by clicking the Insert Layer Folder icon (11). I've labeled my folder "Set" in Figure 6-1.

8. **Layers inside the layer folder:** These are examples of layers inside the layer folder. You can place any layer type inside the layer folder by dragging it underneath the newly created folder. I created three layers and labeled them "Object in Set" in Figure 6-1 as an example.

9. **Insert Layer:** This icon creates a standard layer. You can also create a new layer by clicking the Insert menu at the top of screen, and then select Timeline to see the different layer types.

10. **Add Motion Guide:** This icon inserts a motion guide into the timeline.

11. **Insert Layer Folder:** This icon creates a layer folder.

12. **Delete Layer:** This icon deletes the selected layer in the timeline. It's important to know that if you select a mask or motion guide layer and delete it, the linked layers will be deleted. If it's your intention to delete the entire set, you must delete each individual linked layer, too.

13. **Center Frame:** This button centers the timeline marker (the red vertical line on the timeline) in the middle of the viewable space on the timeline. This works only when you have enough frames on the timeline to exceed the viewable space on your screen in the timeline window.

14. **Onion Skin:** This button activates the onion skin feature, which is extremely valuable in frame-by-frame animation techniques. Flash normally allows you to see only one frame of animation at a time. In some circumstances, you will find it helpful to see an animation sequence on the stage that shows the before and after frame or frames of the animation from the marker position all at one time. *Onion skinning* allows you to see how your animation looks during its movement from one frame to the next.

When you activate the onion skin feature, you will see your animation object look as if it's blurred, and multiple instances of it appear along its animation path. The object will also become slightly transparent, so you can see the animation progress from one frame to the next—showing before and after frames in the animation. Also, on the frame numbers near the top of the timeline, two brackets appear (32), and the numbers in the timeline turn white. The white numbered frames indicate the frames that will be included in the onion skin mode. So, if you have a total of 11 frames selected, then 11 instances will appear on the stage.

> *You can lock the other layers in the timeline so they will not be affected by the onion skin feature. This helps isolate the desired animation. Also, to see the onion skin feature work, you need to scrub the timeline with the marker or playhead. To scrub the timeline, click and hold the marker, and move the marker left and right. Note that a movie clip will not show the animations inside its timeline like a graphic will while scrubbing.*

15. **Onion Skin Outlines:** This button activates a feature that is the same as the onion skin feature, except the full-object animation is replaced by an outlined-only version. This can help you see how your animation is happening in relation to other objects on the stage. This is also helpful if you have a slower computer, because it uses slightly fewer processes.

16. **Edit Multiple Frames:** Clicking this button allows you to edit multiple frames at one time, regardless of where the current marker is, which is sometimes helpful in frame-by-frame animation. With this feature turned off, you can edit only the currently selected frame.

17. **Modify Onion Markers:** Clicking this button reveals a drop-down list with the following options related to onion skinning:

    - Always Show Markers displays the onion skin markers in the timeline header, whether or not onion skinning is enabled.

    - Anchor Onion locks the onion skin markers to their current position in the timeline. Normally, the onion skin range is relative to the current frame pointer and the onion skin markers. By anchoring the onion skin markers, you prevent them from moving with the current frame pointer.

    - Onion 2 displays two frames on either side of the current frame.

    - Onion 5 displays five frames on either side of the current frame.

    - Onion All displays all frames on either side of the current frame.

18. **Current frame:** This indicator displays the number of the frame where the marker currently resides.

19. **Frame rate:** This indicator displays the frame rate, or frames per second, of the Flash project. Here's a nice little shortcut: double-click this area, and the Document Property panel will appear, allowing you to change the frame rate and other document properties.

20. **Elapsed time:** This indicator displays the real time of the animation or Flash movie.

21. **Keyframe:** A keyframe is a blank or occupied frame in which you define a change in an animation or include frame actions to modify your Flash movie.

22. **Shape tween:** A shape tween is created when a shape is animated. A shape tween has some characteristics that a motion tween does not possess, such as the ability to distort from one keyframe to the next.

23. **Motion tween:** This type of tween can be applied only to a graphic or movie clip. It does not support distortion of the object. However, it does allow you to use the new filter features in Flash 8, like Blur, Glow, and Drop Shadow, just to name a few.

24. **Blank frames:** Frames that do not contain any data or ActionScripts.

25. **End keyframe in an animation:** This indicates the end of the animation.

26. **Empty keyframe:** This is a blank keyframe ready to receive content that is different from the frame before it. This essentially is a blank slate for new animation or ActionScript.

27. **Empty keyframe with ActionScript applied to the layer:** Best practice is to create an ActionScript file for the sole purpose of holding ActionScript. This makes debugging much easier.

28. **Timeline options:** This button allows you to modify the look of the timeline to meet your needs. For example, you may have a really long animation sequence and prefer to see more frames than in Normal mode. If you select Tiny or Small, the actual frame size reduces, allowing you to see more frames in the same window space. (As a matter of fact, the Small mode is the one I prefer to use for my work.) Once you click the button, you will see several other options to modify the timeline look as well: Medium, Large, Preview, Preview in Context, Short, and Tinted Frames. Medium and Large simply make the timeline frame size larger. Preview shows a preview of the objects on the stage. Preview in Context shows a preview of the objects on the stage in relationship of the stage itself. Short makes the frame in the timeline shorter. This allows you to view more layers at one time. Finally, Tinted Frames adds color to the animation tweens shown in the timeline making them easier to identify.

29. **Stage scale:** This drop-down list allows you to adjust the scale of the stage from 8% to 2000%.

30. **Edit Symbols:** This button is a shortcut that allows you to jump straight into editing the specified library asset.

31. **Edit Scene:** Another shortcut that allows you to jump from scene to scene.

32. **Onion skin brackets:** These are the start onion skin and end onion skin brackets that allow you to manage which frames will be onion-skinned. These brackets are adjustable. You can grab them and manually move them left or right to increase or decrease the number of frames the animation shows on the stage at one time.

33. **Timeline marker:** This shows where the playhead is currently located while you're editing. Sometimes, it's helpful during editing to scrub the marker back and forth to see the animation sequence play back, and then make adjustments.

34. **Show All Layers As Outline:** When you select this icon, everything in the timeline is drawn as an outline during editing. Sometimes, it's helpful to toggle this mode on and off to find elements on the stage or to see what is happening behind the scenes. Underneath this icon are colored box icons for each layer, which you can toggle to make only individual layers show as outlines.

35. **Lock/Unlock All Layers:** Clicking this icon allows you to lock or unlock all the layers at one time. If you want to isolate only one layer, a timesaver is to lock all the layers, and then unlock that one layer.

> *It's good practice to lock the layers you are not working with to prevent any accidental changes to those layers. This can prevent a loss of work and time.*

36. Scene/asset name: This indicator lets you know if you are editing on the root timeline or if you are inside a movie clip or other asset.

37. Timeline: This button hides or shows the timeline. This is convenient if you need to toggle the timeline off to show more of the working stage.

Whew! OK, now that you know the timeline inside and out, let's get to the goods. Let's explore the most requested and sought-after design element, the gel pill.

A layering example: the gel pill

To explore Flash layering techniques, you'll now create the gel pill shown in Figure 6-2. If you are not familiar with the unofficial design requirements of this button, then let me explain. This button resembles a pill. The pill is supposed to be translucent and shiny. Lastly, any text on the button should reflect to the bottom of the pill.

Figure 6-2. You can create a gel pill like this using Flash alone.

The techniques you'll use here (some of which take advantage of the new features in Flash 8) can be applied to many design elements because the gel pill features many typical important attributes, such as light, shadow, and depth. When used correctly, these attributes can really make your design come to life. Of course, everything you build will not look "gel-ish," but the techniques you will use can be translated to all sorts of styles. However, the main purpose of this exercise is to clearly demonstrate how to effectively use layers to stay organized and how layers contribute to the design process.

So with that, let's get started.

Creating the layers

To begin, let's create our layers and name them. You need to create five layers and name them as shown here.

You want to name your layers according to what object is in them. For example, in our case, we first need to draw the main body of the pill button, so naming a layer Main Pill Body seems appropriate.

Drawing the pill body

Follow these steps to start creating the gel pill:

1. Click the Main Pill Body layer to select it.

2. Select the Rectangle tool. Select the Set Corner Radius button that now appears and give the rectangle a radius of 100. Make sure that the Stroke Color (line) is turned off.

> *If you would rather use my shapes to follow the example, you can find them in the finished version of this example in the code download files available from the friends of ED website (www.friendsofed.com).*

3. Drag out a rectangle (which will look like a rounded edge rectangle) to around 430 × 65 pixels. It doesn't have to be exact.

4. With the main body of the pill drawn, let's fill it with the proper fill gradient. Select the rectangle on the stage and adjust the Color Mixer panel for a Linear gradient with the following colors: #5ABAF3, #66C0E6, #0A4E76. Refer to the following illustration for the layout of the gradient in the Color Mixer panel.

5. More than likely, the gradient will be from left to right. You need to reposition this gradient to be from top to bottom. Choose the Gradient Transform tool from the toolbar and click the pill to select it. You will see the edit handles appear on the pill for the gradient. Click and hold down the rotation handle (which is small white circle), and rotate the gradient so the dark color is on top, as shown in the following image. Having Snap to Objects on (View ➤ Snapping ➤ Snap to Objects) may help you get the gradient perfectly straight on the pill.

Adding the bottom highlight

Next, let's begin working on creating some depth in the pill. We ultimately want the pill to look translucent and to give the idea it has some mass. The goal here is to make a highlight, or glow, on the bottom half of the pill to help give that illusion of depth. Let's build the bottom highlight.

1. In the Bottom Highlight layer, create an object that looks like this:

You can make this shape by creating another rectangle with the same radius properties as the main part of the pill. The color of the shape is not relevant, and I'll explain why in a bit. Then use the Selection tool to select the area that you want to remove and delete it. Finally, stretch the left and right corners slightly to ultimately fill in the bottom of the pill better.

2. Make this shape a movie clip and name it Bottom Highlight. The reason you want to make this a movie clip and not a simple graphic symbol is because Flash 8's new filters work only on movie clips, text, and buttons.

3. Back in the root of the timeline, select the Bottom Highlight movie clip. In the Filters panel, located just below the stage by default, click the plus sign and choose Drop Shadow. At first glance, you might think that the Glow filter would be the one to use; however, the Drop Shadow filter is the best choice in this case, because it handles the outer gradient better and, with the Hide object option, it gives you more control over the effect. The actual color of the shape was irrelevant because we hid the object here.

> Keep in mind that just because the filter you are using is called the Drop Shadow filter does not mean you must use it for that. Keeping an open mind about how to approach a design need is important. As clichéd as it sounds, always think outside the box.

4. Populate the parameters as shown in the following illustration. The hex code for the shadow color is #9CD2F8.

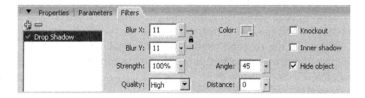

Your shape should now look like this:

The overall pill should look something like this so far:

The gel pill is starting to take shape. So far, we've used two layers. As a side note, it is nice to be able to toggle the layers on and off to see the object take shape and make tweaks where necessary—yet another benefit of using layers in this way.

Adding the top highlight

Now, let's get to the third layer.

1. Select the layer called Top Highlight. In it, create a shape this looks like this one:

You can create this shape by using the Rectangle tool with the same settings as before. Draw a long rectangle, slightly smaller in width than the main pill. Then with the Distort tool (Modify ➤ Transform ➤ Distort, or click the Transform button and select Distort from the set of Transform options that appear below the other buttons), grab the two top edges and pulled them in slightly to give the shape a bend that roughly matches the shape of the main pill.

2. Add the gradient fill to match the pill colors. Make sure the new shape (highlight) is selected. Adjust your gradient fill as shown in the following illustration. The three colors are #E8F4FC, #B5DCF6, and #62B4EC.

3. Once again, you will need to adjust the direction of the gradient by selecting the Fill Transform tool and rotating the gradient where the lightest color is at the top.

At this point, the gel pill should look like this:

The effect of a 3D pill button is really coming together at this point. However, we need to do a few more things to really make this a convincing gel pill. Sometimes, it's the small details that make all the difference—this is no exception.

Creating a translucent shadow

Next, let's create another drop shadow. This will not be just any drop shadow though. A gel pill is translucent, meaning that any light that shines down on the pill will essentially shine through it onto the surface below. This means that the shadow will not be a dark gray or black. The shadow should inherit the main color of the pill: blue.

We will create our drop shadow on the Main Pill Shadow layer.

1. Copy the shape on the Main Pill Body layer and paste it in place on the Main Pill Shadow layer. You may want to hide the other layers for now so you can see the Main Pill Shadow layer. Again, this is a good opportunity to get into the habit of locking the other layers to prevent any unnecessary editing.

2. With the shadow selected, make it a movie clip and name it Shadow.

3. Apply the Drop Shadow filter to the new movie clip. Populate the filter setting as follows. The color is #529FC6.

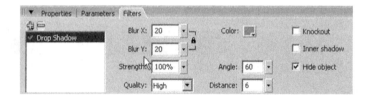

To finish the pill, let's add some text.

Adding text

At this point, we could simply type text over the top of the pill and it might look just fine, but let's take the extra steps to really make the text feel like part of the button. The text should take on some of the highlight of the button on the areas that it covers. After all, it has light on it too, right? So the top portion of the text should be slightly lighter than the lower half of the text.

1. On the Main Text layer, type your text. Use a relatively large font, such as Arial Black at a point size of 46 and the color #333333.

2. Make the text a shape that can be manipulated to create the highlight. Break the text down into a shape. To do this, press Ctrl+B (Windows) or Cmd+B (Mac) twice.

3. With the entire shape/text selected, make it a movie clip and name it Text.

4. Select the Text movie clip to edit it. Once inside the new clip, select the portion of the text (now a shape) that overlaps with the highlight from the pill.

5. With that area selected, fill the color with #555555. You can see this is a slightly lighter shade of gray than the other color in the text. This helps give the illusion that the text lives on the pill shape and also has a highlight reflecting on it.

6. To finish off the gel pill, drill back to the root in the timeline and make sure the Text movie clip is selected. On the Filters tab, add a Drop Shadow effect. Make sure that it matches the following parameters for the glow.

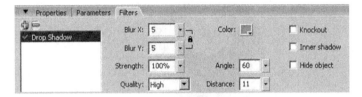

The long distance for the Drop Shadow is intentional to attempt to make the shadow of the text feel like it's showing up on the back side of the pill. This only strengthens the idea that the pill is translucent.

That's it! Your final gel pill button should something like this:

So what have we done? We created a multilayered object that uses multiple layers to keep things organized and therefore makes the design and development phase much more manageable. With layers, you can hide things completely with guides, lock them down to prevent accidental selections, and use outlines to see what is happening below that layer.

Another large benefit is that if you need to make any modifications to the object, you can easily do so. Hiding layers by using the guide layer also allows you to create features in future revisions in the same document. By simply removing the guide, that feature will become active, saving steps and time.

Now that you've had some hands-on experience with using multiple layers, let's look at some of the new features in Flash 8 that are related to layers. The following sections describe blending modes, masks, and motion guides.

Blending modes

If you're a Photoshop user, you are all too familiar with blending modes. If you are not familiar with them, then read on.

Blending modes allow the selected layer to react to the layers below it by compositing images. This is the process of blending colors of two or more layers. Blending modes can also deal with a certain level of transparency. These modes can also add a degree of color or desaturation to the movie clip.

Take a look at the object shown in Figure 6-3. Notice the shadow underneath the ball.

Figure 6-3. A ball with a shadow

What would happen if we placed a background behind the image? Figure 6-4 shows the answer.

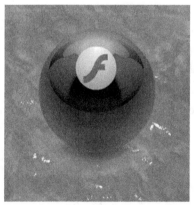

Figure 6-4. After adding a background, the shadow is wrong.

The shadow is clearly not correct. This is because the gradient used to make the shadow has been created to work correctly for a white background.

The easiest way to correct this type of problem is to use blending modes, specifically the Multiply mode. Figure 6-5 shows the same object with the shadow changed to the Multiply blending mode.

To apply blending modes, make sure the object is a movie clip or button. Then select the object and under the Properties tab located at the bottom of Flash by default you will see the option called Blend.

Figure 6-5. The Multply blending mode fixes the shadow problem.

Figures 6-6, 6-7, and 6-8 show a few other different blending modes applied to the ball: Darken, Lighten, and Overlay.

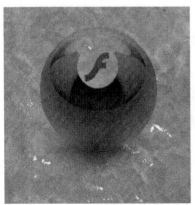 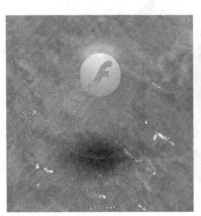 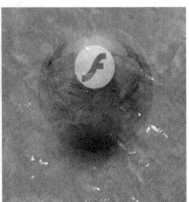

Figure 6-6. The Darken blending mode   **Figure 6-7.** The Lighten blending mode   **Figure 6-8.** The Overlay blending mode

These are just a few of the blending modes Flash 8 offers. It's easy to see how powerful this new feature can be and how it helps the Flash designer by reducing the amount of time it takes to complete several operations. Certain tasks that were normally done in an image editing program like Adobe's Photoshop can now be done directly in Flash.

Masks

Without a doubt, masks are commonplace when creating in Flash. A mask is a way to show only certain areas of an object on the layers below the mask. A mask can be animated, or the object below the mask can be animated, providing great flexibility.

Just about anything can be used as a mask: movie clips, symbols, graphics, and even rasterized images like a JPG or PNG. It's good practice to use vector objects when you can, and it's important to know that images used as a mask will not use the alpha channel that a PNG uses. So a complicated PNG with an alpha layer will show up as only a block of whatever the dimensions of the image are.

A benefit of a using a movie clip as a mask is that you can add ActionScript to the movie clip, thus creating a dynamic mask. The possibilities are limitless, but let's explore a simple use of this technique. Let's create a mask that can be moved around the stage with the mouse to reveal the image below.

1. Set up a mask called Ball Mask and a linked layer called Water Bckgrnd. To set up a mask, create a layer first. Then right-click the layer and choose Mask. Next create another layer under the mask layer and make sure it is attached to the mask as shown here:

   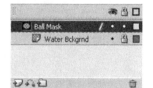

   The objects on the stage look like this when the two layers are not locked:

   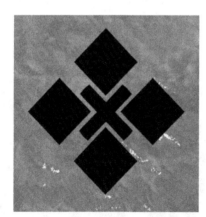

2. Lock the layers. Only the water image shows through the defined mask.

3. Create another layer and make sure that it's at the top of the layer stack. Call this layer Actions.

4. In the Actions layer on frame 1, place the following code:

```
ball.onPress = function(){
   startDrag(this);
}
ball.onRelease = function(){
   stopDrag();
}
```

5. In the Property inspector for the Ball Mask, give it the instance name ball.

That's it! Export the movie and drag the ball around. You can see that the Ball Mask layer reveals different areas of the image below it.

Dynamic masks can be very useful for unique Flash applications of all kinds. I'm certain your ideas are boundless.

Motion guides

Motion guides are a linear way to animate an object along a path. The layer setup for a motion guide is almost identical to that for a mask. You must have at least two layers: one must be the motion guide and the other the linked layer under the motion guide. The motion guide setup looks like Figure 6-9.

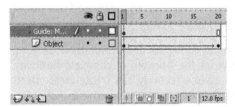

Figure 6-9. The layer setup for a motion guide

109

There are several important things to remember while working with motion guides. The first is that the guide itself must be made from a stroke/outline or use the Pencil tool. The Pencil tool has settings of its own: Straighten, Smooth, or Ink. You can draw the guide using any of the three methods. Straighten will attempt to keep the guide as straight as possible. The Smooth method will attempt to draw the guide with curves. Ink will create the guide as you draw with the Pencil, pixel by pixel with aliasing, without Flash adding any additional corrections to your drawing.

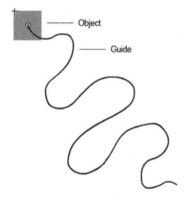

Object

Guide

The object must be a movie clip or a graphic in order to use the guide. In the example shown in Figure 6-10, I made the square a graphic because I did not plan to add ActionScripting, blending modes, or filters to the box. If you plan on using the new features in Flash 8 or add ActionScripting, you will need to make sure the object is a movie clip.

Take note of the box in Figure 6-10. The small circle in the center of the box needs to be "snapped" or locked onto the guide. This is important because that small circle essentially becomes the registration point for the box to follow along the guide. The beginning keyframe and the ending keyframe of the box animation must be locked onto the guide in order for the box to follow the guide. If the object is not locked onto the guide, that object will not follow along the guide; instead, it will just take a straight path to the other end of the animation keyframe.

Figure 6-10. An object and motion guide

Summary

Layers play an essential role during the design phase and when creating effects in Flash. They have several important functions to assist in design. During design, layers are required for the all important mask, alpha channels, the ability to create depth, and other design tools and tasks.

Taking the time to organize your layers at the beginning of a project will dramatically decrease debugging time. Properly labeled layers and a properly grouped set of layers speed workflow.

The use of multiple layers to create complex objects is beneficial in many ways. With multiple layers, you have the ability to turn layers on and off. This is useful during the creation process to hide layers to view work that may lie under the hidden layer. Think of this process like that used by animators to create cartoons on paper. They would layer the acetate paper sheets, one on top of the other, and flip them back and forth to ensure that the animation was playing back smoothly. The same concept applies here to your static objects.

Organized layers and an organized timeline mean organized Flash projects. The results mean faster workflow and productivity, and limitless creativity.

It's easy to see how layers are useful during the design and development process. Masks are essential. The mask layers in Flash 8 allow for the freedom of complete flexibility and control over how the design takes shape. Mask layers, used effectively, can create great effects by hiding or showing elements in a creative way. The mask layer can also be used with ActionScripting for ultimate dynamic control.

Blending modes add a new level of design in Flash 8. Being able to natively control how an image interacts with another image in Flash directly is huge. This type of style could only be performed in another program like Photoshop. This not only speeds up the design process if this technique is needed, but makes making changes on the fly a breeze.

Guides are an effective way to animate an object along a complicated path that you create. Guides are useful for a more linear method of animation.

Chapter 7

WORKING WITH 3D VECTORS

by Michael Kemper and Guido Rosso

Our goal with this chapter (actually the whole book, but specifically this chapter) is to show you all the 3D tips and tricks we've amassed in our years of experience with the wonderfully diverse and powerful application that is Flash.

> *Chapter 5, which covered gradients in Flash, is a must-read before diving into this one, so please either make sure you've read it or are knowledge-able enough already with the art of layers and stacking them to create more depth than you would be able to achieve with flat graphics.*

The way this chapter will work is simple. We'll take you through step-by-step examples on how to create a variety of cool 3D visual effects. We'll be creating many of these objects in Flash, and also utilizing Illustrator to create 3D effects with maximum impact. The ability to increase or decrease the screen size of your graphics without losing any visual quality or information is a feature exclusive to vector art, so it is very important to learn the ropes in vector-based applications to provide a safety net during your production process.

Since collectively as authors we've developed unique techniques for interface design and Flash on separate continents, you can expect some differences between our approaches to certain effects and graphics. We view this not as a detraction, but as a benefit for you: instead of one way to do things, you can see how the same end products can be achieved in different ways. We're very excited to show you what we've picked up through the years, and we hope that you'll get the most out of our collective experience.

OK, let's get started!

Working with real 3D assets

How can we create high-quality 3D graphical assets that we can easily manipulate and animate in Flash? Creating a 3D engine in Flash to draw objects in real time isn't a feasible solution, unless you're making a game and you can dedicate all processing power to that. If you're creating a website interface and need to make a simple icon look 3D, there's no point in wasting all of that power.

A true 3D model created in a program such as Softimage, 3D Studio Max, or Maya is a good solution, but it has to be rendered to a raster image or outputted to vector format for use in Flash. Many 3D programs nowadays have plug-ins (such as Swift 3D, which is available as a stand-alone 3D program and as a plug-in for 3D Studio Max and LightWave) that can output a sequence of vector frames specifically for Flash. You can find more specific information on Swift 3D at Electric Rain's site (www.erain.com).

These plug-ins generally have various settings that you can customize, including the quality of the outputted vector graphic. As you would expect, higher quality means larger file size. Higher quality generally also hinders playback speed of animations. Keep in mind that playback speed for Flash is still entirely dependent on the user's processor, so while it may be very fast on your computer, it might be simply too slow for your target market. You need to find a balance between quality, playback speed, and file size.

The general rules for when to use raster or vector for 3D graphics are as follows:

- If you want to use a very realistic graphic, you should render it to a raster image and import it into Flash. You can do this for a short animation too, but watch out for file size.
- If you need to create a simple graphic and don't require a photorealistic render, use a plug-in to export to vector.
- If your 3D animation is very long, use a plug-in to output a series of vector frames to a SWF file that you can then import in Flash. This keeps file size down, although it won't look as good as a progression of rendered images.

Working with semirealistic 3D assets

Most of the time, we actually don't use real 3D programs such as 3D Studio Max to create graphical assets. This is mostly because we can achieve satisfactory results with Photoshop, Illustrator, or Flash in a much shorter amount of time.

The main advantage to creating assets entirely in vector format is that you'll be able to manipulate and animate those assets in Flash. The new ability to apply filters and blending modes to movie clips in Flash 8 allows us to add many more details to our assets, which would not have been possible in previous versions of Flash. These new features also make working in Flash a lot more similar to designing in Photoshop or Illustrator, possibly one of the first signs we've been able to see, as designers, of the Adobe–Macromedia merge.

Our main method of creating 3D-looking shapes is through gradients, opacity, and shadows. In the next chapter, you'll see how to use similar techniques to actually create an entire interface in

Photoshop. The key to this technique is to really have a strong understanding of what gives depth, what makes objects look closer, farther, smaller, and so on. Always keep in mind that your eyes are your best judge.

To explain our method, we'll demonstrate how to create the three icons in Figure 7-1 entirely in Flash.

Figure 7-1. We had to recently create these icons for a project. From left to right, they represent a user, a domain, and statistics.

User icon

First we're going to explain how to make the user icon. Open up Flash and create a new FLA file, making sure your background is white.

The base shape

Select the Oval tool (press O) and draw two circles as shown in Figure 7-2. You can press and hold Shift while using the Oval tool to constrain the proportions of the oval, making it a perfect circle. First draw the body circle, 37×37 pixels, and then the head circle, 21×21 pixels.

Figure 7-2. Draw two circles in your first layer.

Click the bottom part of the border on the smaller circle and delete it. Your document should now look like Figure 7-3.

Figure 7-3. The body circle and head circle are no longer separated by a line, making the body and head one shape.

Now select the entire object (double-clicking the fill automatically selects also the borders) and scale the shape vertically by 80% through the Transform panel (Ctrl+T on a PC or Cmd+T on a Mac), as you see in Figure 7-4.

Use the Selection tool (press V) to select the lower portion of the shape and delete it, so that just about half of the bottom circle remains, as shown in Figure 7-5. Now use the Line tool (press N) to draw the bottom border of the shape back in.

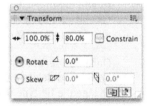

Figure 7-4. Scale the shape.

Select the shape and set its fill color to #005EB3. Set its stroke color to #004584. Now press F8 to convert the shape into a symbol. Name it UserShape and set Behavior to Movie Clip and click OK. With the UserShape movie clip selected, go to the Filters panel and use the plus button to add two Drop Shadow effects. Use the settings shown in Figure 7-6 and Figure 7-7. Notice the second drop shadow is larger yet more subtle (lower alpha) than the first one. Its purpose is to emphasize the icon better, making it feel even more raised from the white background. Although this may seem almost unnoticeable, try enabling and disabling this shadow a few times to compare the different effect it provides.

Figure 7-5. Our object now resembles the shape of a typical user icon.

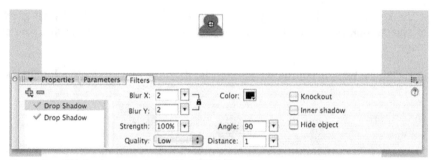

Figure 7-6. This is what your shape should look like with the new colors and Drop Shadow filters applied. Use these settings for the first drop shadow, which immediately makes the shape of the icon feel more 3D.

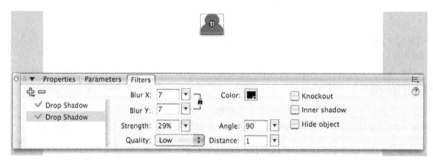

Figure 7-7. Use these settings for the second drop shadow.

The bottom highlight

Now you're going to create a subtle highlight at the bottom of the icon using a transparent gradient to add depth. First you want to copy your initial shape so you can use it for the highlight. Copy the UserShape movie clip (Ctrl+C or Cmd+C), create a new layer above the original one, and paste it in place (Ctrl+Shift+V or Cmd+Shift+V). Press Ctrl+B or Cmd+B to break apart the duplicated symbol.

Once you've broken apart the shape, select just its border and delete it so that only the fill remains. Now change the fill type from Solid to Linear. This creates a linear gradient. Set both color stops to white, but set the alpha of the first one to 43% and the alpha of the second one to 8% (from left to right). Your icon should now look like Figure 7-8. Pay particular attention to the Color Mixer and the gradient stops. You'll notice that the selected gradient stop, the one on the left, is the one with 43% alpha. At this point, however, the order of these doesn't matter, as you'll be rotating the gradient later.

The highlight isn't complete. You still need to fix up the alignment of the gradient, but first you're going to modify this shape so it aligns with the bottom of the icon.

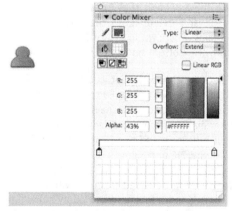

Figure 7-8. Using the Color Mixer to make a transparent gradient fill for our new highlight

Select the Oval tool (press T) and set its fill to empty. Refer to Figure 7-9 if you don't know how to do this.

Now draw an oval exactly as we did in Figure 7-10, making sure you have the layer with the new highlight shape selected.

Figure 7-10. Draw an oval with an empty fill on the same layer as the highlight shape.

The reason you're doing this is that the highlight shape is now actually split in two shapes by the stroke you just created, as you see in Figure 7-11.

Figure 7-11. The oval stroke splits the highlight shape in two and allows you to select and manipulate either of these.

Notice that you can select the top or the bottom shapes. Select the top, as in Figure 7-11, and delete it. The oval stroke has served its purpose, so you can delete that also.

Figure 7-12. Rotate the gradient 90 degrees counterclockwise using the Gradient Transform tool.

Now select what's left of the highlight shape and use the Gradient Transform tool (press F) to first rotate the gradient 90 degrees counterclockwise, as in Figure 7-12, and then scale the gradient to match the height of the highlight shape, as in Figure 7-13.

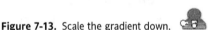

Figure 7-13. Scale the gradient down.

Figure 7-9. Set fill to empty.

Depth with inner glow

The icon is starting to look 3D, but it still needs more depth. You're going to use the new Glow filter to achieve this. Select the initial shape, copy it, and paste it into a new layer (using Paste in Place) as you previously did with the highlight layer. Remove the two Drop Shadow filters (click the minus button) and add a Glow filter. Use the settings in Figure 7-14 for the glow, making sure you check the Knockout and Inner Glow options.

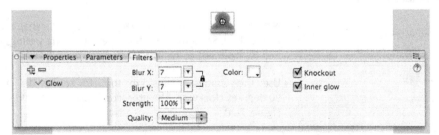

Figure 7-14. Use these settings for the Glow filter. This is what your icon should look like now.

Under the Properties panel, find the new Blend option and set it to Add, as shown in Figure 7-15. This is exactly like using blending modes in Photoshop or After Effects. Your icon should now look like Figure 7-16.

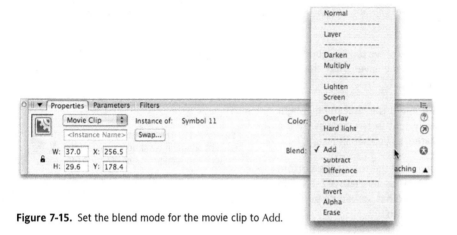

Figure 7-16. This is what the icon should look like now that you've applied the blend mode to the glow. (*A full-color version of this figure is available in the color insert.*)

Figure 7-15. Set the blend mode for the movie clip to Add.

Adding gloss

The icon is looking a lot better now, and it just needs one final touch. You're going to add a glossy effect to make the icon look as if it were made of glass. The key to this effect is getting the opacity of the gradient just right. The contrast between the soft glows and the hard edges of the gloss is what ultimately makes the overall effect work.

To create the gloss layer, copy and paste into place the initial shape into a new layer above all the previous ones. Break the movie clip apart and delete the stroke so that only the fill remains. Now create an oval stroke, as shown in Figure 7-17. You're going to use this the same way you did with the bottom highlight to cut the shape.

Delete the right portion of the shape and the oval. Your shape should now look like Figure 7-18.

Figure 7-17. Using the Oval tool to cut the gloss shape

Figure 7-18. The gloss shape. We colored it here to make it more evident. (*A full-color version of this figure is available in the color insert.*)

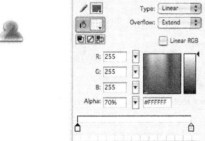

Now go to the Color Mixer panel and give the shape a linear gradient fill. Set both stops to white with alpha settings of 70% and 8% from left to right, as shown in Figure 7-19.

Use the Gradient Transform tool to rotate the gradient 90 degrees clockwise. The user icon is done! It should look like Figure 7-20.

Figure 7-19. Apply a gradient to the gloss shape.

Figure 7-20. The finished user icon with gloss

Domain icon

As you can see, it's very easy to make something realistic and complex looking with very simple shapes and techniques. We'll now explain how to create the domain icon; however, we won't show the entire process step by step, as it would be redundant. You'll pretty much be using the exact same tools and effects you used with the user icon.

Creating the shadow

Start by opening a new file in Flash. As before, make the background white. You're going to start by creating the shadow of the orb first. Create a circle, give it a radial gradient fill, and make both of the stops black. Make the outer stop fully transparent with a 0% alpha. Make the shadow a symbol (press F8, either a graphic or movie clip will do), and scale it down a little vertically. Play with the alpha value of the symbol to make it as close as possible to Figure 7-21.

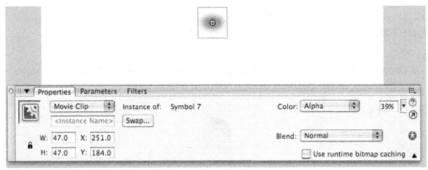

Figure 7-21. Use the radial gradient to create a shadow.

Creating the orb

To create the orb, simply draw a circle using the Oval tool. Set its stroke color to #E3E3E3 and its fill is a linear gradient. It has three color stops with values #4B040A, #291222, and #10568C from left to right. Use the Gradient Transform tool to rotate the gradient 90 degrees clockwise so that the red is on top and blue on bottom as in Figure 7-22.

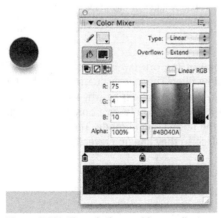

Figure 7-22. The orb shape with a gradient applied

119

Next, add a Bevel filter to the orb shape to create a more rounded blue glow from the bottom. As you see from the settings in Figure 7-23, the color for the highlight is fully transparent with a 0% alpha, and the shadow color is #3A6AB4 with a 73% alpha.

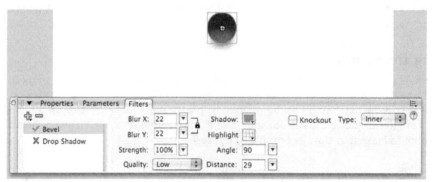

Figure 7-23. The orb shape with a Bevel filter applied

Also apply a Drop Shadow filter to this shape, as shown in Figure 7-24. It creates a better sense of depth for the orb shape, as will become more evident at a later stage.

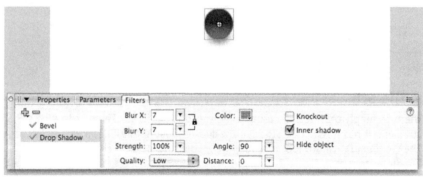

Figure 7-24. Apply a Drop Shadow filter to this shape.

Outer glow

The outer glow is simply a copy of the orb layer. You create this by deleting the Bevel and Drop Shadow filters and adding a Glow filter. The color value to use is #80C3FF, as you see in Figure 7-25. Make sure you check Knockout. If you're wondering why we didn't have you simply add a Glow filter to the orb shape, it's because we wanted you to give only the outer glow a Hard Light blend mode. This way the orb shape keeps the normal blend mode. The layer is positioned directly above the orb layer. Be sure to paste it into place so they line up correctly.

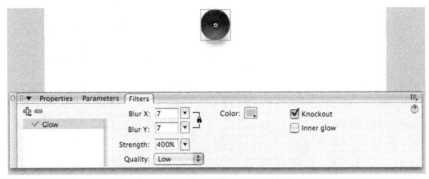

Figure 7-25. The outer glow layer has a Glow filter applied to it.

Inner glow

The inner glow is again a copy of the orb layer, in the same position. It also has a Glow filter, but this time you check the Inner glow option and give it an Add blend mode. The color is pure white. Take a look at Figure 7-26 for the specific settings to use.

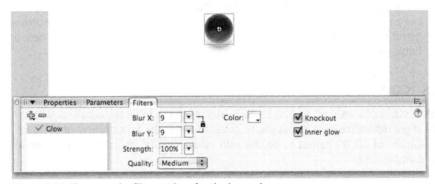

Figure 7-26 These are the filter settings for the inner glow.

Stars

To create the stars, use the Oval tool to make six random circles. With all of the stars selected, press F8 and convert them into a movie clip. Give it an Overlay blend mode and duplicate the layer. Now give the bottom star layer a Glow filter. Use the settings in Figure 7-27.

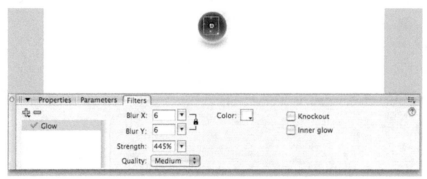

Figure 7-27. The two star layers both have an Overlay blend mode. The bottom star layer only has a Glow filter with these settings.

Adding gloss

Similarly to the user icon, the final step here is the gloss layer. Create the shape with the Oval tool and use the technique we explained earlier to cut the shape with another oval. Follow the steps you did for the user icon to add gloss, starting with Figure 7-15. Your final effect

Figure 7-28. The final domain icon with the gloss effect

should look like Figure 7-28. There are actually two gloss layers in our example. The bottom one has an Overlay blend mode, while the top one has a Normal blend mode with 59% alpha. These two layers are placed between the two stars layers.

Statistics icon

To create the statistics icon, you're going to use pretty much the same techniques as with the last two icons. One slight difference here is that you're going to tweak the four borders of the base shape to create the illusion of 3D. It's easiest to do this with square shapes, which is why this icon works very well as an example here.

The base shape

Create a square with the Rectangle tool (press R) and rotate it 45 degrees. Scale it down vertically a little to give it some perspective. It should look like Figure 7-29.

Figure 7-29. Rotate and scale the base shape.

Next you're going to give the base a gradient fill. Use the settings in Figure 7-22 for this. Then modify the color of each one of the four strokes to achieve the 3D look in Figure 7-22. Imagine that the light source is above and slightly behind your shape, and just a little bit to the left. As a result, the top-left border is the lightest and the bottom right is the darkest. The specific color values you should use are top left, #F2F2F2; top right, #EDEDED; bottom right, #666666; and bottom left, #999999. Remember that there's no real mathematical formula to stick to here; you're doing what looks good and what looks convincing enough to deceive a human eye into believing that you have a real 3D object. Next, apply a gradient to the fill color, using the gradient stop values, from left to right, of #E3E3E3, #FFFFFF, and #EEEEEE, as you see in Figure 7-30.

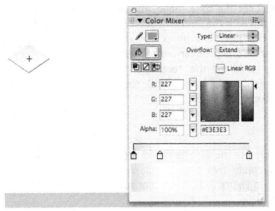

Figure 7-30. The base shape starts to look 3D.

Convert the base shape into a movie clip and apply a Drop Shadow filter. Use the settings in Figure 7-31.

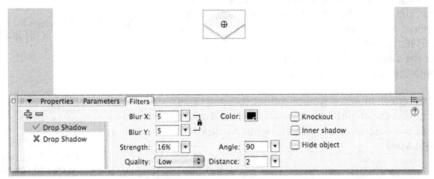

Figure 7-31. A subtle drop shadow works very well when creating depth. It's important to not make it stand out too much. You want people's reactions to be "Wow, that looks very realistic" instead of "Wow, that has a shadow."

Now add a second Drop Shadow filter to the filters list and use the settings in Figure 7-32.

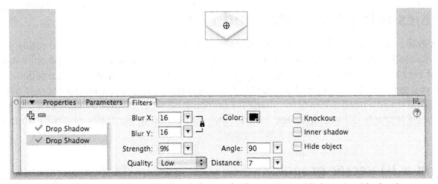

Figure 7-32. This second Drop Shadow is larger, farther away, and lighter. It adds depth without losing the detail of the smaller original shadow.

As a very subtle last effect for the base shape, you're going to copy the movie clip with the Drop Shadow filter, paste it in place in a new layer, and break it apart. Now move the entire layer up one pixel (arrow key up). Change the bottom-left stroke of this rectangle to #E5E5E5 and the bottom-right stroke to #C2C2C2. Your object should now look like Figure 7-33.

Figure 7-33. The detail added by this new layer is probably too subtle to show up in print, but it makes the object look just a little more complex and realistic on screen.

The graph

To create the graph, simply use the Line tool and create three strokes. Then create two circles and plot them along the stroke as in Figure 7-34. The color for the fills and strokes is #426396.

Figure 7-34. The graph is simply three strokes and two circles.

The reflection

Duplicate the graph and flip it vertically to create the reflection as shown in Figure 7-35. Select all three strokes and give them a linear gradient as in Figure 7-33. The gradient colors stops are both #426396. The first has 100% alpha and the second has 0% alpha. Use the Gradient Transform tool to rotate the gradient, as you did with the user icon in Figure 7-12.

Figure 7-35. The shape for the reflection of the graph

Convert the reflection into a symbol and set its alpha to 14%. Add a layer mask by copying the original base layer and pasting it above the reflection layer. Break the base layer copy apart, right/Ctrl-click it in the timeline, and set it to Mask.

Now that you've created the mask layer, the reflection layer below it should have automatically become part of the mask. If it didn't, simply drag it into the mask layer as seen in Figure 7-36.

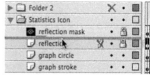

Figure 7-36. Drag the reflection layer into the mask layer to add it to the mask.

That's it! Your final statistics icon should look like Figure 7-37.

Figure 7-37. The completed statistics icon

3D graphics using Illustrator and Flash

Many designers don't realize that Adobe Illustrator has a fairly robust 3D engine for creating static 3D graphics. By static, we mean the final product is the equivalent to a single frame of animation. The process of creating 3D images in Illustrator and porting them over to Flash might seem tedious at first, but once you get used to the workflow and see the final product, it's clear that the process pays off in the end. So when you need a 3D vector image for comping up what COULD be an entire sequence, or you just need a simple 3D vector image for the final output, using Illustrator could be your perfect solution.

Creating a 3D vector graphic

Now, we'll walk you through creating a static 3D logo in Illustrator and then import the graphic to use in Flash. During this process, we'll cover creating the 3D image from a vector logotype in Illustrator and making a reflection of that image, and some additional drawing techniques you can use on any project.

First, draw your shape in Illustrator. For this example, we'll show you a vector logotype we created for a furniture company (see Figure 7-38). If you have several shapes in your image, you want to make sure they are grouped before continuing. To group your illustration, select all of the shapes and then press Ctrl+G (Cmd+G). Now if you select them, they all move together. You can apply and modify the stroke and fill colors of your graphics later if you wish to wait, but otherwise feel free to apply whatever line stroke and/or fill color you want.

Figure 7-38. This is the logotype we'll be converting to a 3D image by using Illustrator and Flash. All of the shapes are grouped together.

Select your shape using the Select tool from the toolbox, then click about 30 pixels below your selected shape(s). This has established the center point for Illustrator to use to reflect your selected image over. Now click your illustration, then hold down the Option and Shift key on your keyboard and drag down vertically to reflect your object directly under your original image. Let go of your mouse. You'll now have a copy of your image mirrored underneath the original, as demonstrated in Figure 7-39.

Next, group both of the illustrations so that all of your graphics can be moved together. Select your grouped images and choose Effect ➤ 3D ➤ Extrude And Bevel from the Options menu. The 3D Extrude & Bevel Options window will appear. Check the Preview option so you can see your 3D manipulation happen in real time as you tweak the settings. Now you'll see the default off-axis position applied to your vector illustration on the canvas (see Figure 7-40). If you have another setting in mind, use the Position drop-down menu to browse and apply different positions, or simply click and drag the cube in the position preview to tweak it manually. Click and drag the edges of the cube to change the z- or y-axis position; and drag the surface of the cube for a free-form manipulation.

Figure 7-39. This is our logotype reflected.

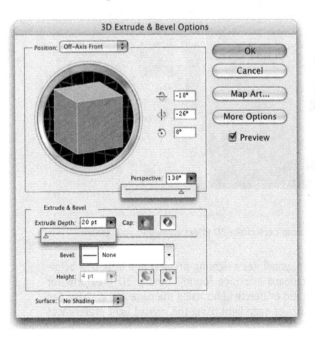

Figure 7-40. You can see your extrude and bevel effect as it is applied by checking the Preview check box.

We have a simple formula for tweaking these settings that we generally start with for the purposes of static vector 3D images; then we tweak the settings to perfect the effect. Depending on the effect you're trying to achieve, you have available an unlimited number of combinations using the options in this panel to generate standard 3D graphics. For your logo, you want your perspective to be more extreme than the default 0, so make your perspective 138 degrees. You'll get inconsistent results from the Bevel options, so typically you won't want to apply a bevel. Also, keep in mind that this is a RAM-intensive effect, so the more complex your settings are, the more likely you are to lose your preview or activate "processing" windows that will negatively impact your workflow. On this logotype, you don't want such an extreme extrude depth as the default 50 points, so change that to 20 points, as Figure 7-40 demonstrates.

Click the More Options button to reveal the Surface options for your image, as shown in Figure 7-41. We rarely use the wire frame surface with graphics we intend to import into Flash because the result is a very complex batch of lines. We either use None or the Plastic Shading Surface option.

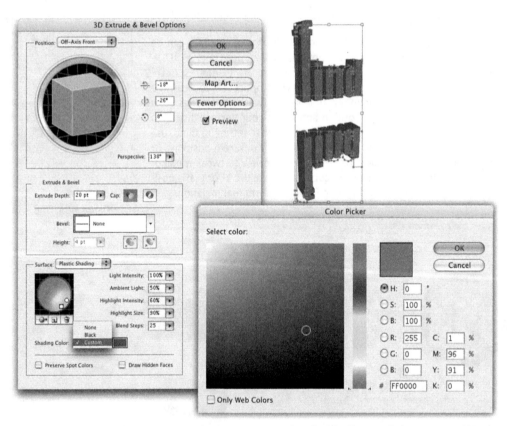

Figure 7-41. By using the More Options button, you can perfect the 3D effect applied to your graphic.

Once you select the Plastic Shading Surface option, you'll get a lighting preview in a little box below the Surface drop-down menu. This is a pretty standard interface found in many 3D programs for determining lighting effects on objects. It's easy to add or delete lights using the page and garbage can icons below the light box; you can tweak the settings of each light using the myriad light preferences to the right of your light box. To change the position of your lights, simply click and drag them in the light box to where you want them.

Sometimes we find it hard to get the perfect shading color from using the default Black fill setting, so we typically choose Custom in the Shading Color drop-down list, and then click the color preview swatch that appears and grab a better color to work with. By using this option, you get a standard color picker, which we find extremely helpful.

A note on the mapping feature: this is a really cool feature that enables you to map an object from the Symbols Library to your 3D graphic—but for the purposes of Flash design, we do not recommend using this feature in the 3D Extrude & Bevel Options dialog box for three reasons. The application is VERY tedious because you have to apply the art separately to each surface of your graphic (ARGH! There goes good workflow. . .); and since this is for a Flash project, once the final image is imported into Flash, the result is a complex mix of library symbols and masks. Finally, if you want to map an image to the object (especially if this image is a bitmap), then it is easy enough to apply a mask layer to the bitmap in Flash over the 3D image. So beware when using this feature—it is not recommended for Flash design. Once you have the effect you want, click OK to render your 3D vector graphic.

It's time to bring your graphic into Flash. Export the image out of Illustrator as a SWF file and then import that SWF into a Flash file. For more detailed guidance on this process, follow the instructions in the Chapter 5 section "Moving From Illustrator to Flash," and then continue to the next step in this chapter.

Now you should have your 3D graphic placed on the stage in Flash. Depending on how complex your graphic is, you should notice that Flash has created some Library symbols from your graphic (see Figure 7-42). If you double-click those symbols to edit them from your Library palette, you'll notice that they are shapes from your graphic that have been masked by duplicates of themselves. This is a minor inconvenience since you can see your graphic appears in Flash exactly as it did in Illustrator. But to maintain a clean file, you must fix the image to contain no Library symbols.

Go into each symbol by double-clicking it in the Library palette. Delete the layer mask (see Figure 7-43). As you go through each library item, make sure the remaining graphic in each symbol is grouped. Edit these in this order to maintain the coloring options on each object and to prepare for the next step in the process.

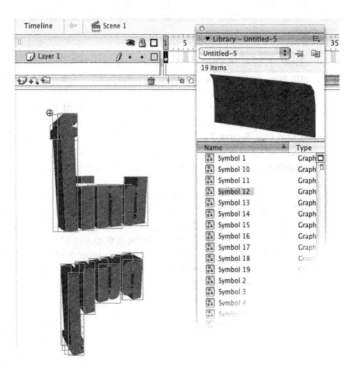

Figure 7-42. Our imported vector artwork in Flash. You can see by the selection that Flash has grouped it into many shapes. In the Library palette, you can also see that some of these shapes are graphic symbols.

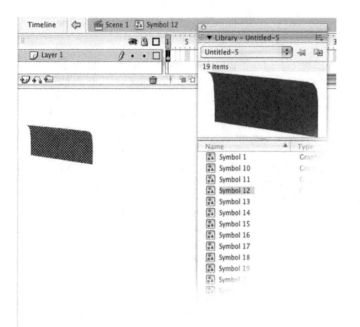

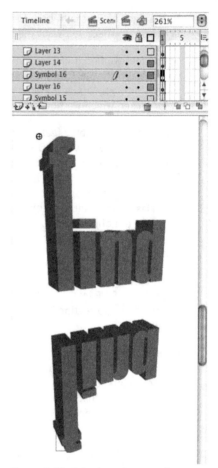

Figure 7-43. Inside one of the default Library symbols, converting the mask layer to a regular layer in Flash. Notice we've already deleted the layer mask.

Next, return to your root timeline by selecting the Scene 1 tab on your Flash document window. Select all of the objects in your cluster of images and symbols and distribute them to layers by pressing Ctrl+Shift+D (Cmd+Shift+D). Now all of the images and symbols in your cluster are on individual layers named after them (see Figure 7-44). The images that aren't symbols will just have a "Layer x" label in the Layers palette, and the layers with a symbol on them will have a "Symbol x" label in the same palette.

Figure 7-44. Selecting a layer on the root timeline with a symbol on it and breaking that symbol apart so that is is just a grouped graphic

Select all of the images on each layer by pressing Ctrl+A (Cmd+A), then break all of the graphics in your cluster apart until they are ungrouped images. You can break apart images and symbols quickly by selecting them and pressing Ctrl+B (Cmd+B). Now, group everything once by pressing Ctrl+G (Cmd+G) on your keyboard. Now you have an image on each layer and no Library symbols on your stage. Delete all of the symbols that were created for your 3D image from the Library palette by dragging them to the garbage can in that palette.

Again, select all of your images on the stage, copy them to a new layer, and delete the long list of layers you used during this last production cycle. You should have one layer with all of your grouped images on it intact (see Figure 7-45). Click and drag to select the upside-down copy of your image and make it a movie clip symbol—this is going to be your reflection.

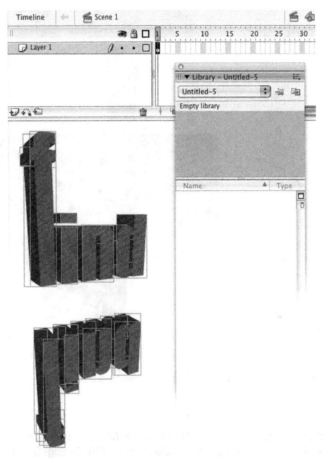

Figure 7-45. Now that all of the production layers are gone and we've eliminated the need for all of the random symbols created by the import process from Illustrator, the file is a simple single-frame FLA.

Next, you want to make a surface for your logo to rest on. Make a new layer and place it under the layer with your image on it. On the layer, create a gradated rectangle with no stroke. Adjust the gradient in the fill to run vertically, dark to light, as shown in Figure 7-46.

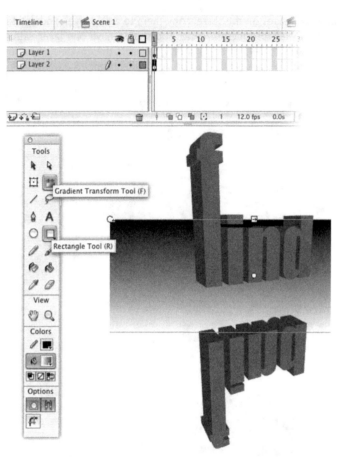

Figure 7-46. To create a surface for the logo to rest on, draw a rectangle with a gradient fill.

Now, you want to make the rectangle appear to be a plane on the z-axis. Select the rectangle with the Free Transform tool and activate the Distort option by holding down Ctrl+Option+Shift (Cmd+Option+Shift). Now grab the top-left corner of the bounding box around the rectangle and drag it into the shape until you have the correct perspective (see Figure 7-47).

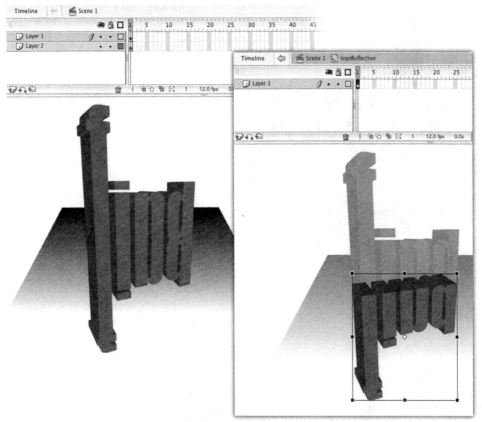

Figure 7-47. Create perspective by using the Distort feature of the Free Transform tool.

Now, bump up the reflection movie clip to fit under the top logo image. You'll most likely need to tweak the reflection image inside the reflection movie clip using the Free Transform tool to get it flush with the top logo image (see Figure 7-48).

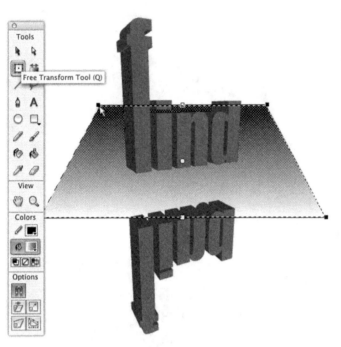

Figure 7-48. First bump the reflection movie clip up to fit along the bottom of the logo image. Then tweak the reflection graphic inside the movie clip so it would fit flush with the bottom of the logo image.

The final step to finishing off your 3D vector graphic is treating the reflection to have the proper transparency. Select the reflection movie clip and apply an alpha of 30% or less and also apply an Overlay Blend mode to the movie clip in the Property inspector. The final product is a perfectly rendered 3D image complete with surface reflection, as you see in Figure 7-49.

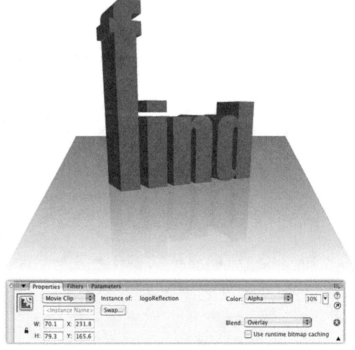

Figure 7-49. After treating the reflection movie clip, the final product is a realistic vector 3D logo in Flash.

Summary

In this chapter, you got your feet wet and started doing some real design work with the theories and design techniques discussed in all the previous chapters. Through our examples, we've tried to emphasize the simplicity of creating complex-looking, realistic objects. You don't need to spend hours creating a perfect 3D model that will only end up giving you a headache when it comes to importing it into Flash and animating it. Our techniques show you how to save file size and preserve the highest quality of graphics that can be scaled, animated, and transformed in Flash without limits.

Having said that, in our next chapter, we're going to depart a little from this mentality and shift our focus to Photoshop, which is a program that runs on a raster engine. Photoshop is one of the most powerful tools in our industry and an invaluable tool for interface designers, even if it does require a little extra work to integrate with Flash.

In this chapter, you've learned the following lessons:

- The Shape tools and gradient fills are your most powerful assets when designing objects in Flash.

- Your eyes are your best judge. Learn to trust them and understand why things are appealing and others are not. Remember that everyone can make mistakes and that a short break from work can help you catch these mistakes without wasting an excessive amount of time.

- Working with 3D software to create real 3D models can help you achieve incredibly detailed and photorealistic graphics, but there can be complications when importing these into Flash.

- When exporting graphics from 3D software, you can render a bitmap to import in Flash or use a plug-in to export a flat vector file. Exporting to vector can keep file size down; however, a complex vector can slow down playback more than a sequence of bitmaps. Flash has introduced a bitmap-caching feature to improve playback of complex vectors. This is a handy tool that stores in memory a bitmap image of vector graphics inside movie clips—which helps the Flash renderer process it faster for playback. Note that this is most effective with static graphics.

- Creating semirealistic 3D graphics directly in Flash allows you to save a lot of time, maximize compatibility, and achieve excellent quality results.

- The new filters and blend modes bring designing in Flash closer than ever to designing in Photoshop. These new effects can help you achieve convincing looking objects that are ready to be manipulated and animated at your whim.

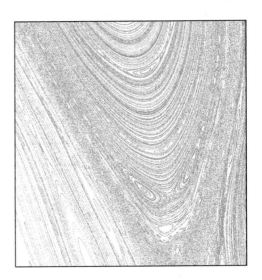

Chapter 8

USING VIDEO IN FLASH

by Michael Kemper

One of the most exciting innovations with Flash over the last couple of versions is the improved integration of video. As video content and the Internet continue to converge, Flash will no doubt be a primary vehicle for video delivery in the foreseeable future. You'll find many benefits to choosing Flash for delivering online video content, the most practical being compression. FLV compression has been simply the most flexible and dependable video format for the file size out there—and it just got a lot better with the On2 VP6 codec available in Flash 8. Flash video is now also one of the best video formats for deploying online video because of its improved import workflow. Designers and programmers alike now have complete control over video content in Flash, and that gives us the freedom to produce just about any interactive video concept for web deployment. Couple this new freedom with the versatile array of design resources available, and you can see why we as interface designers are being enlisted to shoot, edit, and animate for the video format. It's pretty common now for a Flash interface designer to use After Effects, Final Cut Pro, some flavor of sound design application, and Flash all in the same day. In this chapter, you'll see how to leverage all these new capabilities to enhance your design work and help make the Flash interfaces you create even more enjoyable and immersive experiences.

> *In case some of the video-oriented terms in this chapter are unfamiliar to you, I've included a glossary at the back of this chapter. Terms appearing in the glossary appear bold on first mention throughout the text.*

The product **shoots** I'm referencing in the pictures and examples, like the one you see in Figure 8-1, come from a series I did for a furniture company to use on their website. For each piece of furniture in their catalog, Find Furniture wanted a video of each product to be interactive on the site. Users can spin each piece around to view it from every angle, along with measurements and a short description of each piece. This chapter explains my video production process for distribution of this type of content and more in Flash.

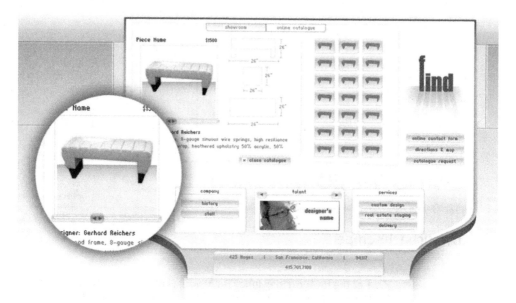

Figure 8-1. Interactive video of a product on the Find Furniture site

Video content for Flash

For many of us, "video producer" is a new hat to wear, and one that we're willing to try on. Much of the Flash video I see online tends to be tutorials or tours. These productions typically put talent (or the actors/spokespersons) over a single color (usually white) background and have them attempt to sell you one thing or another. This type of experience exemplifies why I get so excited about the possibilities of interactive video in Flash. It reminds me that we're still at the ground floor of possibilities for Flash and video. These types of experiences affirm to me that there is a next BETTER thing; and as Flash interface designers, we're perfectly positioned to create it. There are many parallels between the tools of Flash and video production such as using timelines, keyframes, movie clip management—the list goes on. As a Flash designer/animator, you're already primed for working with video. With a solid understanding of basic video productions and some practice, you can create and deploy professional interactive video solutions in Flash starting from the ground up.

Shooting video content for the Web: A basic guide

As visually creative people, interface designers are very observant. If put to the task of creating a video, most would no doubt reflect on what they have seen in movies or television and generate workable concepts to shoot. I encourage that type of creative spark. Combine this with basic procedural video production knowledge, and your next interactive project will teach you volumes about the power of video presentation on the Web. And it might even be the most compelling Flash piece you've ever created.

Equipment basics

You don't need extremely expensive equipment to generate professional video for online broadcast. The realities of video compression coupled with the advances of digital video technology create a pretty even playing field when considering what equipment is best for you. In fact, interactive video is a great medium for getting your feet wet doing video productions for just that reason. Since it doesn't have to cost a mint to get the basic gear, you can wean your way into doing professional video projects. As you learn more about video productions, there will very likely be a project in your future that will justify making additional purchases. Before you know it, you'll have a full production outfit ready to produce any number of professional videos.

For many of us, a decent digital video camera isn't too far out of reach, if at all. Following is a list of basic camera features you should keep in mind when considering purchasing a camera for shooting web-bound video:

- **Format:** There are many new high-definition digital video (HD DV) cameras on the market that are nice to have but not absolutely necessary. MiniDV is a must. You can use Final Cut Pro, Adobe Premiere, Adobe After Effects, etc., to capture MiniDV format with little instruction, and the tapes are inexpensive and easy to find as well. If you get a HD DV cam, you will most likely need special tapes to utilize that feature—meaning you can't run to the corner store for an extra tape if you need one quickly. Use 3**CCD** cameras—they are more expensive but well worth the extra money. The quality in color and resolution (especially for camera pans and arcs) far surpasses lesser CCD cameras.

- **Design:** When I was starting out, it was important for me to have something small enough to store easily in a compact bag, and this might be a consideration for you, as well. Many "prosumer" cameras (professional-quality cameras under $2,000) that fit this requirement don't allow for professional audio equipment, so make sure you purchase something that you can hook a microphone up to. Another important consideration is having an LCD panel. Chances are that unless you have a crew to help you on your shooting engagements you're going to play the role of camera operator, director, set **grip**, gaffer, etc. If you can't get a camera with an LCD panel, consider purchasing a small, cheap, portable TV so you can see what you are shooting without getting stuck behind a viewfinder.

- **Lens:** You will want at least a 10X fixed lens or greater and optical image stabilization. It is pretty common to find affordable cameras with 20X lenses. Interchangeable lens systems are nice to have, but not necessary.

- **Connectivity:** The sound you capture is likely just as important as the video you're shooting, so you will need at least one microphone jack. If you anticipate needing more than one microphone at a time, you can purchase an inexpensive dual-microphone kit with **lavaliere mics** and regular mics that work with most single-mic prosumer cameras. Make sure there is a headphone jack to do sound checks.

Having a decent tripod for pans, tilts, arcs, and other steady camera movement is absolutely necessary—there is no way to fix a bumpy video pan in postproduction.

Invest a little cash in a decent camera bag to hold everything. Chances are you'll need to have mics, cables, batteries, lens wipes, etc. during your shoot, and it's almost impossible to remember all this stuff unless it's all together. When you get your bag, get one a third larger than you need to fit all the extra scripts, pens, tapes, etc. I got my first camera bag at a Wal-Mart for $30. It was a pretty good deal considering similar bags at camera stores sell for $90 to $150.

As I stated earlier, sound is extremely important. The ideal microphone for capturing dialogue on a small production is a wireless lavaliere microphone, or lav mic. These mics are easily hidden in the collar of your subject's shirt, and you don't have to pack around cables. Lav mic kits can be purchased for $150, and they are well worth it. If you use the directional (or shotgun) mic that comes on your camera, your biggest sound problem will be ambient sounds you will pick up. You can try to edit this stuff out of your sound, but it's a long, tedious process and isn't always a consistent or reliable fix.

Another important investment is a basic lighting kit. Many kits are available with numerous combinations of lamps, stands, bulbs, etc. The basic video lighting configuration to achieve *base light* (even set lighting) consists of three different lights: **back light**, **fill light**, and **key light**. A basic affordable lighting kit that will serve your purposes should contain a spotlight (or hard light), floodlight (or soft light), and a broad (usually with barn doors) lamp complete with **stands**, **gels**, **lighting cables**, **umbrellas**, **clamps**, and other general rigging equipment. These types of kits are available for as little as $700 online.

Figure 8-2 illustrates the basic three-point lighting positions. The main idea with using this combination of lighting is to create pleasant contrast on the subject and also an even base light over the whole scene. If you are intending to use an editing program to "knock out" your subject from the background, purchase some **green screens** to place behind and under the subject. In lieu of having green screen, I've blasted walls with light behind my subject and used a high-contrast setting on my camera to shoot the subject against an artificial white.

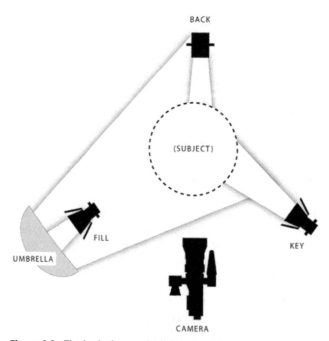

Figure 8-2. The basic three-point lighting positions

Figure 8-3 shows a variety of standard camera handling techniques for shooting **takes: arc**, **dolly**, **pan**, **pedestal**, **tilt**, and **truck**.

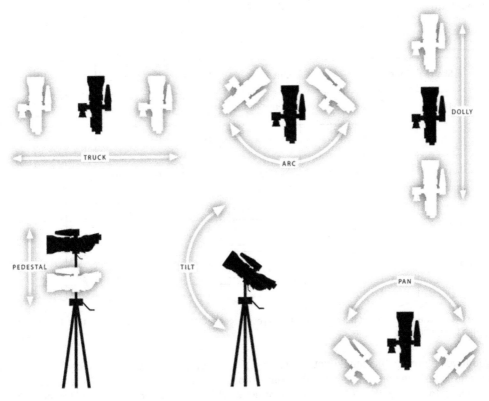

Figure 8-3. Standard camera handling techniques for shooting takes

A practical (and free!) necessity for your video projects is a shot log, like the one you see in Figure 8-4. This is basically an itemized list of all the footage captured during a shoot. It's common for the camera operator to call out the **time code** of a shot before recording footage and as soon as the camera stops recording so that someone can accurately record the quality of the take. Once you are ready to start editing footage, you can use the shot log to skip over all of the "junk footage" and spend your time capturing/saving the good footage. This saves a lot of time during the editing process.

Production Title

Shoot Date

Scene	Take	In	Out	Notes	OK	NG
1A	1	01:03:26	01:05:56	Shutter and skipped line		X
1A	2	01:06:00	01:08:14	False start		X
1A	3	01:08:15	01:11:03	Perfect turn—best take	X	
		_ _ : _ _ : _ _	_ _ : _ _ : _ _			
		_ _ : _ _ : _ _	_ _ : _ _ : _ _			
		_ _ : _ _ : _ _	_ _ : _ _ : _ _			

Figure 8-4. If you are shooting talent (people), it is recommended that you keep a shot log to help you get through the editing process more efficiently.

If you haven't already, this should get you started piecing together the basic equipment you need to do professional video productions for the Web. Through my own research, I discovered that a beginner wanting to put together a basic equipment list would spend around $3500. And remember: you can always rent lights and other equipment if you aren't able to splurge on all of this gear. The most important thing is to get a reliable camera and do more research before making any of these purchases. A search on Google for "digital video equipment" will provide you with ample information for online research. Do your homework and good luck!

Shooting and editing basics

There are many application options when it comes to editing digital video. I prefer to use a combination of Final Cut Pro and After Effects. I use Final Cut Pro because it makes logging and capturing footage and editing that footage together easy. Whatever program you decide to use for your editing, make sure it has a **batch capture** option for capturing your footage from the camera and saving it digitally to your computer. This will literally save you hours during the editing process.

After Effects is great for creating every type of video animation, even effects that can be used in Flash, but it is also a really great keying tool for knocking out green screen. This provides an even solid color in the background that makes **keying out** the subject much easier. Keying is a technique used in video editing applications to cut out people or objects based on the color around them. This is very similar to using the wand tool in PhotoShop and deleting the selection. If you plan on keying out your background and utilizing the new alpha channel capabilities in Flash, make sure that when you shoot your video, the background of your subject is blown out with plenty of light to save time keying it out. Be careful, though, because lots of light also means a lot of color spill on surfaces of your subject. I have had good results using the DV Matte Pro plug-in for After Effects, which is shown in Figure 8-5.

Figure 8-5. After Effects is a great tool to use for keying out green screen.

In the past, excluding art films, editing professional video consisted of three basic main narrative elements: beginning, middle, and end. There are variations on this, but that's pretty much the rhythm. The video boom created by amateur video enthusiasts, offline and online, have turned that standard on its head. I attribute online video to being more like the *Choose Your Own Adventure* books I grew up with. In these books, you would finish a chapter and select an option from a key at the bottom of the page, which would tell you the page to flip to in order to complete the story. One short book was full of dozens of different stories because it was interactive. Today's online video experiences are very similar. The narrative possibilities are extensive when creating an interactive video project, and understanding some traditional fundamentals will most likely enhance your final product.

Planning for continuity is one of the most basic things you should keep in mind while shooting video. This means making sure clothing, props, subject, and location are consistent throughout your filming assignment. This way if you decide you want to edit in a **clip** of your subject from day 3 of your filming to a clip from day 1, you don't have to worry about something like the subject wearing colored pants for one cut that are different from what the subject is wearing for the rest of that segment. Also, always keep the narrative of your video in mind when considering transitions. Flash is a great delivery tool for interactive video because you can plan to animate transitions in Flash instead of in your video editing application, or use a mixture from both. Planning continuity starts before you edit, but you will feel its impact most when you are sitting in front of your editing station trying to put the final piece together.

You don't need a degree in video production to create great video for online consumption, but having some fundamental knowledge will make your work more professional and competitive. If you are interested in learning more on the subject of video productions as it relates to Flash, I recommend *Foundation Flash 8 Video* by Tom Green and Jordan Chilcott (friends of ED, 2006). I strongly encourage you to also research online so your final product is as good as possible.

A note on format and standards

Every video editing application was created for editing and exporting video format for TV and movies. And thus, the standard digital format for video has traditionally been NTSC and PAL. NTSC is the standard in the Americas and Japan; PAL is used in the EU and in Asia. These formats differ from web-standard formats in that they utilize rectangular pixels (Pixel Aspect Ratio) to display content, while computer monitors use square pixels. Since computer monitors are based on square pixels, the frame size for what is traditionally used on other screen formats differs from what is appropriate for computer monitors. For instance, NTSC image ratio is 720×480; PAL is 720×576, whereas the comparable computer image ratio standard is typically 640×480, 1024×768, 1280×1600, etc. Another major difference between these standards is that NTSC and PAL is an **interlaced** *display method, and a computer uses a progressive method to display content. This difference is not readily noticeable to the naked human eye. If you have ever seen video footage taken of a computer monitor, then you have seen this difference in action. You would have noticed a constant line flickering vertically across the computer monitor screen as it "drew" the content. Many video editing programs like Final Cut Pro, After Effects, and Adobe Premier have export settings to compensate for interlaced footage. When exporting video for a computer monitor, make sure you are exporting it using a de-interlaced or DV setting; this will format your video using square pixels, so your images don't appear squished on a computer monitor.*

Final Cut Pro basics

I am a huge fan of Final Cut Pro, and I use it as much as possible to edit my digital video projects. It's a typical Apple application: it's easy to use, works well, and looks great doing it. I have also extensively used Adobe Premiere to edit video on a PC, and the good news is that Adobe Premiere now looks and behaves a lot like Final Cut Pro. Unfortunately, there are still hard-to-find presets that drive me crazy, but Premiere will do in a pinch. My point is that you can take much of the knowledge from this section and use it for both applications, but the following is done in Final Cut Pro.

Batch-capturing video

Once you have all of your footage and your ins and outs marked on your **production log**, it's time to capture your footage so you can edit **sequences** or even key out the background. When you are logging and capturing your footage, it is important to note that the time code of the DV tape in your camera is the backbone of this operation. This impacts the logging and capturing process deeply. For instance, if you have 10 minutes of tape with recorded footage on it, and then for some reason you **zeroed out** the tape before continuing with the remainder of recorded footage during your shooting, Final Cut Pro will get confused when trying to find specific times before and after the point where the tape is zeroed out. To avoid this happening and having to relog your footage, you can take a couple of preemptive steps. First, you could record black on each DV tape before using it on your shooting assignments. This basically means recording dead space on the tape, typically done by letting the camera record a tape all the way through with the lens cap on. Then rewind it and use it just like you would a fresh tape. This makes a time code impression for the tape that will remain consistent throughout the tape with no breaks. Another tip is to never fast-forward on a fresh tape beyond the point of recorded footage during your shooting assignments. Most cameras add 1 to 2 seconds of blank tape space before recording again after having been stopped/rewound/fast-forwarded. If there isn't a time code impression on the tape at the point where it starts recording again, the tape starts at 0 again. Preventing time code breaks on your DV tape during the shooting assignment will save many headaches during the logging and capturing process.

Start by connecting your MiniDV camera to your computer with a FireWire cord. Open Final Cut Pro. Once the application has booted, select File ➤ Log and Capture. A window appears with all of the tools you need to grab snippets of your recorded DV tape and batch capture them to save into your project.

The main part of this window is dedicated to the DV preview, as shown in Figure 8-6, where you can see the footage as it plays on your camera. If your Caps Lock feature is on, the preview will be disabled.

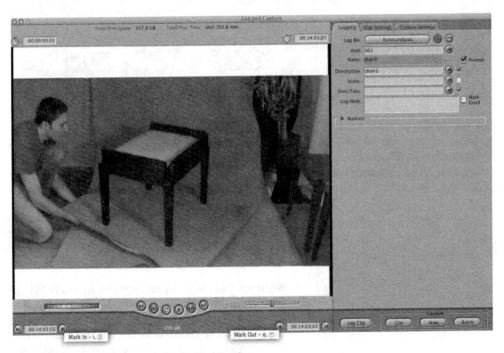

Figure 8-6. Log and Capture window in Final Cut Pro

Along the left of the window is the different log and capture preference tabs. The Logging tab allows you to enter clip titles and other notes about each clip. You can also expand the **markers** arrow to create or delete editing markers as you **log clips**. The Capture Settings tab, shown in Figure 8-7, provides you with input drop-down menus where you can define NTSC for your capturing format and allocate your **scratch disk**.

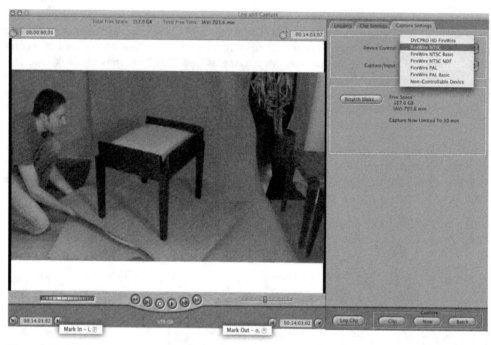

Figure 8-7. Capture Settings options in Final Cut Pro

Along the bottom of the window you have all of the manual controls to navigate through the tape, like rewind and play buttons. Also along the bottom are your logging controls to mark the in and out points of each clip. You can play the video and click the in and out arrows as you see fit, or you can manually type in the time code you wish to capture. Once you have the timing you desire, simply click Log Clip and it will be added to your clip logging bin window as a temporary clip until you capture it.

Figure 8-8. Confirmation window for clip logging in Final Cut Pro

Each time you log a clip, the application will prompt you to confirm the clip settings, as shown in Figure 8-8. Enter your title for the clip, click Mark Good if you prefer that clip, then click OK.

When you have logged your clips and are ready to import or capture them from your camera, click the Batch button in the Capture area on the bottom right. The Batch Capture window, shown in Figure 8-9, will prompt you to confirm your capture settings. Use DV NTSC 48 kHz for your capture preset. This is the most flexible format for final output to the web. NTSC refers to the western video standard, and the 48 kHz is the setting for the sound. You can choose to capture all or just selected items in your logging bin; typically I do my entire log and capture for a project at once, so I select All Items in Logging Bin. To eliminate logged clips, just delete them from the logging bin. You can also press Option on your keyboard and select only clips you want to capture and then click the Items Selected in Logging Bin option. Click OK, and Final Cut Pro will rewind and capture all of the logged footage from your camera to your clip browser in your project.

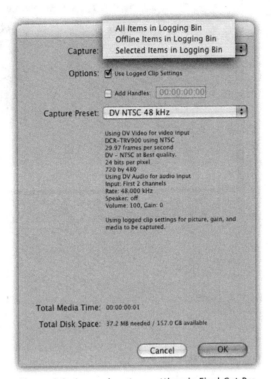

Figure 8-9. Log and capture settings in Final Cut Pro

Once all of your clips are captured, make sure to save the project before creating and editing sequences.

Editing basics

Now that all of your footage is in Final Cut Pro, you are ready to edit your sequences together. Let's get familiar with the interface. Take a look at Figure 8-10 before reading on.

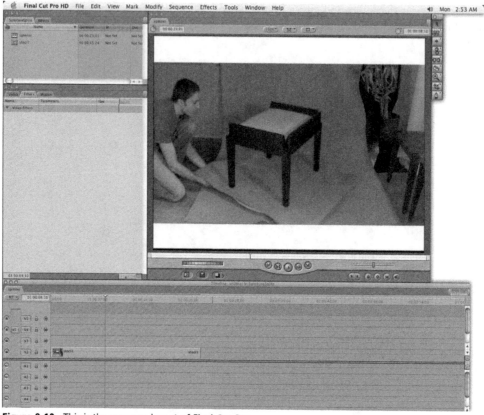

Figure 8-10. This is the program layout of Final Cut Pro.

Many of the same paradigms of asset management and timeline editing in Flash are similar in video editing programs including Final Cut Pro. In Final Cut Pro, you create sequences and then drop your video clips onto the timeline of those sequences. You can double-click clips in the clip browser window to create in and out points, or you can use the Razor tool to slice them up once they are placed on the sequence timeline. Your canvas shows the video preview of your clips as you edit them together. If you **scrub** the timeline, the canvas updates in real time to the **playhead** scrub. The timeline is divided into video and audio tracks. Place your video clips on the top portion and your audio for each track will automatically be placed on the bottom tracks.

You might find that you need to color correct your footage and give it slightly more contrast or tweak its color balance to make the colors more or less vibrant, depending on the effect you are going for. There are more filters than you could possibly need in the Filters tab, usually grouped with the clip browser. Typically when I am keying footage out in Final Cut Pro, I up the brightness and contrast slightly to help make my subject pop off the green screen, as you see in Figure 8-11, and make the green screen easier to select.

Figure 8-11. Applying a Color Correction filter to footage on the sequence timeline in Final Cut Pro

To apply a filter to a clip, you can double-click it from the clip browser or the timeline after it's been placed, and that clip will appear individually in a preview window.

Click the Filters tab in the preview window to view filter preferences as you add them. Then, click and drag filters from the Filter palette into the clip's Filters tab. Adjust these filters, and you'll notice the similarities to how filters in PhotoShop work, many of which are even called the same thing. Keep in mind that with many filter applications, your rendering and exporting time will increase. If you are correcting footage with people, a good tip is to use skin tones as your guide to finding proper contrast and hue adjustments—backgrounds and props can be believable if they are a little off, but skin tones look either right or wrong.

To key out backgrounds in Final Cut Pro, start by using the Color Key filter. I generally need to apply between 5 to 10 of these in subtle variations before getting the perfect combination of clean contours and definition (see Figure 8-12). You can use the Eyedropper tool in the Color Key filter dialog box to grab colors off of the canvas preview, or you can select a color from the Color Picker window by clicking the sample color swatch. The effect of your color key won't be apparent until you adjust the tolerance lever in the Key Filters dialog box. Remember that if you are keying out an image in your video, scrub to many parts of the clip to make sure lighting changes don't modify the **junk video** around your image enough to warrant additional color keys before you output the video. Also, it most important to just get a **clear key** (or crisp contour) around the space of your subject; don't worry about imagery that can be cropped out by using the Flash Video Encoder crop options, which I cover later in this chapter.

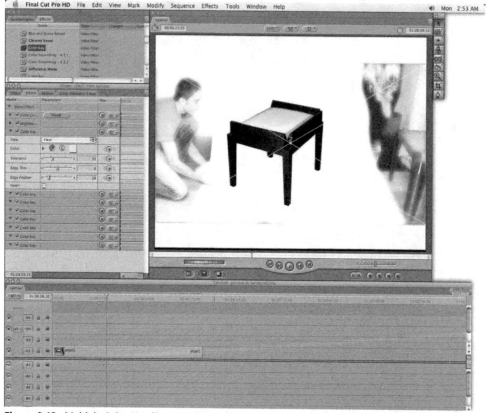

Figure 8-12. Multiple Color Key filters applied to a clip on the sequence timeline in Final Cut Pro

Since this is for web distribution, keep in mind that the effects of optimization will have deep impact on long fades and other custom transitions you add to your video. I talk more about this later in this chapter.

Exporting your sequence

Once your sequence is edited and ready to go, it's time to export your video and prepare it to bring into Flash. Since I am on a Mac and therefore most familiar with QuickTime formats, I export my sequences as QuickTime files; but if you are on a PC, AVI is also a usable format to compress in the Flash Video Encoder used later in this chapter.

Go to File ➤ Export ➤ Quicktime Movie. The first step in this process is to name your file and choose where on your computer to save it, as you see in Figure 8-13. Since we know we are going to compress this using the Flash Video Encoder, it's best to export it out of our video editing program with as much data as possible to limit the number of life cycles of compression on our final optimized video. In other words, compressing a video multiple times usually degrades the final quality, so just doing it once will give you better results for the file size. So we want to export as much data as possible to discourage any loss of video quality during this step in the process. Export the video in the same format you captured it in, in this case DV NTSC 48 kHz.

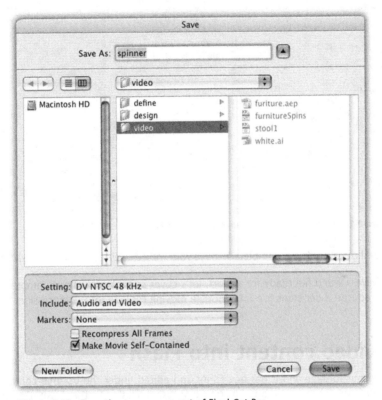

Figure 8-13. Exporting a sequence out of Final Cut Pro

You can customize this setting by selecting Customize from the Setting drop-down list (see Figure 8-14). This is the same preferences window you get when you are modifying sequence settings.

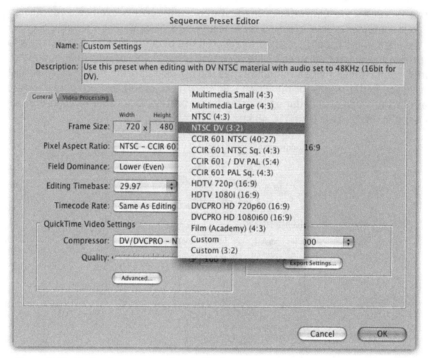

Figure 8-14. Customize export settings in Final Cut Pro.

Once you have all of your settings completed, make your movie a self-contained movie, then click Save.

Now that we have a video file ready for export, let's cover some basics about compression that will help you make educated decisions for your footage moving forward into compression.

Bringing video content into Flash

After you have your footage and it has been shot and edited under the optimal conditions for web delivery, it's time to compress it and distribute it using Flash. At the Flash Developer Center (www.macromedia.com/devnet/flash/), you'll find several articles on best practices for Flash distribution of Flash video, and I recommend reading these as well as the following to get a broader understanding of the capabilities Flash offers for video delivery. Among the best articles are

- "Encoding Best Practices for Prerecorded Flash Video"
- "Delivering Flash Video: Understanding the Difference Between Progressive Download and Streaming Video"

Formats and compression

At times, video compression seems more like an art than a science. I suppose this is because there are so many combinations of settings you can apply to any given video, and each video is different due to varied lighting techniques and subject matter. Fortunately, most compression tools provide many default settings so that you can get started easily and learn the ropes through testing variations on these settings. And even better yet, applications like Sorenson Squeeze let you save your favorite settings to use in other projects and even on other computers.

Of the many different options you have for outputting video from most video editing programs, currently FLV (Flash Video) is not one of them. Until the Flash Video Encoder came out, I used Sorenson Squeeze to compress digital video for use in Flash. For me, this involved exporting a file from Final Cut Pro as a QuickTime video (.mov) and then running that file through Sorenson Squeeze. Squeeze is a versatile program because it lets me tweak my settings using many different default options as a starting point. The myriad presets are helpful if you are still learning about video compression. Another great feature of squeeze is the ability to set a *watch folder*. This enables Squeeze to automatically compress any compatible video files in that folder and output it in the same location, which saves you a lot of time if you are batch exporting several clips from your editing program.

The Flash Video Encoder has many of the same options as Squeeze—and better yet, IT'S FREE with Flash. Clearly the biggest advantage to using the new VP6 Flash Video Encoder is the ability to save an alpha channel in your compressed file. Even though you still need to key out your alpha channel in a video editing program prior to using this feature in order to get a clean channel, it's another great tool at your disposal to create innovative video solutions with Flash. Output quality has also been greatly enhanced with this new compression tool. The two-pass encoding allocates the bits within the file far more intelligently, resulting in increased quality throughout the video. When you compare this new technology to older versions of Flash video, you will notice the older version seems pixilated, even blocky; and the newer compression appears a lot smoother and clear.

There are pros and cons to using the new Flash Video Encoder depending on what you are trying to achieve. When considering overall quality and file size for Flash 8, using the VP6 compression will usually be your best option. I get inconsistent results with the Sorenson Spark compression option when exporting for Flash 7–compatible projects. In those instances when I need to consider Flash Player 7, I still use Sorenson Squeeze so I can tweak the many more options it offers for lesser Flash Player versions.

Generally speaking, here are some best practices you want to keep in mind when going through your compression workflow:

- Whenever possible, always encode a file from its uncompressed form so that there are fewer "lifetimes" of compression on the video, and the final quality is better. In other words, only optimize your video once.

- When your video contains lots of motion, it will be tougher to compress for lower-bandwidth users. When you are compressing footage with a lot of motion, it will require a larger bit rate and more keyframes to maintain a clean image; and that adds to file size.

- Using lots of fade- or wipe-intensive transitions in your editing will also increase the number of pixel changes in the video content. Again, this will require a higher bit rate and more keyframes to pull off—and in turn, increase file size along with user download times.

Encoding the video

Once you have your footage edited and exported, it's time to compress it to use in Flash. The Flash Development Center has a good online tutorial on how to use the general functionality of the Flash Video Encoder, and I encourage you to take advantage of that resource. I will cover additional insight

I have gained by my personal experience with the tool. Also, we will discuss Sorenson Squeeze in comparison to the new Flash Video Encoder.

To begin, open the Flash 8 Video Encoder that shipped with Flash. Click the Add button on the upper-right side of the screen. Use the directory browser to locate your video file and open it up. Now you will see a new source file added to the queue, as shown in Figure 8-15, with a "waiting" status. Select this item in the queue and click the Settings button on the right side of the screen.

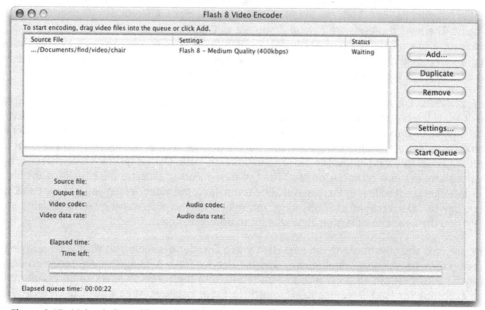

Figure 8-15. Main window with a queue list of the Flash Video Encoder

> **A note on importing video for FLV conversion**
>
> *You may experience problems if you are trying to convert MPEG files to FLV. The issue is that some MPEG files are muxed or multiplexed. In a muxed MPEG, the audio and video tracks are mixed together. Typically, this is common with MPEG1 and MPEG2 video formats. Ironically, MPEG1 is the most common QuickTime compression for online video: it is a high-quality/small-size (and quick download time) format perfect for viewing video using the QuickTime plug-in installed on most browsers. In other words, this is most likely the format you would get if you requested video from a production person and all that person knew is that it is for online distribution. You will not be able to convert a muxed video to FLV: the result will most likely be an FLV file that looks great but has no sound. If you must get an MPEG, then make sure whomever you get it from understands the best format for converting to FLV is MPEG4 (not muxed), MOV, or AVI files.*

As you can see in Figure 8-16, the default settings for the video are the medium-quality settings (400 kbps—or kilobits per second). This may be fine for a video using a streaming service, since it will play in bits as it downloads (as long as your target audience is expected to be viewing the content using a high-speed broadband connection), but even then I recommend further optimizing your video to increase its performance. You definitely want to tweak the optimization settings if you plan on bitstreaming or embedding the video. Click Show Advanced Settings to bring up the dialog box shown in Figure 8-17.

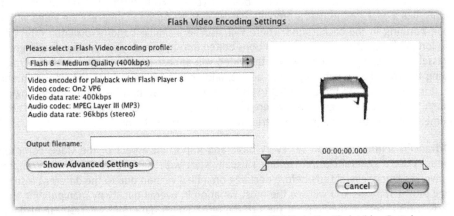

Figure 8-16 Basic default settings for a medium-quality FLV file in the Flash Video Encoder

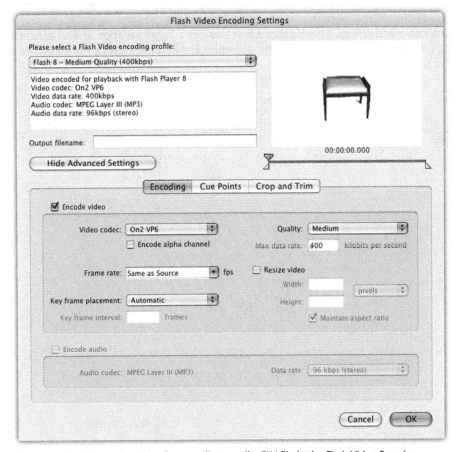

Figure 8-17. Advanced settings for a medium-quality FLV file in the Flash Video Encoder

It's important to note that your settings will vary depending on the video content you are optimizing. Good optimization starts with proper lighting and camera technique at the outset of your project, which is why I covered those basics previously in this chapter. You simply can't compensate for poor footage during the editing and compression process. If you are compressing video with many **dithers** or gradients, like a background that is omni lit, it's going to be hard to compress the video without at least some **banding** in the background. There will also be a similar banding/pixilated effect if your video has long fades or other dithered transitions edited into it, comparable to what you might see in a compressed GIF file. You will notice that the video will appear just fine until it hits the transition, then during the transition a banding effect occurs, and goes away as soon as the transition ends. In Squeeze, it is possible to use the 2-Pass VBR setting to avoid this somewhat. What this setting does is run through the footage and remember where those trouble spots are. When Squeeze runs through a second time, it anticipates those spots and tries to compensate for them.

In the Advanced Settings, you can set every basic and important aspect of the video compression. These settings are a general Custom setting I usually start with (see Figure 8-18). My compression process involves doing several tests before deciding on a final version due to the different results I get depending on the footage. You will see the most variation in overall quality by manipulating the data rate. This is also the setting that impacts file size the most. Lower data rates will result in pixilation on the video or even larger artifacts that distort the video image, similar to what you might observe in a compressed JPEG image. Frame rate modifies how many frames appear per second. I never go less than 12 fps because that is when the final output typically starts to appear jumpy or choppy. 15 fps is a standard web video setting. I have noticed that you get a larger variation in final output size by increasing the frame rate with a high data rate. But with a low data rate, varying the frame rate doesn't impact file size as much.

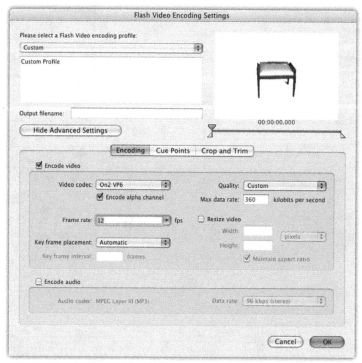

Figure 8-18. Modified advanced settings for an FLV file in the Flash Video Encoder

Using the alpha channel option is simple. Make sure you are using the VP6 codec, and then just click the Include Alpha Channel check box. When you key out colors of the video in your video editing application, this information is saved in the color depth of the file. The Flash Video Encoder will automatically read that data and use it to generate the alpha channel.

A cool additional feature in the Flash Video Encoder is the ability to crop and resize your video during the compression process, as you see demonstrated in Figure 8-19. Click the Crop and Trim button in the Advanced Settings dialog box. You can tweak the screen size of your video by modifying the left, top, right, and bottom edge positions as indicated in the crop panel (see Figure 8-20).

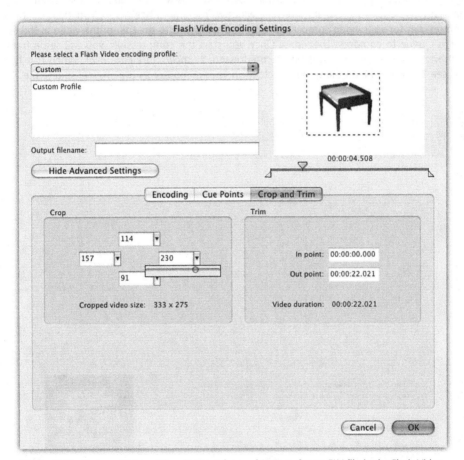

Figure 8-19. Crop and trim settings in the Advanced Settings for an FLV file in the Flash Video Encoder

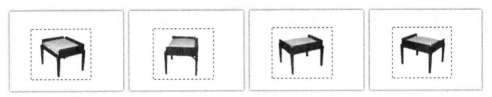

Figure 8-20. Trying out different positions with the playhead of the video while cropping its screen size

155

I generally set this and then scrub the playhead in the preview to make sure my image isn't exceeding the new bounds of the video before continuing. You can also set the in and out points of your video. This is handy if you are modifying the frame rate on a video that should seamlessly loop. If you take out too many frames in the frame rate, the end of your video will sometimes "pop" back to the beginning instead of looping smoothly. To avoid this, I use footage that gives me a little leeway at the beginning and end, then after tweaking the frame rate I edit the in and out points to make sure the video picks up at the beginning where it leaves off at the end. You can manually input the timing for your video trim, or you can scrub the handles on either side of the video preview scrubber to find the right timing.

Once you have selected your preferred settings, click OK. This will close the Advanced Settings dialog box and take you back to the main interface window. You will notice that if you changed the compression settings for your video compression, it will display next to the title of the video in the list box. Click Start Queue to compress the video. Once you start the compression, you will see a frame-by-frame preview of your video as it is being compressed, as shown in Figure 8-21. When it is finished, you will see a new FLV file in the same directory on your computer as the original source file.

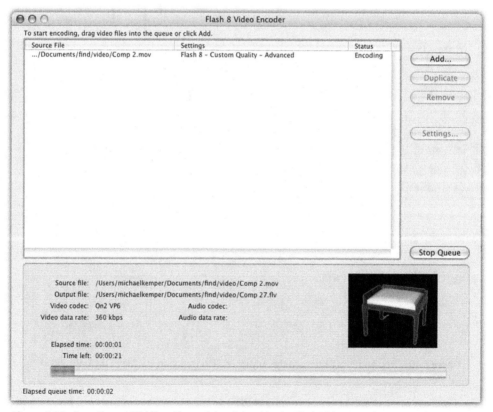

Figure 8-21. Exporting an FLV file with an alpha channel in the Flash Video Encoder

Using video in Flash

It is very easy to deliver your video content using Flash in a few different ways. Depending on the control you anticipate needing for the video content, you will want to select the option that also works best in your server environment. There are three main ways to deliver video using Flash:

1. **Bitstream:** Also known as *progressive download*, this method is commonly used on many of the Flash video sites online now. This basically means that video content is being progressively loaded into a Flash interface using a basic HTTP request in a way similar to how you would load a movie clip or bitmap image off of the server using the loadMovie method. The content is buffered until enough data has loaded to play. The amount of video content that is loaded before it plays can be set using ActionScript (setBufferTime();). This method allows you to switch out video content without having to open the FLA and do additional production/ programming work. Using the bitstream method keeps your SWF file size down because the video file is loaded externally. This impacts many architecture concerns positively, as it means navigation, animation, and other interactions are accessible to the user without having to wait for a huge video file to download. This method has limited playhead seek capabilities where you would want a scrubber or playhead in your design to allow your users to jump to sections of the video—but this is only in circumstances where the video isn't completely downloaded from the server. Also, this method actually downloads the FLV content onto the user's machine, and if that user is knowledgeable about browser caching, he could potentially save it and reuse it for his own purposes—I have never actually seen or heard of this happening, though. The other side of this argument is that when a user returns to the site without clearing the browser cache, the video content will play instantly because it is being read locally from the browser cache folder. This is Flash Player 7 and 8+ compliant.

2. **Streaming:** Many of us are familiar with streaming media technologies. Whatever service you decide to use for streaming FLV content, it will most definitely be some flavor of Flash Communication Server. There are specialized services that are even Flash authorized, like VitalStream, to stream FLV content into Flash interfaces. All of the benefits to using this and other Flash video streaming services start with the fact that the video content plays as it's loaded, so the user doesn't have to wait for a buffer or preload. VitalStream can also detect bandwidth, and your account can be set up to vary the quality of your video so that your users don't have to wait too long to view the content regardless of their connection speed. Streaming services are hands down the most advantageous to users when you anticipate serving up large amounts of video content. From a user perspective, the video will play sooner, download faster, and allow her functionality like full seek (jumping to sections of a video before it completely downloads), live video feeds, video capturing and recording, and more. From a developer's perspective, the server and network resources are more efficiently utilized and many streaming services like VitalStream provide in-depth tracking and reporting with their server packages. This is Flash Player 6, 7, and 8+ compliant.

3. **Embed:** This technique is widely used for very small video clips that are viewed in navigation rollovers or complex screen transitions. The main reason why this technique is restricted to small video clips is because it actually embeds the video into the SWF file and increases its file size considerably. Another reason is because once the video is embedded into the FLA, you can

scrub it like a graphic set to play once/loop. This is helpful because it provides additional control to help you determine button states or transition timing more accurately than if you had to consider loading the video externally. When using embedded video in this way, it is a good practice to make sure your FLA frame rate is the same as the video you are importing—they don't have to be, but you will get mixed results if these vary. Embedded video content is tougher to update than the other options because it requires someone to actually open the FLA to replace the video with new content. This could mean modifying timeline effects, keyframing, and other timeline-intensive production. If you choose to embed your video, you have the option of using a QuickTime format, but I recommend using FLV files to maximize performance and optimize download time for your users. This option is only recommended when you absolutely need the video to be in the same file as the SWF file and the video is short and small. This technique is Flash Player 6, 7, and 8+ compliant.

If you aren't sure what options are best for you, here are some basic guidelines you can use to make the right decision:

Solution	Bitstream	Stream	Embed
Video has a small screen size (less than 200×200 pixels) and is 10 seconds or less			✔
Video is between 10 seconds and 1 minute	✔	✔	
Video is longer than 2 minutes		✔	
Low viewership expected	✔		
High viewership expected		✔	
Needs bandwidth profiling for variable quality and size		✔	
Extra security for intellectual property		✔	
Instant start		✔	
Live video, video recording		✔	

The preceding chart is based on one published by Adobe, but is much more forgiving to the bitstreaming option. Of course, you will run into server problems if you serve up hundreds of megabytes of video to thousands of simultaneous viewers unless you purchase a streaming server solution like Flash Media Server. But in my experience, bitstreaming functions just fine for most video content online: short interviews, demo reels, trailers, etc., that you anticipate a general number of viewers for in any given period of time.

Bitstreaming video

To create a bitstream Flash Interface for your video content, open a new Flash file. Open up your Components Library and drag the FLVPlayback component to the stage, as you see in Figure 8-22.

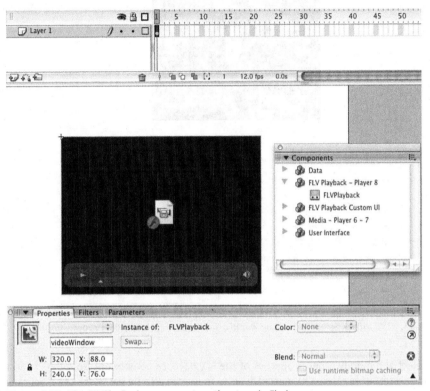

Figure 8-22. The FLVPlayBack component on the stage in Flash

One really cool feature of Flash 8 is the Library of default player controls for the FLVPlayback component. To select the best skin for your needs, click the Parameters tab in the Property inspector and scroll down to Skin. Click the small magnifying glass beside the default SWF selected as your skin. The Select Skin dialog box, shown in Figure 8-23, will appear with a preview of the selected skin set from the drop-down menu. Navigate through the skins until you see the one that best works for your design, then click OK.

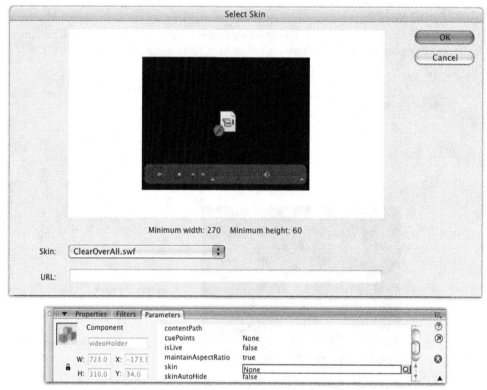

Figure 8-23. FLVPlayBack Select Skin dialog window and Parameters tab in the Property inspector

You can select and modify other properties of the FLVPlayback component from the Property inspector like autoSize, bufferTime, skinAutoHide, etc. These can also be easily set using ActionScript.

Now you will see the same video component with your selected skin, as in Figure 8-24. Give your component an instance name to use when loading your video content. In this example, we will call it videoWindow. At this point, I always make the video component a movie clip so that I can apply movie clip control functions to place, show/hide, fade, or anything else you would typically be able to do to a movie clip using ActionScript but not be able to apply as easily to a component. Give the movie clip an instance name so you can reference it in ActionScript; in this example, I will call the movie clip containing the video component movieHolder.

Figure 8-24. A movie clip containing the FLVPlayBack component

On the _root timeline, create a new layer called actions. Select the first keyframe and open your actions palette. In the actions palette, enter the following:

```
movieHolder.videoWindow.contentPath = "chair.flv";
movieHolder.videoWindow.skinAutoHide = true;
movieHolder.videoWindow.autoSize = true;
movieHolder.videoWindow.autoPlay= true;
movieHolder.videoWindow.autoRewind = true;
```

This line of code is calling the file chair.flv as the video content for movieHolder.videoWindow. All of the other lines are simply setting properties for the component. It's easy to see how this can be integrated into a function; chair.flv could even be a variable so the video title could be loaded dynamically. There are many possibilities. Now preview the FLA, and you should see your video content playing in the FLVPlayback component (see Figure 8-25). If you choose to use one of the preskinned player controls, your FLA will publish two SWFs: one containing your work and one containing the assets. These assets are loaded into the component at runtime, so both SWFs need to be in the same relative directory as your FLA in order to display the controls.

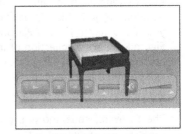

Figure 8-25. The final out put showing the FLVPlayBack component's player skin. This shows a video being bitstreamed with a transparent background utilizing Flash video alpha channel capabilities.

161

You can also create custom controls such as play, pause, and rewind buttons. To do this, draw your button graphics and make them movie clips with instance names. The following code provides basic control over video playback:

```
// This assigns a onPress action to a movie clip on the root timeline
 that tells the video component to pause its content
pauseBtn.onPress = function() {
 movieHolder.videoWindow.pause();
};
// This assigns a onPress action to a movie clip on the root timeline
 that tells the video component to play its content
playBtn.onPress = function() {
 movieHolder.videoWindow.play();
};
// This assigns a onPress action to a movie clip on the root timeline
 that tells the video component to rewind and play its content
rewindBtn.onPress = function() {
 movieHolder.videoWindow.playheadTime = 0;
 movieHolder.videoWindow.play();
};
```

Additionally, it's also very easy to track the playhead time of the video through the following code. This can be used for tracking web stats, triggering events in animation, or loading external files.

```
// onEnterFrame handler constantly checks the playheadTime of
the video component
movieHolder.onEnterFrame = function() {
 //vidTime is a textbox on the root used to display the playheadTime
  vidTime = movieHolder.videoWindow.playheadTime;
 //outputs the playheadTime in the output window for testing
  trace(movieHolder.videoWindow.playheadTime);
};
```

Creating custom UI assets for video playback is one of the major benefits to using Flash for video delivery. Flash has a set of easy-to-skin components available for download to help you further customize your video player. The FLV Playback Custom UI components, shown in Figure 8-26, are a collection of individual video controls that can be associated with an FLVPlayback instance. The custom UI components can be edited like standard movie clip symbols. They include hard-to-script features like the seek bar, volume slider, and buffer handling.

The following code shows properties available in the FLVPlayback Custom UI component set as they would apply to our preceding example.

Figure 8-26. FLVPlayback Custom UI component set

```
// NOTE: you need to make sure there isn't a skin selected
for the video component in order for these to work...
movieHolder.videoWindow.playButton = playBtn;
movieHolder.videoWindow.pauseButton = pauseBtn;
movieHolder.videoWindow.playPauseButton = playpauseBtn;
movieHolder.videoWindow.stopButton = stopBtn;
movieHolder.videoWindow.muteButton = muteBtn;
movieHolder.videoWindow.backButton = backBtn;
movieHolder.videoWindow.forwardButton = forBtn;
movieHolder.videoWindow.volumeBar = volBar;
movieHolder.videoWindow.seekBar = seeker;
movieHolder.videoWindow.bufferingBar = bufBar;
```

Now, upload your SWF files to your server along with the FLV file. When the FLV file format first came out, I ran into problems bitstreaming FLVs because the MIME type for FLV files weren't defined as a video file in my server settings, so the content wouldn't play. I don't think that would be a problem anymore, but if you can view the video locally on your computer, but not on your server, that might be the issue.

I think it should be noted that you could use the Import Video Wizard to set up bitstream video in Flash. This is a simple way to load a single video into a video component. I believe this option is intended for people who don't know or need to learn too much about Flash. It will basically place the component on the stage and set up preferences in the Property inspector for you. If you are bit-streaming video into an interface, I strongly recommend doing it manually and controlling the component properties using ActionScript as described earlier, because it will give you more control overall throughout your development workflow.

Embedding video

There are many instances when the option to actually embed a video into the timeline makes sense—for example, if you are going to use a short video effect you created in After Effects as the rollover animation of a button, or if you have a very short video of a product spinning that you need very tight control of. These videos would be very small in file size and make sense to be embedded into your final SWF file. Of course, the longer and less compressed your file is, the larger the file size of your output SWF. It's not recommended to make your SWF files too large because it will "bog down" the viewing experience. This happens because your SWF file is stored on a computer's RAM while it's being viewed, so the more RAM your SWF takes up, the less RAM there is for other computer operations at the same time. If your SWF is too large, the computer begins to "chug," and everything becomes slow.

To embed a video file into Flash, begin by opening a new file in Flash. Press Ctrl+R (Cmd+R) to import your video file. Select the file you want to embed into your FLA as shown in Figure 8-27, and click OK.

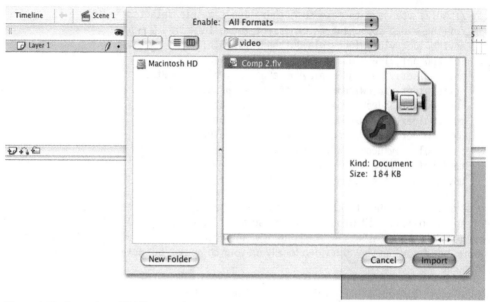

Figure 8-27. Importing a FLV file onto the stage in Flash

The first screen of the Import Video Wizard will appear to confirm the file path, as you see in Figure 8-28. Confirm the path and click Continue.

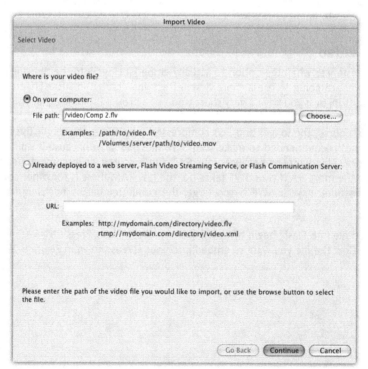

Figure 8-28. The Import Video Wizard in Flash

Next the Deployment screen appears, as shown in Figure 8-29. This is where you confirm that you want to embed the file into your timeline. Select Embed video in SWF and play in timeline and click Continue.

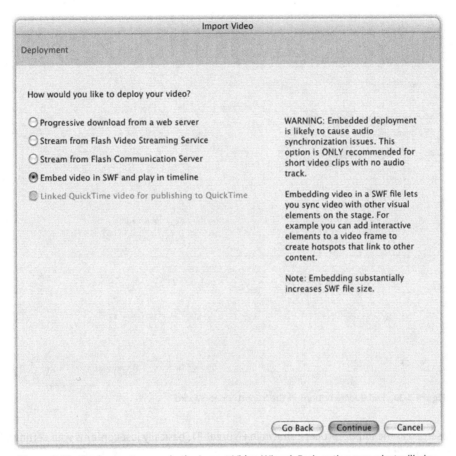

Figure 8-29. Deployment screen in the Import Video Wizard. Each option you select will give you an overview of each choice along the right of the window.

The Embedding screen, as shown in Figure 8-30, will appear next. Here you can choose to embed your video as a graphic or movie clip symbol as well as an embedded video. If you select Movie Clip from the Symbol type drop-down menu, your video will still be embedded into the timeline, only it will be nested inside a movie clip. This might be a good option if you intend to apply a filter or blend mode to the video. If you select this and then later decide you just want it on the _root timeline, you can simply break it apart by selecting the movie clip and pressing Ctrl+B (Cmd+B) on your keyboard. Embedding the video into a graphic gives you the ability to use the graphic loop or play once options. This is especially handy if you intend to sync your video with animation on the _root timeline, or if you intend to control the playhead of the _root timeline and want the video inside the graphic symbol to follow at the same pace. Make sure the Expand timeline if needed option on the Embedding screen is selected so that the timeline will push out to the length of your video once the embed process is complete. If you embed the video inside a movie clip or graphic symbol, the timeline will push out accordingly inside those nested instances of the video, too. For this example, I choose Embedded Video.

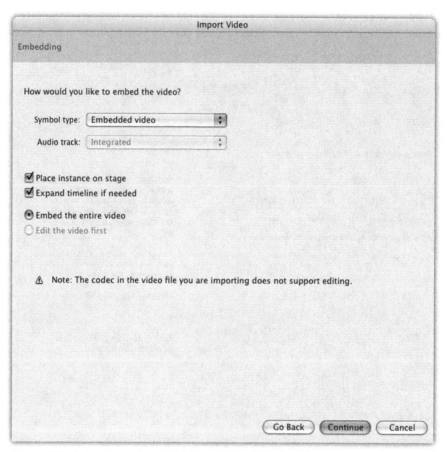

Figure 8-30. Embedding options in the Import Video Wizard

The final screen in the import process, shown in Figure 8-31, basically just confirms your settings. Click Finish to complete the setup.

Figure 8-31. Confirmation of settings in the Import Video Wizard

After the video imports into your library, you should see the video on your stage and placed in your timeline. The video will appear in your Library palette as a small video camera icon. The Property inspector gives you the file size and length of the embedded video. If you scrub along the timeline, you can see that your video previews in real time. If you have an alpha channel saved in your FLV file, it will be preserved upon import into Flash. You can see in Figure 8-32 that a black background indicates the alpha channel. Simply place your layer containing the video object above any layer containing graphics or animation, and the content from the lower layers will show through the alpha channel.

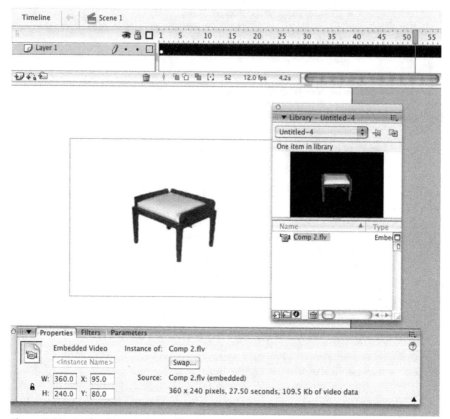

Figure 8-32. A video imported onto the stage in Flash. You can see the video represented in the Library palette as a video camera icon.

Now that you have the video embedded into your FLA and it is accessible from your library, you can employ it on nested timelines in movie clips for use as buttons and transitions.

Summary

If you didn't already know how to do video productions for the web, now you have a solid understanding of the fundamentals involved and how to get started. You discovered what equipment to purchase and some additional helpful tips to use while on shooting assignments. You also learned how to import, edit, and export your digital video out of Final Cut Pro complete with color correction and keying effects. Now that you have gained insight into the different ways to optimize and import video into Flash, you can use video for timeline effects in your interface design and even distribute/stream your client's video projects or your own short films using Flash.

Now that you've read this chapter, you've learned the following lessons:

- You don't need a Hollywood-sized budget to create professional video projects for online distribution. Much of the equipment is accessible for many of us at reasonable prices.

- Understanding the process and theory behind video productions is easier said than done. Before you produce professional video—even for online distribution—you will need to get the hang of the on-set workflow. Using tools like a shot log and understanding how to operate a decent camera and light your subject will become second nature after you have a few shoots under your belt.

- Understanding the difference between video format standards will help you make educated decisions about what format to shoot and edit in.

- Much of what you already know about using Flash and Photoshop can be applied to using video editing programs, as well. Timelines, asset management, color correction, and more use the same basic controls across application types.

- To achieve a crisp, clean key in your final video product, you need to key out your desired colors in a video editing program prior to generating an alpha channel using the Flash Video Encoding tool.

- Compressing video for use in Flash has never been easier than it is now because of the Flash Video Encoder tool that ships with Flash 8. For instances where you need to compress FLV content that is Flash Player 6 and 7 compliant, you can use the Sorenson Spark option in the Flash Video Encoder or opt to use Sorenson Squeeze for additional control over your image quality.

- Depending on the application for and quality and file size of your video, there are a few different options you have to use Flash as your distribution vehicle. Flash can utilize video as embedded animation or stream longer, higher quality videos as primary content.

Glossary

arc

Camera shot: swiveling the camera around the subject horizontally on a center point.

back light

A light that is positioned to illuminate the back of a subject to separate it from the background.

banding

An undesirable effect caused by overcompressing gradated colors on bitmap images and video.

batch capture

A method in most video editing applications that allows the user to enter all of the ins and outs of good takes on a tape and capture them automatically. Without batch capture, you would have to rewatch every single good take just to input each of them into the computer. Batch capturing saves a lot of time.

CCD

A charge-coupled device (CCD) is a digital sensor for recording images and video. CCDs convert incident light into an electrical (video) signal, and then the recorder encodes the video signal into a storable form.

clamps

Most professional lighting kits come with clamps to temporarily rig lights onto unstable surfaces.

clear key

Achieving a nice crisp contour around a subject by using filters and effects in video editing software. You can get plug-ins for most applications to help manage generating a clear key, and Adobe After Effects is a great program for creating a clear key. Although there are lots of tools at your disposal for generating a clear key during the editing process, the process begins with proper lighting during the shoot where the footage is captured.

clip

Most video editing software organizes each captured take into a library of clips. This is the same basic methodology as using movie clips and graphics in Flash.

dither

Commonly seen in GIF images, this is a technique used in computer graphics to create the illusion of color depth in images with a limited or fixed color palette (known in the web world as a *clut*). Although this is not noticeable on web graphics to most people, it can be a distracting side effect of overcompression to digital video.

dolly

Camera shot: moving the camera towards or away from the subject.

fill light

A less-intense light positioned to soften shadows on the front of the subject.

gels

Transparent colored plastic sheets to place on front of lights used to achieve special lighting effects.

green screen

A green fabric placed behind the subject of a video during filming. This provides an even, single color background for keying out in a video editing application.

grip

A person who rigs lighting, props, and general "stage" setting. In the movie industry, grips typically make up the department that works with electricians and lighting setups.

interlaced

A method for displaying images in which the display alternates between drawing the even-numbered lines and the odd-numbered lines of each frame. The result is a flickering unnoticeable to most people. This is how traditional TVs display images. NTSC, which is the standard western video format, typically draws 59.94 fields per second, or 525 lines.

junk video

Refers to the color being deleted in a color key. This is also footage recorded between good takes during a video shoot. It's basically any footage or piece of footage that isn't usable.

key light

An intense light positioned to cast shadows and define features of a subject.

key out

A method of removing color in video footage to "cut out" the subject of the shot.

lavaliere mic

A small inconspicuous microphone (sometimes wireless) that talent can hide on their shirt collar.

lighting cables

Professional lighting kits come with industrial insulated cables that you need to plug into the lights as well as an outlet.

log clip

Terminology used to enter an in and out point of a take in preparation to batch capture footage from a tape into video editing software. Most applications, like Final Cut Pro and Adobe Premier, have a Log Clip button for the user to use in order to add a time code sequence to the batch.

markers

Video editing applications use markers to indicate the beginning and end of clips. Generally the user can drag markers to modify the in and out points of each clip in the library.

pan

Camera shot: turning the camera horizontally from side to side on a center point.

pedestal

Camera shot: raising or lowering the camera vertically.

playhead

The current state on a timeline. This is the same as the playhead in Flash. It is also a term used to describe the current visible frame on a DV tape.

production log

An itemized list of each take during a video shoot. The more helpful production logs document the quality of the take and the ins and outs of each take.

progressive scan

This is the alternative to interlacing where the image is displayed line by line. Progressive scan is used in most CRTs that function as computer monitors. High-end television equipment is often capable of performing de-interlacing so that interlaced video can still be viewed. When exporting video for modern televisions or computer display, always export using a de-interlaced or progressive mode to attain the best quality during compression.

scratch disk

A hard drive used to store files. Video editing applications generally set the computer's hard drive as the default scratch disk, but it can also be manually reset to an external hard drive.

scrub

Terminology for grabbing the playhead on a timeline and moving it to preview content.

sequence

A series of edited movie clips on a single timeline. In Final Cut Pro and Adobe Premier, users create sequences in the library to place movie clips onto. This is similar to using scenes in Flash in that they are separate timelines in the same project. Usually you can nest sequences inside sequences in video editing apps just like you would nest movie clips inside one another in Flash.

shoot

A scheduled session where footage is shot for a production.

stands

Items that hold lights and umbrellas for lighting. Most light kits include these.

take

A complete sequence shot with a video camera.

tilt

Camera shot: swiveling the camera vertically across the subject.

time code

The sequence of time as it is recorded onto a tape during recording. You can use the ins and outs of time code to document good takes, then use the same time code to speed up capturing the video to your computer using video editing software. "Making an impression on time code" means that there is recorded space on the tape.

truck

Camera shot: sweeping the camera horizontally from side to side.

umbrellas

Most professional lighting kits come with umbrellas for deflecting light. This is helpful if you need to soften a light to use as a fill.

zeroed out

Refers to DV tapes displaying a 00:00:00 time code when nothing is recorded on them. It also refers to the beginning of recorded space on a DV tape.

Chapter 3

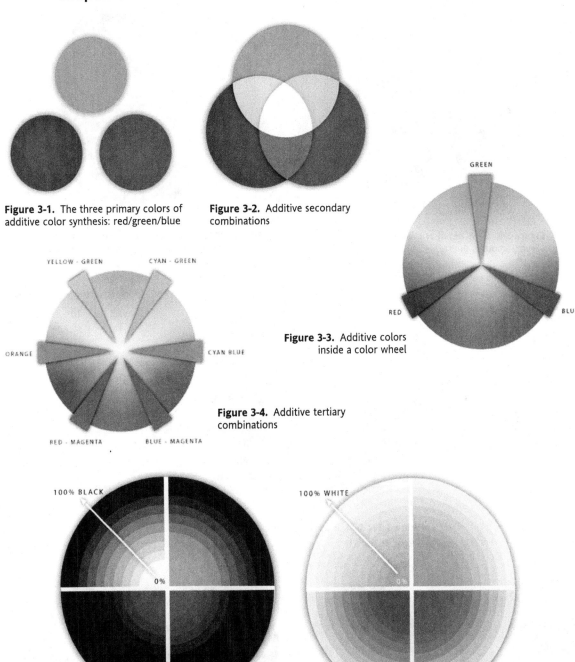

Figure 3-1. The three primary colors of additive color synthesis: red/green/blue

Figure 3-2. Additive secondary combinations

GREEN

RED   BLUE

Figure 3-3. Additive colors inside a color wheel

YELLOW - GREEN   CYAN - GREEN

ORANGE   CYAN BLUE

RED - MAGENTA   BLUE - MAGENTA

Figure 3-4. Additive tertiary combinations

100% BLACK

0%

100% WHITE

0%

Figure 3-6. Multiple shades of the primary hues

Figure 3-7. Multiple tints of the primary hues

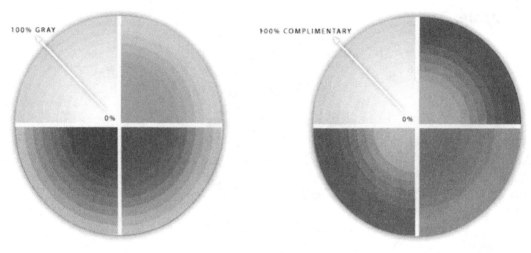

Figure 3-8. Swatches of primary hues with varying amounts of gray

Figure 3-9. Swatches of primary hues with varying amounts of complementary hues added

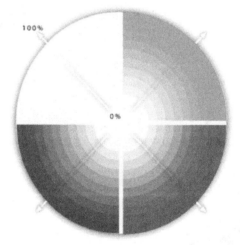

Figure 3-10. Demonstrating color alpha with the primary hues

Figure 3-11. Example of vibrating color

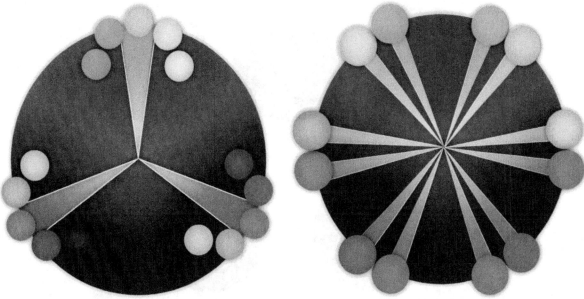

Figure 3-12. Monochromatic scheme

Figure 3-13. Analogous scheme

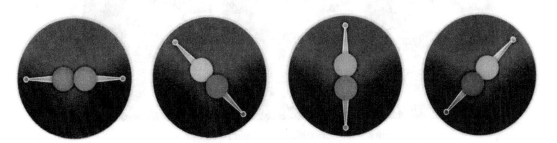

Figure 3-14. Complementary scheme

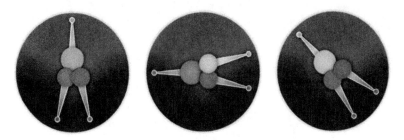

Figure 3-15. Split complement scheme

Figure 3-16. Triadic scheme

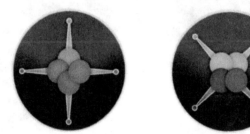

Figure 3-17. Tetrad scheme

Figure 3-18. Comparing 8-, 16-, and 24-bit color

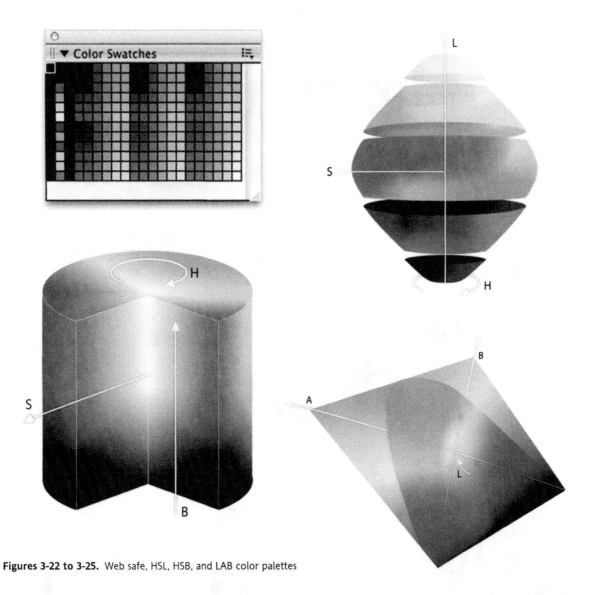

Figures 3-22 to 3-25. Web safe, HSL, HSB, and LAB color palettes

Figure 3-26. Color-coded zodiac with corresponding gems and metals

ARIES
THE RAM
RUBY
IRON

TAURUS
THE BULL
EMERALD
COPPER

PISCES
THE FISH
AQUAMARINE
PLATINUM

GEMINI
THE TWINS
OPAL
MERCURY

AQUARIUS
THE WATER BEARER
AMETHYST
ALUMINUM

CANCER
THE CRAB
MOONSTONE
SILVER

CAPRICORN
THE SEA GOAT
DIAMOND
LEAD

LEO
THE LION
TOPAZ
GOLD

SAGITTARIUS
THE ARCHER
SAPPHIRE
TIN

VIRGO
THE VIRGIN
AGATE
NICKEL

SCORPIO
THE SCORPION
GARNET
STEEL

LIBRA
THE SCALES
JADE
BRONZE

SIGN
SYMBOL
GEM
METAL

Figure 3-27. Color wheel with cool colors highlighted

Figure 3-28. Color wheel with warm colors highlighted

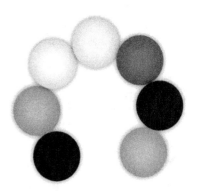

Figure 3-29. Color swatches of neutral colors

Chapter 7

Figure 7-22. This is what the icon should look like now that you've applied the blend mode to the glow.

Figure 7-24. The gloss shape. We colored it here to make it more evident.

Chapter 9

Figure 9-34. The completed Shading layer, after erasing the middle

Figure 9-68. The final interface with sample states for the buttons

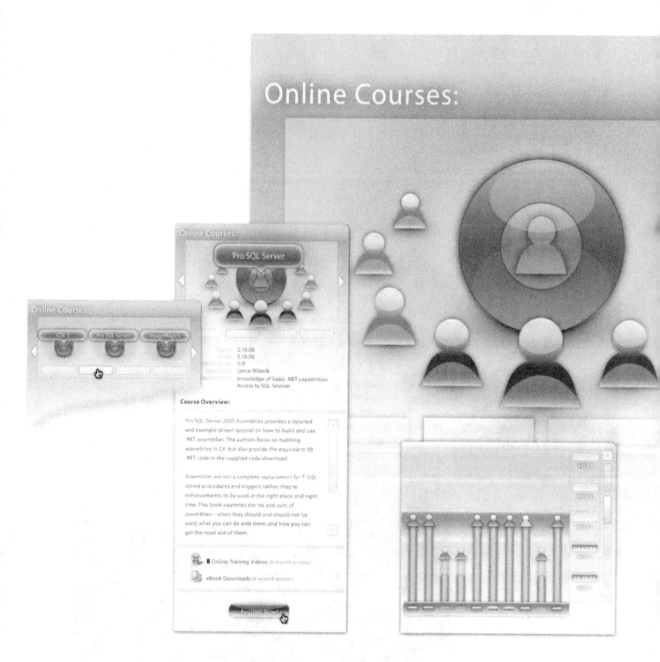

Interface design concept for on-demand e-learning application
Design, Motion Graphics: Michael Kemper
Programming: Metaliq

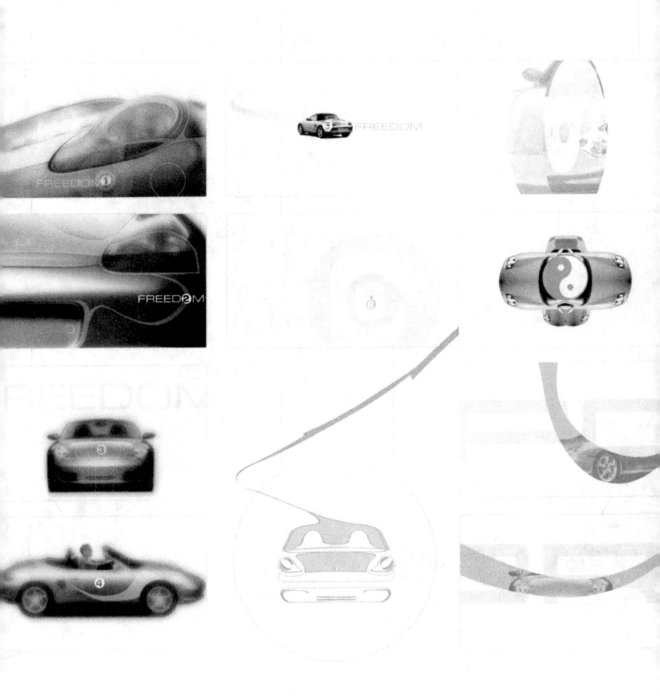

Motion sequence for Porsche America
Design, Motion Graphics: Michael Kemper

CD-ROM interface for Paramount Parks
Design, Motion Graphics, Programming: Michael Kemper

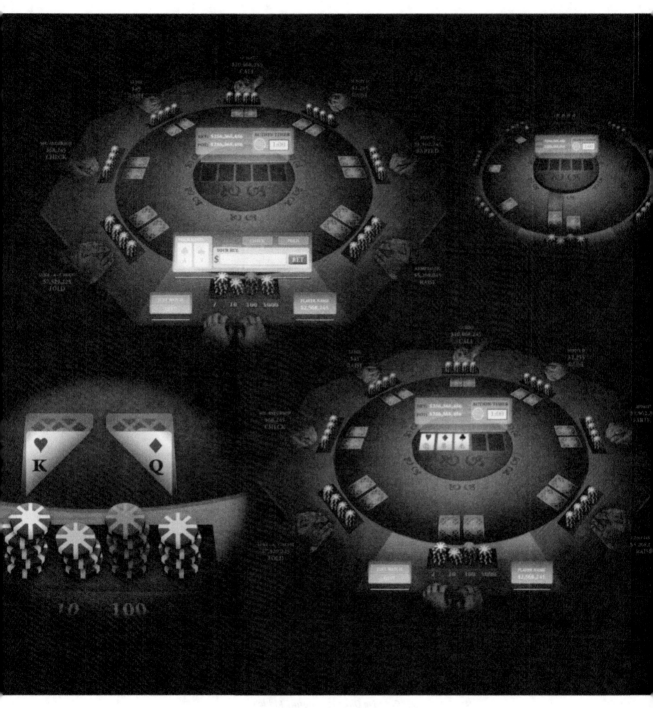

Texas Holdem' multiplayer game interface for Web 2.0 conference

Design, Animation: Michael Kemper
Programming: Beau Ambur
Hands: Danny Riddell

mVID online streaming media tour for salesforce.com

Creative Direction: Danny Riddell
Interface Design: Michael Kemper
Motion Graphics: Michael Kemper, Guido Rosso
Video Producer: Eric Anderson
Programming: gskinner / Metaliq

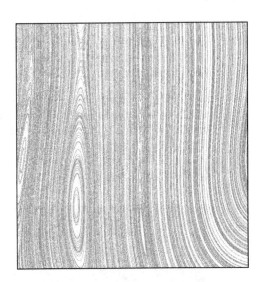

Chapter 9

PHOTOSHOP TECHNIQUES

by Guido Rosso

The previous chapters covered how to create and put together vector-format shapes for your interface using tools such as Illustrator, Freehand, and Flash. In this chapter, I'll explain how to construct your interface in Photoshop, the industry standard in all things raster.

I started using Photoshop many years before I got into Flash, which is in part why to this day I still prefer to start designing in Photoshop before moving to Flash. Other designers prefer to start immediately in vector format. Neither way is right or wrong; you need to experiment with both techniques and decide for yourself which one better suits your style and workflow.

My way of doing it means I often end up having to re-create many of my layers in vector. This may seem inefficient, but I find Photoshop to be much more powerful than Flash when it comes to putting together the shapes for an interface, structuring them into layers, manipulating colors, and tweaking everything until it's as close to perfect as possible.

The *tweaking everything* phase in Photoshop is the part of the design process that I enjoy the most: it's the point where the core of the static design is done, the interface matches the specifications detailed in your planning documents, and you've satisfied the requirements of the client. But you still see ways to make the design better.

You have to be careful when you enter this phase. I tend to get stuck in an endless tweaking cycle, because I want my work to be as perfect as possible; yet I never seem to achieve perfection. For this reason, I've never been 100% satisfied with any of my work, but I've come to understand that this is a good thing. While it's important to learn to accept things when they're "good enough," otherwise you end up losing a lot of valuable time in our fast-paced industry, it's even more important never to lose the desire to always perfect your work. It's what drives you to constantly improve.

In this chapter, together we're going to develop an interface for a made-up game development studio, which I've very inventively named *Imaginary Studios*. I'm going to demonstrate how to develop the interface in Figure 9-1 entirely in Photoshop, starting with only the wireframes and sitemap from Chapter 4. I'll explain as much as possible and will go step by step through the more complex parts. At the end of this chapter, I'll outline how to move your work over from Photoshop to Flash, with a more detailed walkthrough of the process to follow in Chapter 10.

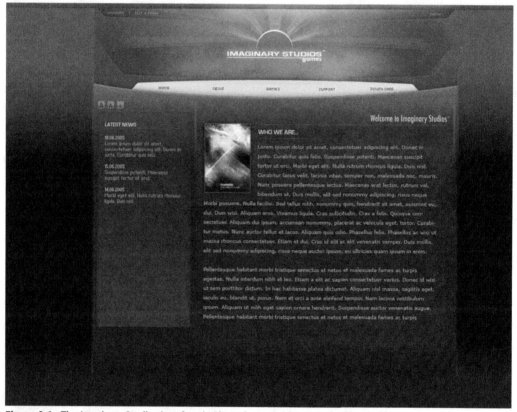

Figure 9-1. The Imaginary Studios interface in Photoshop

Photoshop overview

Before jumping into the tutorial, you should familiarize yourself with Photoshop and its main tools. This shouldn't be the first time you're opening Photoshop, but it never hurts to go over a few basic points. If you're already an expert, you might want to skip this section.

To follow this tutorial, you should be familiar with layers, and you should know how to create, modify, and use them comfortably. I'm going to go over a few basic things before going ahead, just in case.

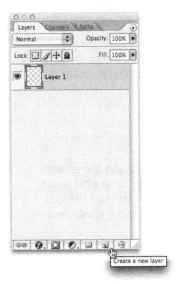

Take a look at Figure 9-2, which shows the Layers palette, the Photoshop palette you'll be using most throughout the tutorial. Get comfortable with the buttons at the bottom: from left to right, their functions are to link layers, add a layer style, add a mask, create a new fill or adjustment layer, create a new group, create a new layer, and delete a layer.

You'll also quite often need to select multiple layers, which you can now do in Photoshop CS2. To select multiple layers, hold down Ctrl (or Cmd on a Mac) to select the layers you want one at a time, or hold down Shift to select a range of layers. You can now move the selected layers by pressing V or free transform them by pressing Ctrl+T (or Cmd+T).

Photoshop has improved a lot over the years in helping designers modify layers in a nondestructive way. Adjustment layers are an example of this: they let you apply certain filters, modify color balance, edit levels, and play with brightness/contrast settings without actually changing any of the original layers, as an adjustment layer affects all the layers below it. To disable the effect, simply hide the adjustment layer by clicking its eye icon.

Figure 9-2. Photoshop's Layers palette, with buttons that let you link layers, add a layer style, add a mask, create a new fill or adjustment layer, create a new group, create a new layer, and delete a layer

A great new feature in Photoshop CS2 in keeping with the nondestructive theme is the ability to create Smart Objects. When pasting a vector shape into Photoshop, you can now choose to keep its vector content. In previous versions, once you paste the vector shape into Photoshop, it becomes a raster graphic. This means that if you later want to increase the size of that graphic, it will appear pixelated instead of smooth, as you can see in the example in Figure 9-3.

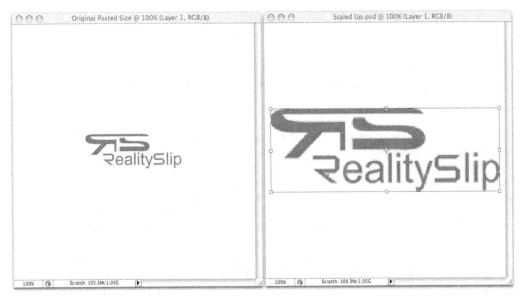

Figure 9-3. Scaling up this raster graphic, which was originally pasted from a vector shape, causes it to become pixelated.

Once you've pasted a vector graphic as a Smart Object, you're free to transform it as much as you like without losing quality. Keep in mind that Photoshop is still a raster program, meaning zooming in won't reveal more details of the Smart Object as it would with a vector file in Illustrator or Flash. Photoshop simply uses the vector data stored in the Smart Object to update the graphic when you scale it.

If you decide to change the color or shape of the Smart Object, you can simply double-click the layer it resides on and it will open it up in Illustrator. Any changes you make will automatically update the Photoshop file.

Setting up your file

Open up a new file by going to File ➤ New or pressing Ctrl+N (Cmd+N on a Mac). Use the settings shown in Figure 9-4. I chose to use 1024×768 as my image size because I like to have some extra space around my interface as extra workspace and to give a better idea of what the final interface will look like in a browser. This doesn't mean that we'll be designing the interface for users with a screen resolution of 1024×768 and above only, however.

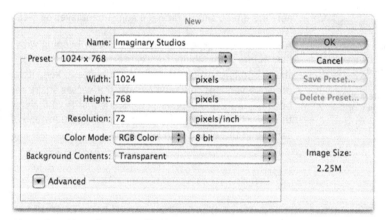

Figure 9-4. Photoshop's new file dialog window. Use these settings to create the tutorial file.

You should always consider your target market when making choices that could affect usability of the site. Many designers, and even some fairly large companies, have started making the minimum width of their sites around 1024 pixels. This is a mistake—it's still too early to be doing this. Unless you're producing a website exclusively for designers, chances are a good 30–50% of your viewers (depending on the type of site) will still be using a screen resolution of 800×600. I know what you're thinking: "If it's only 30%, then why should we bother? After all, that number is only going to get smaller with time." The problem is that you're hampering the usability of the site for a large percentage of your users who are going to have to use two sets of scrollbars, vertical and horizontal, to view all the content of the site. Users might miss important information and are likely to leave the site simply because it annoys them. You can avoid this altogether by sticking with 800×600 as your minimum target resolution; this way both high- and low-resolution users can see all the content on your site without horizontal scrollbars.

Another way to get around this issue is to make your interface scale proportionally with the width of the browser. This requires a little extra work in HTML, but quite a bit more work in Flash. There are still problems with this, mainly for legibility. Shorter line lengths are generally easier to read, with 40 to 60 characters being the recommended number per line. If your interface scales with the width of the browser, users with very high resolutions will be seeing paragraphs as just a few lines.

Also, with CSS you can set a max-width value, which works very well for this specific issue. The interface width scales up and down in proportion to the browser; however, once the browser window exceeds the max-width value, the interface stops scaling. Compare Figure 9-5 to Figure 9-6 for an example. In Figure 9-5, you can see the interface at www.mozilla.org, which scales with the browser width so that even users with low-resolution screens don't see horizontal scrollbars. Figure 9-6 shows the interface at www.mozilla.org again; this time the browser window has been stretched to 1100 pixels wide. Notice how the interface width scaled up as well, but it doesn't stretch all the way to the left and right borders as it did in Figure 9-5. This is because it has a max-width setting, which stops the interface from stretching to any value above the max-width. This keeps all users happy by eliminating horizontal scrollbars for low-resolution users, without wasting the screen space on high-resolution users, and without sacrificing legibility.

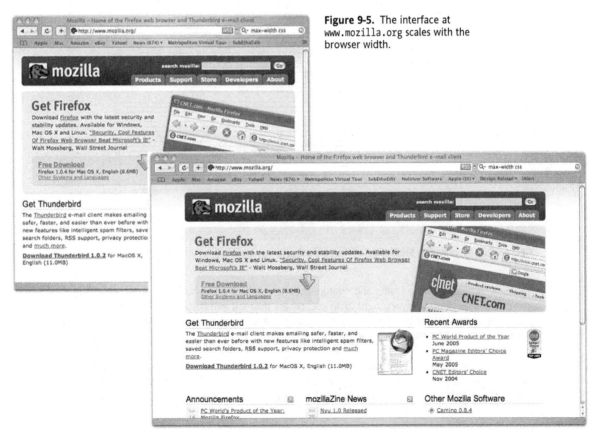

Figure 9-5. The interface at www.mozilla.org scales with the browser width.

Figure 9-6. The interface at www.mozilla.org again, this time with the browser window stretched to 1100 pixels wide

Let's get back to our file. Your first step should always be to import the wireframe for the home page of your site. I generally keep it in my background until I've finished constructing the actual interface layers. It serves as a foundation and helps you keep track of what you still need to add to the interface. How you add the wireframe will vary depending on what you used to build it. If it's in vector format, you can just place it (File ➤ Place), or copy and paste directly from Illustrator. Otherwise, just take a screenshot with the Print Screen key (or run Grab on Mac) and paste it into a new layer (Ctrl+Shift+N on a PC, Cmd+Shift+N on a Mac). The wireframe for this tutorial, shown in Figure 9-7, is already in raster format, and you can download it at www.friendsofed.com.

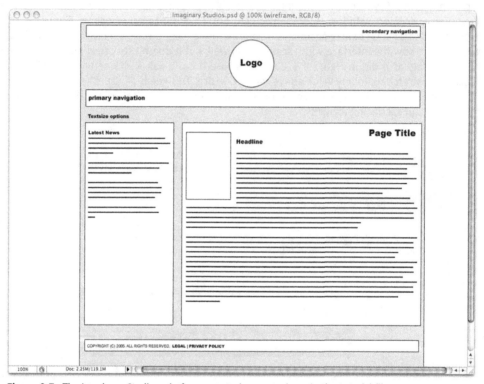

Figure 9-7. The Imaginary Studios wireframe, pasted as a new layer in the tutorial file

Double-click the name of the layers and change them to Background and Wireframe, respectively. I'd recommend always naming layers, right after you create them. It will help you a lot later when you've got too many to remember them all. I'm not very good at doing this and always end up hiding layers by trial and error to find the one I'm looking for. Incidentally, one quick way to find the layer you're looking for is to right-click the workspace using the Move tool. This pops up a context menu, shown in Figure 9-8, with the list of layers that appear on the specific spot you right-clicked. Clicking the layer you desire selects it for you in the Layers palette. With Photoshop CS2, you can also select layers directly by clicking them while pressing the Shift key (or Cmd on a Mac) with the Move tool activated.

You might want to activate the Layer Edges feature (View ➤ Show ➤ Layer Edges) to help you see what you're selecting.

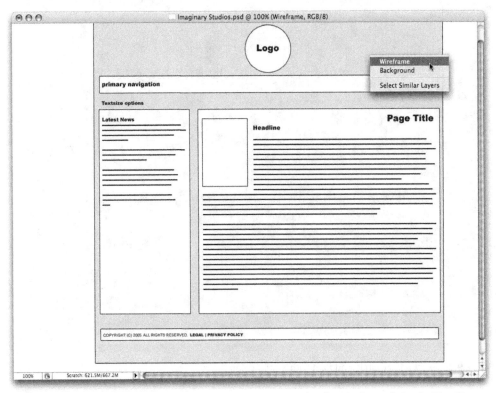

Figure 9-8. Right-clicking the workspace opens a context menu that lists the layers that coincide with where you clicked.

Creating the background

First let's give some color to the background. Hide the Wireframe layer and fill the Background layer with color value #1462C0. To quickly fill a layer, use Ctrl+Delete to fill with your current background color and Alt+Delete to fill with your current foreground color. (On a Mac, that's Cmd+Backspace and Option+Backspace, respectively.)

Light source

Create another layer and name it Light. Now select the Elliptical Marquee tool (press M and then Shift+M to cycle through the different Marquee tools) and place a large filled circle in the center of your document, as shown in Figure 9-9, which will be our light source. It doesn't matter what fill color you use at this stage, as we'll be changing it in the next step by using a gradient overlay.

Figure 9-9. Select a large circle and fill it with a solid color.

Double-click the Light layer in the Layers palette, or right-click and select Blending Options. You should now be looking at the Layer Style window, shown in Figure 9-10. When I'm not using adjustment layers, this is what I use to color and style my layers.

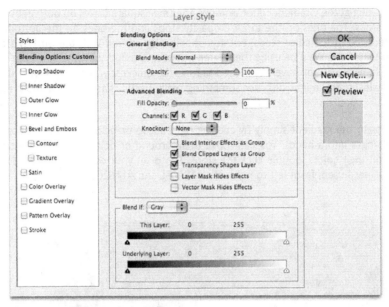

Figure 9-10. The Layer Style window

Click Gradient Overlay from the menu on the left. Your circle should now have a white-to-black gradient from top to bottom. Set the style to Radial and click the gradient to edit it (see Figure 9-11).

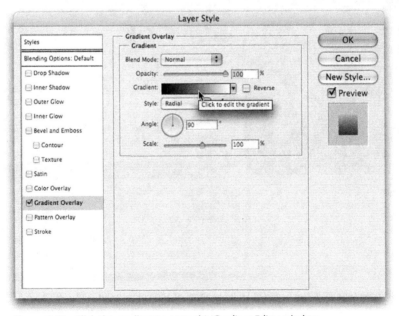

Figure 9-11. Click the gradient to open the Gradient Editor window.

You should be looking at the Gradient Editor window. The small square boxes on both ends of the gradient are called *stops*. The ones on the top are opacity stops and the ones on the bottom are color stops. We're interested in the color stops, but you should play around with the opacity stops if you don't know how they work. We'll be using them later, but keep in mind that whenever you find something you're not familiar with or have never used before, the quickest way to learn what it does is to just experiment with it. You might discover something really useful that you wish you'd found a lot sooner.

You can add stops to the gradient simply by clicking right above or below it (you'll notice that your mouse cursor changes into a hand). You can move them around or delete them simply by dragging them away. To edit their colors, double-click the stops. Try to set your color stops like I did in Figure 9-12. The color values I used, from left to right, are #15A0FE and #1462C0.

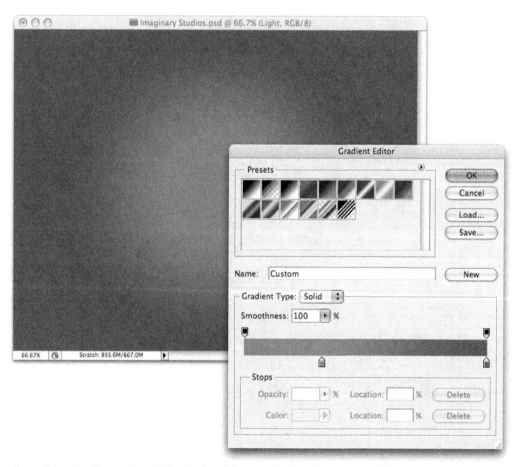

Figure 9-12. Use these settings in the Gradient Editor window to add color to our light source.

Click OK and return to the workspace. Move the Light layer up with the Move tool until about half is showing, as the rest of it is off the top of the image—you should be able to see a semicircle of light (press V). Use the Shift+Arrow keys to nudge 10 pixels at a time.

Background depth

Now we're going to give the background some depth by using a gradient. Create a new layer above the Light layer and name it Background Depth. Double-click the Background Depth layer in the Layers palette to open the Layer Style window. Go to Gradient Overlay and open the Gradient Editor window (this time leave the style set to Linear). Drag the stops to match the locations in Figure 9-13. As you can see, this time we're also using the opacity stops. Set both color stops to black. The opacity stops' values I used, from left to right, are 79%, 100%, 100%, and 0%.

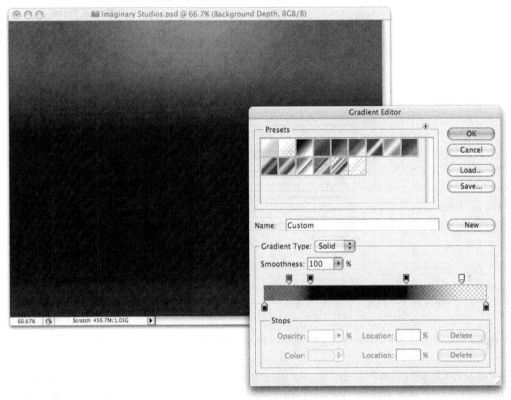

Figure 9-13. Use these settings in the Gradient Editor window to add color and depth to the Background Depth layer.

Foundation shapes

In the next steps, we're going to create the basic shapes that will form the core of our interface; that is, they'll serve as containers for our content. These shapes will be the foundation base, its borders, and ultimately its shadows.

Foundation base

We're now going to create the foundation shapes for the interface. Create a new layer above the Background layer and name it Foundation Base. Unhide the wireframe layer and draw a selection as shown in Figure 9-14 using the Rectangular Marquee tool (press M). You can check the width and height of your selection in the Info palette. (Make sure the Info palette is showing units in pixels. To do this, click the small arrow on the top-right corner and select Palette Options. Now set Ruler Units to Pixels.) I made the selection 735 pixels wide and 517 pixels high. The maximum width you want to use for your entire interface is 774 pixels; anything above that will likely result in horizontal scrollbars for low-resolution users. Using 735 pixels leaves 39 extra pixels for shadows and details that might be wider than the Foundation Base layer of the interface.

Figure 9-14. Draw this selection using the Rectangular Marquee tool.

Fill the selection in your new Foundation Base layer. Now hide the Wireframe layer and double-click the Foundation Base layer to open the Blending Options window. Select Gradient Overlay from the menu on the left and click the gradient to open up the Gradient Editor window. Drag the stops to 0%, 100%, 100%, and 0%. The color stops are set to #135FBB and #1147A6, as shown in Figure 9-15.

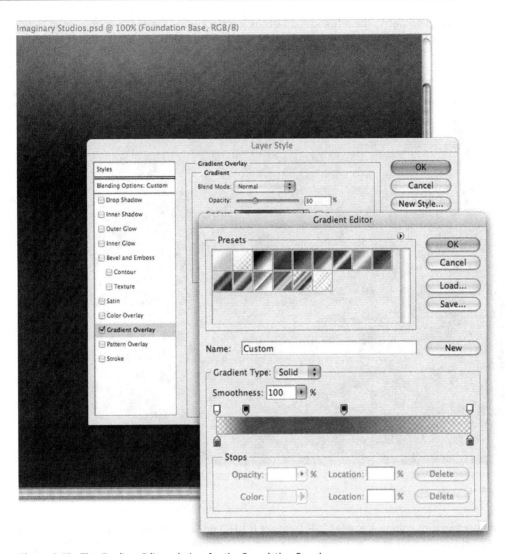

Figure 9-15. The Gradient Editor window for the Foundation Base layer

Foundation borders

To make the Foundation Base layer stand out a little more, we're going to create borders for it. Create a new layer below the Background Depth layer and name it Foundation Borders. Remember that you can move layers quickly up and down using Ctrl+[to move it down and Ctrl+] to move it up (Cmd+[and Cmd+] on a Mac).

Select a three-pixel border to the left and right of the interface using the Marquee tool, as in Figure 9-16. Keep in mind that after making a first selection, you can hold Shift and add to that selection.

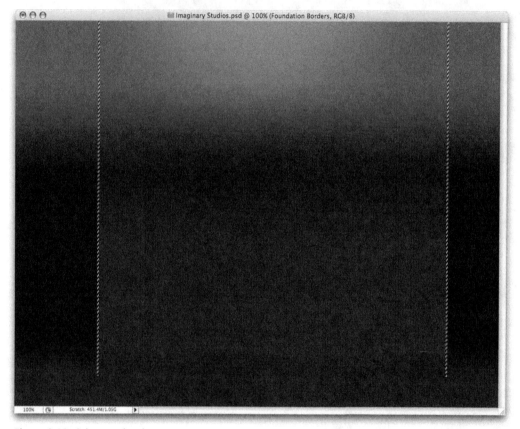

Figure 9-16. Select two borders.

Fill the selection with color value #5ABDFF. Deselect (Ctrl+D or Cmd+D) and activate the Eraser tool (press E). Set your brush size to 200 pixels, flow to 40%, and delete the top part of the borders. Try to make it smooth, as if they're fading into the blue on top.

Background shadows

We're going to add some more depth by creating shadows. Create a new layer, call it Top Shadow, and select a rectangle that spans across from left to right, leaving a little space at the top. Look at Figure 9-17 for an example.

Figure 9-17. Use the Marquee tool to make this selection.

Fill the layer and open up its Layer Style window. Click Drop Shadow and give it the same settings as shown in Figure 9-18.

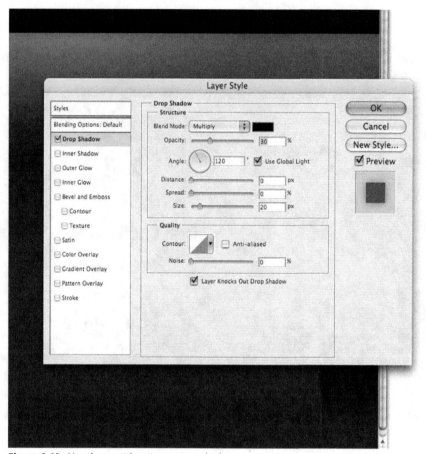

Figure 9-18. Use these settings to create a shadow.

Go back to the Blending Options window by clicking above Drop Shadow, where it says Blending Options: Custom. We want to hide the layer so that only the shadow is visible. To do this, drag the Fill Opacity to zero.

Now we're going to flatten this layer so we can manipulate or erase the shadow with Photoshop's tools. Right now we can't do this. We can only control the shadow through the Layer Style window.

Create a new empty layer below the Top Shadow layer. Select the Top Shadow layer and press Ctrl+E (Cmd+E on a Mac) to flatten the layer. This actually merges the layer with the one below it, but in so doing it converts the layer effects into a flat layer that we can manipulate. Select the Eraser tool (press E) and delete the bottom half of the layer so that only the shadow at the top remains as shown in Figure 9-19.

Figure 9-19. This is what your shadow should look like after merging and erasing.

Now duplicate the Top Shadow layer by pressing Ctrl+J (or Cmd+J). Hide the original shadow layer and use the Eraser tool again. This time you're going to erase the edges so that this shadow matches the top interface within the Interface Borders layer.

Unhide the first shadow layer. It isn't quite as dark as we want it to be yet, so duplicate the first shadow layer again. You can now merge down these three layers. Select them in the Layers palette while holding Shift and press Ctrl+E (or Cmd+E).

Experimenting with colors

Now is a good time to experiment with the colors of the interface. I'm happy with the colors I've been using so far, but you should always try changing hue and brightness settings around to have something to compare to, especially if you've been looking at the same thing for hours. Create a new adjustment layer by clicking the Create new fill or adjustment layer button at the bottom of the Layers palette. This will pop up a menu with a list of different layers you can create. Click Hue/Saturation and experiment with the sliders. Notice that you can also activate the Colorize check box option. Instead of shifting the hue value of the layers below, this will apply the same hue value to all the colors in the layers below the adjustment layer. This can be very useful when working with a monochromatic interface.

The great thing about adjustment layers is that they are layers! That means you can apply the effect to only a specific set of layers, you can mask it, you can run filters on it, and you can pretty much do anything that you'd be able to do with a normal layer. One great technique is to create multiple Color Balance or Hue/Saturation adjustment layers. Find colors that complement each other, and then fill the mask of your adjustment layers with black so that all of the effects are disabled. Select the Brush tool with a low flow setting and start painting the masks of your adjustment layers one at a time. You can achieve some great color contrasts with this technique.

Try creating a Levels adjustment layer as well. Modifying levels is generally associated with image editing; however, it is a very important technique for interface designers as well! When used properly, this adjustment layer can help you achieve a perfectly smooth interface with just the right contrast. Not only will great contrast dramatically increase the usability of your site (which should always be our first concern as interface designers), it will also make your site look a lot better.

A Levels adjustment layer will help you notice if your interface is lacking contrast. Use the histogram to see whether your darkest color is in fact a black and whether your lightest color is in fact a white. Be careful about overstretching your levels settings, as this can result in tone jumps, which means your gradients won't be perfectly smooth anymore. That's why when you're creating an interface from scratch, where you're actually controlling all the color and brightness settings yourself in Photoshop, it's best not to use Levels as a production tool. What I mean by this is that your final interface should not have a Levels adjustment layer applied to it unless you're working with some source material that you have no control over.

In projects similar to this tutorial, where we're creating all the colors in Photoshop, you should use a Levels adjustment layer to tweak the contrast until it's perfectly balanced. Once you see that something needs to be fixed, disable the adjustment layer and add contrast to a gradient manually by editing its color stops.

Adding the logo

Let's get back to the tutorial. Before we go ahead with the interface, let's import our logo, the EPS file available in this chapter's folder in the code download at www.friendsofed.com. You can either open the file in Illustrator and copy and paste it into Photoshop, or you can use File ➤ Place. You might also want to turn on the wireframe layer first, to position it correctly. Your screen should now resemble Figure 9-20.

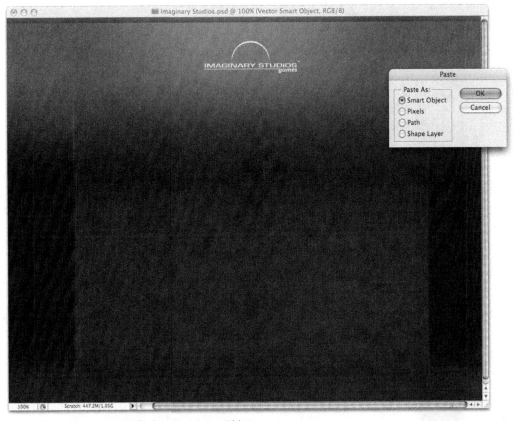

Figure 9-20. Place or paste the logo as a Smart Object.

Once you've placed the logo, open up its Layer Style window and activate Outer Glow. Use the settings in Figure 9-21. The color overlay should be pure white.

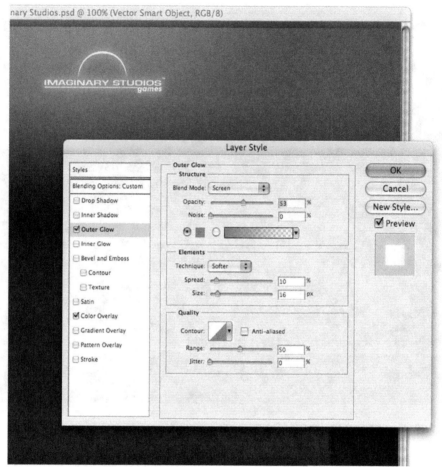

Figure 9-21. Apply layer effects to the logo.

You'll notice that in my later screenshots the logo looks a little different. I wasn't very convinced about using the glow, as it looked just a bit too evident. To correct this, I masked the entire logo aside from the Imaginary Studios text. I then duplicated the layer (Ctrl+J or Cmd+J), inverted the mask (Ctrl+I or Cmd+I), and removed the glow from the Layer Style *window. The final effect is that only the Imaginary Studios text has a glow now. Make sure you select both layers and click the* Link *layers button on the bottom of the* Layers *palette so that if you move or scale the logo, both layers will transform together.*

Creating the interface layers

Now we're going to create the layers for the actual shape of the interface. Since the company doesn't really exist, we're going to pretend their flagship product is a first-person game where we see the world through the visor of a character. Therefore, we're going to try and make the shape of the top part of the interface a little curvy, to give it perspective and to make it resemble a futuristic visor.

Visor shape

To give an initial shape to the visor, we're going to create a shadow. We want the navigation bars to fit in the visor, so first let's unhide the wireframe layer. Create a new layer above your other layers and name it Visor Ellipse. Use the elliptical marquee tool to make a selection as similar as possible to the one in Figure 9-22.

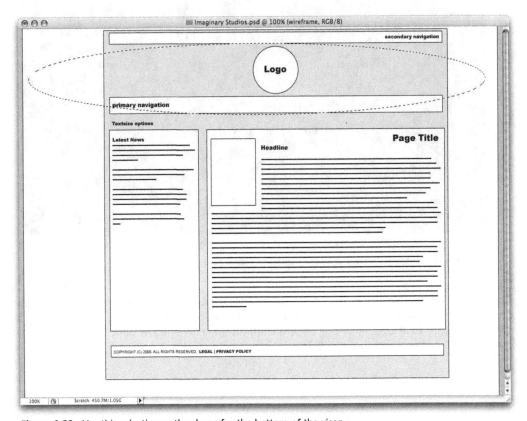

Figure 9-22. Use this selection as the shape for the bottom of the visor.

Fill the selection with any color. We want this to be centrally aligned with the Foundation Base layer as you see in Figure 9-23, so Ctrl-click (or Cmd-click) on the Foundation Base layer in the Layers palette. This will select the perimeter of the Foundation Base layer (Photoshop calls this *Load Selection*). Now select the Visor Ellipse layer in the Layers palette and click the Align Horizontal Centers button in the Options palette on top.

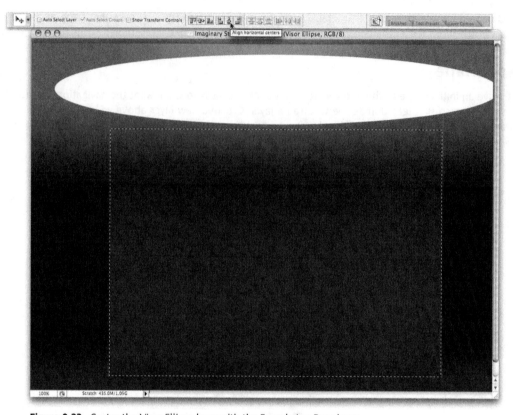

Figure 9-23. Center the Visor Ellipse layer with the Foundation Base layer.

Make a copy of the Visor Ellipse layer by pressing Ctrl+J (or Cmd+J). Name the new layer Visor Main Shadow and hide the Visor Ellipse layer. Open up the Layer Style window for the Visor Main Shadow layer and specify a Fill Opacity setting of zero. Turn on the Inner Shadow option from the menu on the left and use the settings in Figure 9-24.

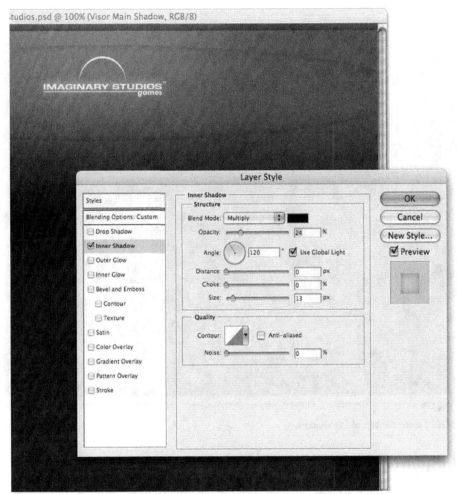

Figure 9-24. After setting Fill Opacity to 0%, use these settings for Inner Shadow on the Visor Main Shadow layer.

Now create a blank layer below the Visor Main Shadow layer. Merge the Visor Main Shadow layer with the new blank layer to flatten it, like we did with the Top Shadow layer. Now use the Rectangular Marquee tool to delete the top part and the side parts of the Visor Main Shadow layer, so it looks like Figure 9-25 and matches the rest of the interface.

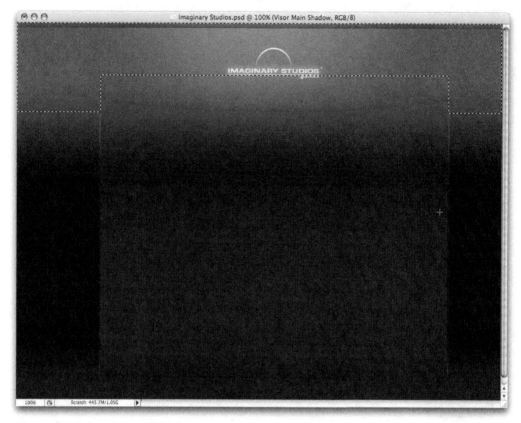

Figure 9-25. Delete the top of the shadow.

Body highlights

This is starting to look more 3D now, but it still needs some highlights to look more realistic. Create a new layer and name it Body Highlight. Use the Elliptical Marquee tool to make a selection as in Figure 9-26. Fill it with any color. Try to align it as close as possible to the Visor Main Shadow layer, as shown in Figure 9-26. (Remember to use the Align function to center it to your Foundation Base layer.)

Figure 9-26. The initial shape for the Body Highlight layer

Do a Load Selection of the Visor Ellipse layer (Ctrl-click or Cmd-click the layer in the Layers palette) and delete this selection on the Body Highlight layer. Use the Rectangular Marquee tool to select and delete any extra parts of the shape if your layer doesn't look like Figure 9-27.

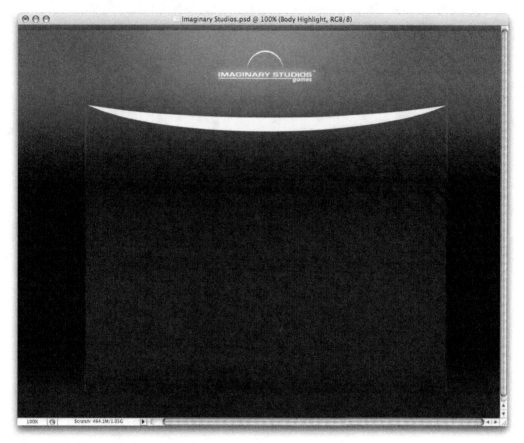

Figure 9-27. The final Body Highlight shape

Open up Layer Style window, set Opacity under General Blending to 36%, set Fill Opacity to 0%, and activate Bevel and Emboss for this layer. Set the style to Inner Bevel, give it a Size of 3 pixels, disable Use Global Light, set Angle to 90°, and set the Opacity for Highlight and Shadow to 18% and 0%, respectively. Your Layer Style window settings should match those shown in Figure 9-28.

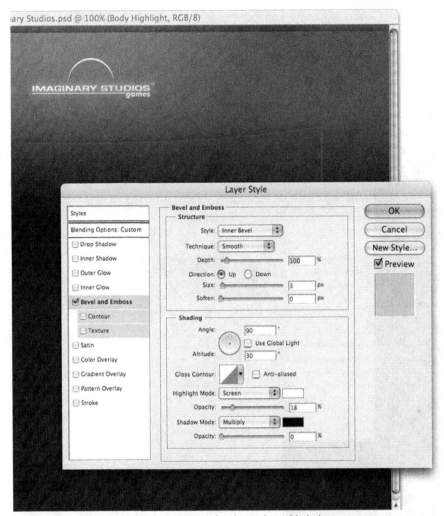

Figure 9-28. The Bevel and Emboss settings for the Body Highlight layer

Activate also Gradient Overlay in the Layer Style window. Set its Blend Mode to Linear Dodge, Angle to 90°, and Opacity to 21%. Click the gradient to open the Gradient Editor window and apply the following settings for the opacity stops' values: 5%, 41%, and 76%. The color stops are both set to white. Your Layer Style window should resemble that in Figure 9-29.

201

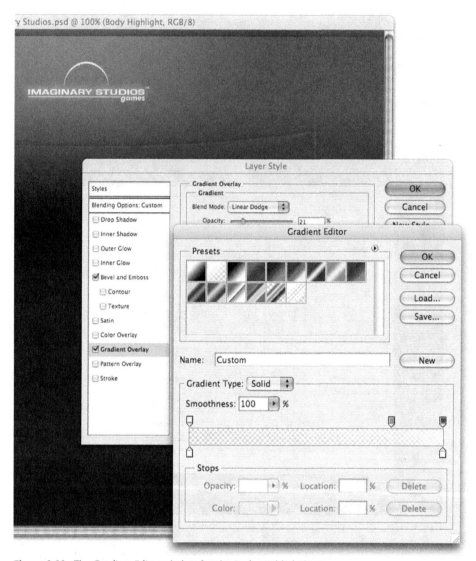

Figure 9-29. The Gradient Editor window for the Body Highlight layer

Click OK and return to the workspace. Create a new layer below the Body Highlight layer and name it Body Highlight Large. Do a Load Selection on the Foundation Base layer and fill the Body Highlight Large layer. Nudge the layer up (Shift+up arrow key) until it's just a little higher than the Visor Main Shadow layer. Do a Load Selection on the Visor Ellipse layer and delete the selection on the Body Highlight Large layer. Use the Elliptical Marquee tool to make a selection similar to the one in Figure 9-30, and then delete this selection on the Body Highlight Large layer.

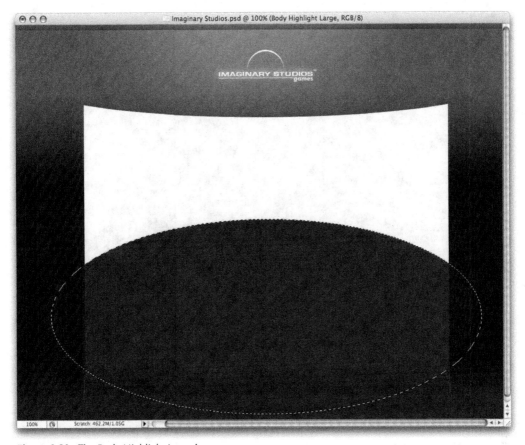

Figure 9-30. The Body Highlight Large layer

Right-click the Body Highlight layer in the Layers palette and select Copy Layer Style. Now right-click the Body Highlight Large layer and select Paste Layer Style. Open its Layer Style window and set the Opacity under General Blending to 100%.

The visor top group

We're now going to create the top of the visor. Create a new layer group (folder on the bottom of the Layers palette) and call it Visor Top. Do a Load Selection on the Visor Ellipse layer. Now use the Rectangular Marquee tool while holding down the Alt key (or Option) to subtract a selection from the top, left, and right of your current selection so it looks like Figure 9-31.

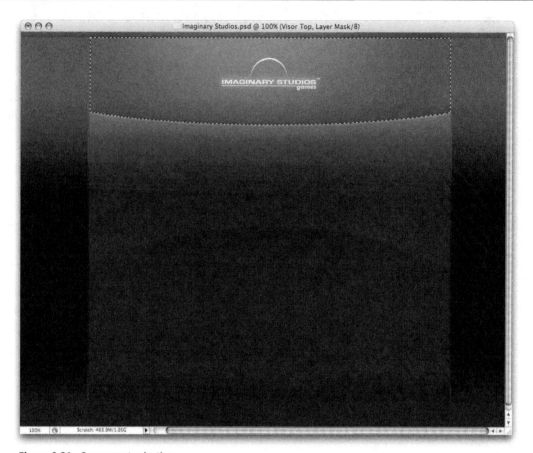

Figure 9-31. Our current selection

Click the Add layer mask button on the bottom of the Layers palette. There should now be a black-and-white mask thumbnail next to the folder icon of the Visor Top group, as you see in Figure 9-32.

Figure 9-32. The Visor Top group with a layer mask enabled

Visor shading

The first thing we're going to do in this group is create some shading for the visor. Make a new layer in the Visor Top group and name it Shading. Fill it with the same selection you used to create the layer mask for the Visor Top group. You can get that selection back by Ctrl-clicking (or Cmd-clicking) the layer mask thumbnail from Figure 9-32—exactly how you'd do a Load Selection on any other layer.

Now open up its Layer Style window and set Fill Opacity to 0%. Activate Drop Shadow using the settings in Figure 9-33. Also activate Color Overlay with color set to black and 11% opacity.

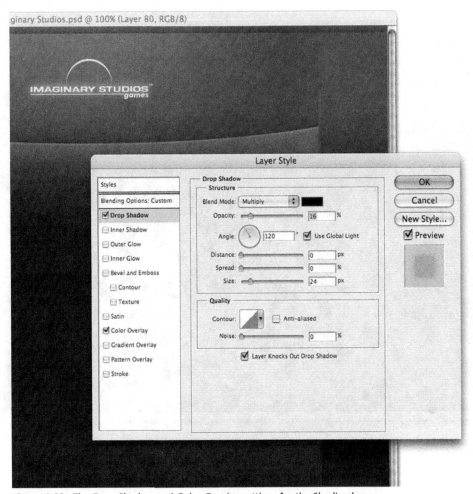

Figure 9-33. The Drop Shadow and Color Overlay settings for the Shading layer

Click OK. Now use the Eraser tool (press E) with a brush diameter of about 500 pixels to delete the middle of the Shading layer. Your screen should look like Figure 9-34.

Figure 9-34. The completed Shading layer, after erasing the middle *(A full-color version of this figure is available in the color insert.)*

Seam

Create a new layer in the Visor Top group and name it Seam. Use the Single Row Marquee tool (click and hold the Marquee tool until the pop-up menu with other tools appears) to create one black and one white line through the logo as shown in Figure 9-35 (the dark line should be above the white one to create the illusion of a 3D seam).

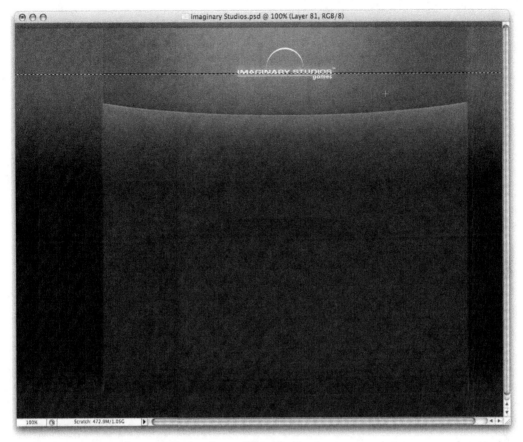

Figure 9-35. Make two lines, one black and one white, to create a seam.

Use the Eraser tool and lower the opacity to make the seam look like Figure 9-36.

Figure 9-36. This is what the final seam should look like.

Adding gloss

Next, we're going to add a gloss effect to the visor. Create a new layer above the Seam layer and call it Gloss. Use the Marquee tool to make a selection like the one in Figure 9-37. Use the Rectangular Marquee tool and then the Oval Marquee tool to subtract from the selection (hold Alt or Option while dragging the Marquee tool to activate subtraction while dragging).

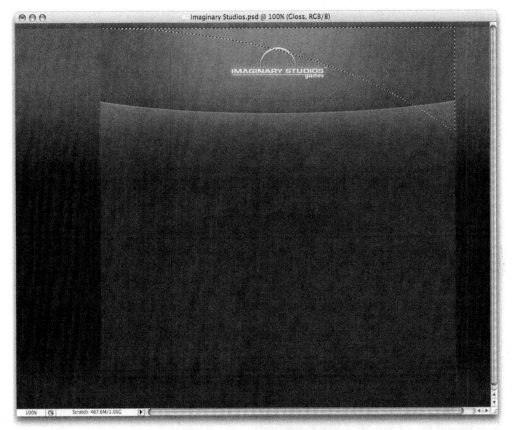

Figure 9-37. We're going to use this selection to add a gloss effect.

Tip: It might be difficult, depending on the resolution you have available, to accomplish this selection in two Marquee tool actions. Keep in mind that you can start by making a rectangular selection and filling it. Then create a new layer, make an oval selection, and fill it also (preferably with a different color from the rectangular layer so that you can distinguish the two). Now you can correctly position the oval shape, do a load selection, and delete that selection from the original rectangular shape. This process adds a few steps, but gives you finer control.

Fill the Gloss layer and open up its Layer Style window. Set Fill Opacity to 0%, activate Gradient Overlay, and use the settings in Figure 9-38. Note that the color stops are both white, whereas the opacity stops are 0% and 13% from left to right.

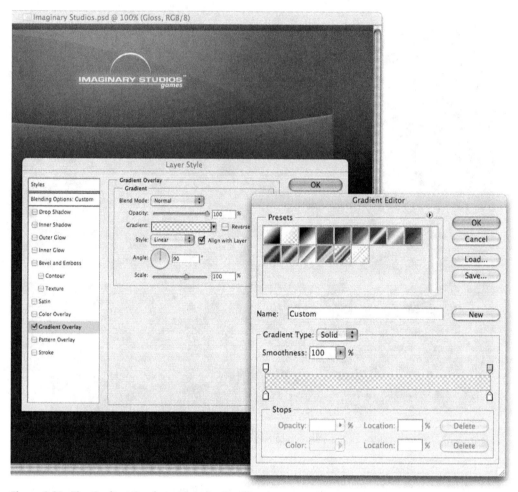

Figure 9-38. The Gradient Overlay settings for the Gloss layer

Now activate Stroke in the Layer Style window. Use the settings in Figure 9-39; specifically, the color stops are both black and the opacity stops are 0% and 64% from left to right. This is a very subtle detail, but makes the gloss stand out a little more and increases the realism.

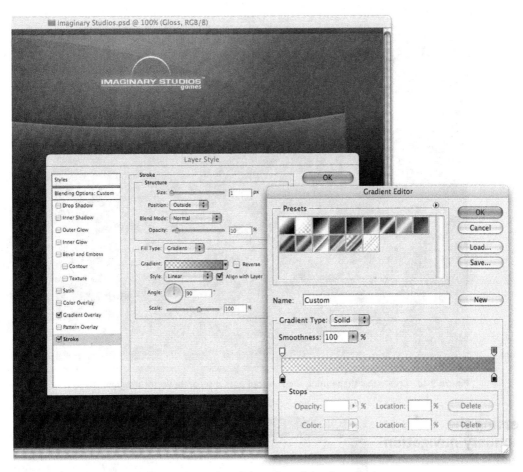

Figure 9-39. Use these settings to create a very subtle outline of the gloss effect.

The visor inset shape

Next we're going to create a new shape to use for the visor. We'll use it to build the navigation menus and to add detail. Create a new layer (outside of the Visor Top group, preferably above it so it's easier to see) and name it Visor Inset Shape. Now create the shape in Figure 9-40 using the Pen tool (press P) or your preferred vector software. (I originally made this in Illustrator, but I was easily able to re-create it using the Pen tool in Photoshop.) Try to get it as similar as possible. If you're using the Pen tool in Photoshop, keep in mind that you should use the Convert Point tool to smooth out the edges (click and hold down the Pen tool until you get a pop-up list with more drawing tools, including the Convert Point tool). Use the Path Selection tool to move vertex points (Shift+A).

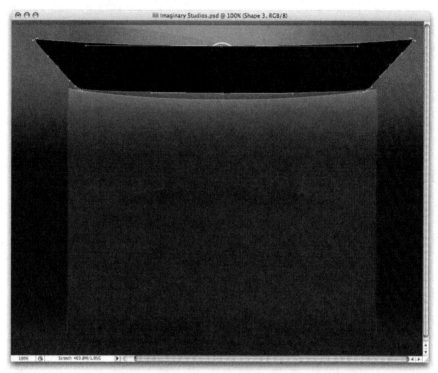

Figure 9-40. Create this shape using the Pen tool or in a separate vector program.

Creating the secondary navigation area

Now copy the Visor Inset Shape layer and hide the original. Name the new one Secondary Nav. Open up the Layer Style window and set Fill Opacity to 0%, apply Inner Shadow (see Figure 9-41—notice that Use Global Light is unchecked), Bevel and Emboss (in Figure 9-42 you can see the color value for Highlight Mode under Bevel and Emboss is #59ABF7), and Gradient Overlay (specifically, opacity stop values in the Gradient Editor window, from left to right, are 100%, 0%, 0%, and 100%, and the color stop values are both #0C3D77, as shown in Figure 9-43).

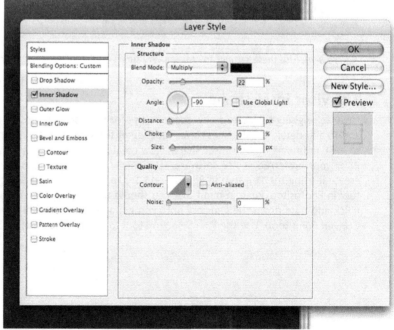

Figure 9-41. The values for Inner Shadow

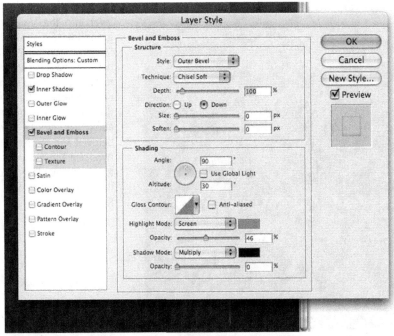

Figure 9-42. The values for Bevel and Emboss

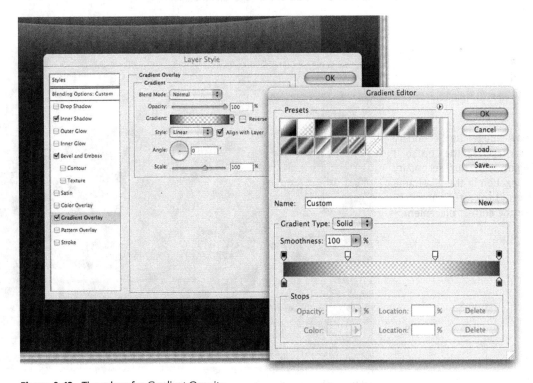

Figure 9-43. The values for Gradient Opacity

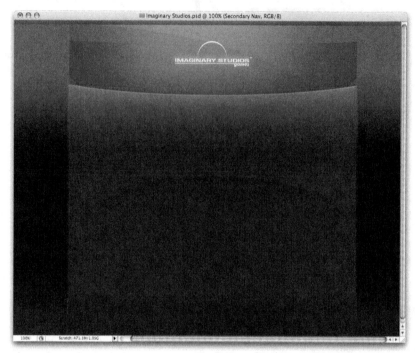

Drag the Secondary Nav layer into the Visor Top group (place it above the Shading layer). Notice how the mask we applied to the entire group immediately takes effect. Flatten the layer effects by creating an empty layer below it and merging the two. Use the Eraser tool to make your layer look the same as the one in Figure 9-44.

Figure 9-44. Flatten the layer effects and erase a little bit of the edges and the middle part of the layer.

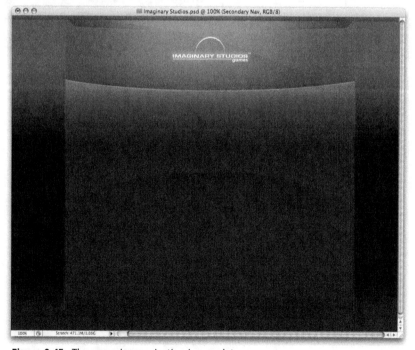

Now nudge the Secondary Nav layer to the top so it aligns with our secondary navigation in the wireframe layer. Look at Figure 9-45 for the correct placement.

Figure 9-45. The secondary navigation is complete.

Adding details to the visor

Now copy the Secondary Nav layer and press Ctrl+T (or Cmd+T) to activate the Free Transform tool. Scale the layer down a bit horizontally and flip it vertically to make it look like Figure 9-46. You'll have to use the Eraser tool on the edges and on the bottom to make it look like Figure 9-47.

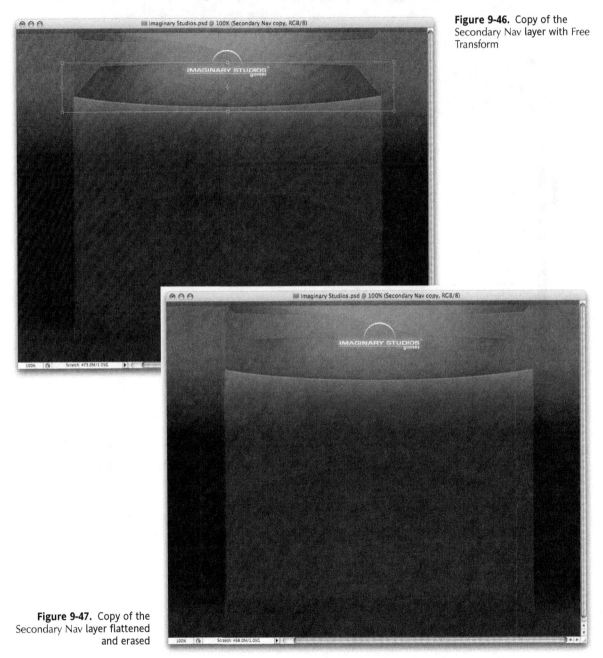

Figure 9-46. Copy of the Secondary Nav layer with Free Transform

Figure 9-47. Copy of the Secondary Nav layer flattened and erased

We also need to duplicate the Visor Inset Shape layer, flip it horizontally, scale it down, and make it white to add a highlight. Refer to Figure 9-48 for details on this.

Figure 9-48. The color stops are both white for this gradient. The opacity stops are 17% and 25% from left to right.

Copy the Secondary Nav layer again and activate Free Transform again. This time scale it only horizontally. Use the Eraser tool once more to make this layer look like what you see in Figure 9-49.

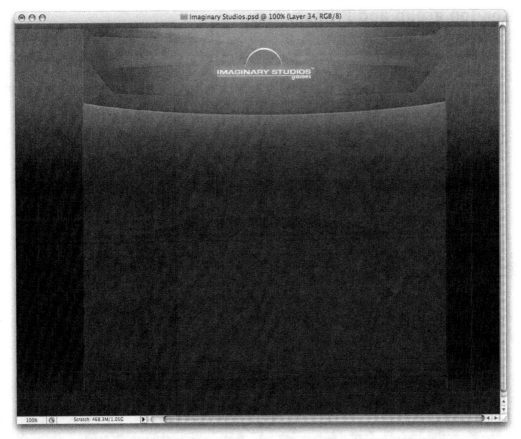

Figure 9-49. More copying and transforming to add details

Creating the primary navigation

In the next sections, we're going to shift our focus to the main navigation bar and area of the site. We will call this the Primary Nav, and it will ultimately be the container for the main links of the site. In the next chapter, you're going to look at re-creating this part of the site in Flash with vector graphics, which will allow you to animate it smoothly. For now, however, we need to design a concept that will allow us to quickly transition to Flash without having to do too much experimenting. You want to enter the Flash design phase with a very clear goal of what you have to do. Anyway, on to the next steps!

Visor Top group and Primary Nav

We're going to reuse the Visor Inset Shape layer to make the primary navigation bar. First create a new layer group, above the Visor Top group, and name it Primary Nav. Now create a new layer in the Primary Nav group and name it Nav Bar. Do a Load Selection on the Visor Inset Shape layer and fill the Nav Bar layer. You should notice that the shape looks way too big; that's because we have to apply a mask to the Primary Nav group, like we did with the Visor Top group.

Now select the Primary Nav group in the Layers palette. Do a Load Selection on the Visor Top group's layer mask (as you normally would, but click the black-and-white mask thumbnail). Now press the Add layer mask button at the bottom of the Layers palette to mask the Primary Nav group.

Go back to the Nav Bar layer and flip it vertically. The results should resemble Figure 9-50.

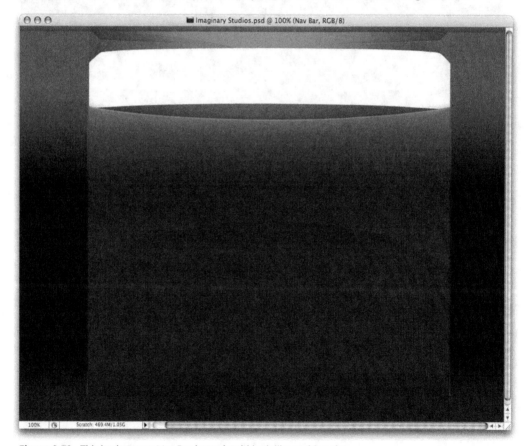

Figure 9-50. This is what your Nav Bar layer should look like at this point.

> *Note that if you're using Photoshop CS2, you can copy a layer mask from one layer to another using drag and drop. Drag the layer mask thumbnail (on the right side of a layer in the* Layers *palette) while holding the Option key from your masked layer to the layer you want to apply the mask to.*

Nudge the layer down to line up the top part with the top of the primary navigation rectangle in your wireframe layer. Apply another free transform to this layer and scale the width down to 80% as in Figure 9-51.

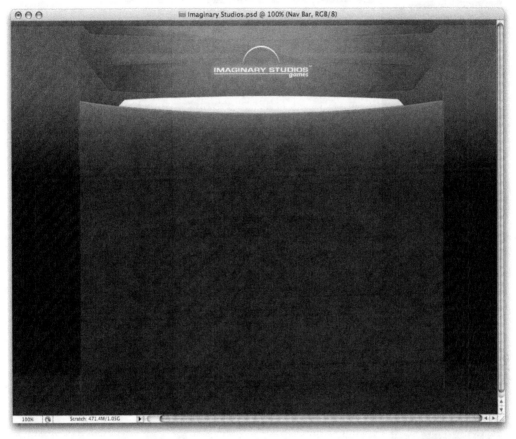

Figure 9-51. The properly sized Nav Bar layer

Open up the Nav Bar layer's Layer Style window and activate Drop Shadow (see Figure 9-52) and Bevel and Emboss (see Figure 9-53). For Gradient Overlay, the color stop values, from left to right, need to be set to #B9E2FE, #DEEDFE, #B9E2FE. Also set the color midpoint of the first color stop to location 5%, as shown in Figure 9-54.

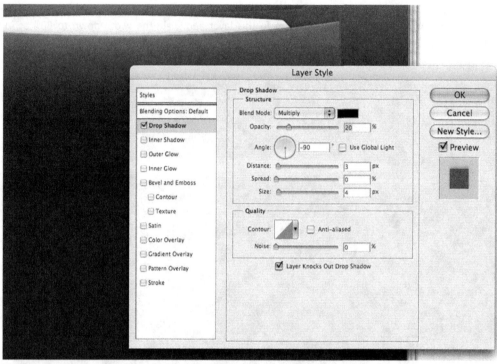

Figure 9-52. The settings for the Nav Bar layer's Drop Shadow effect

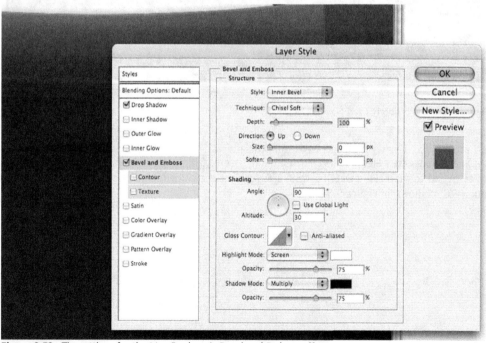

Figure 9-53. The settings for the Nav Bar layer's Bevel and Emboss effect

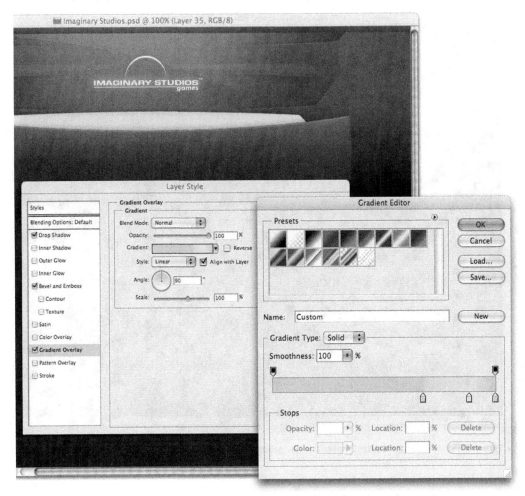

Figure 9-54. The color stop values and the color midpoint of the first color stop setting

Adding a highlight

You can also make a copy of the highlight layer I demonstrated in Figure 9-48. Drag it into the Primary Nav group and place it above the Nav Bar layer to create a gloss effect. Also give this layer a stroke to create a subtle outline of the gloss effect, similar to what we previously did in Figure 9-39. This lends a better 3D feel to the navigation bar, as Figure 9-55 illustrates.

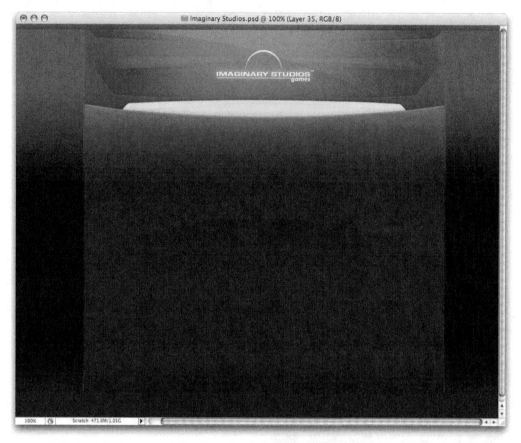

Figure 9-55. A subtle gloss effect makes the navigation bar look more 3D.

Navigation bar shadow

To improve the 3D effect and add even more depth, we're going to create a shadow on the navigation bar. Create a new layer above the last gloss layers we made and name this layer Nav Shadow. Do a Load Selection on the Visor Ellipse layer and fill the Nav Shadow with the selection. Open its Layer Style window, set Fill Opacity to 0%, and activate Inner Shadow. Use the settings in Figure 9-46. (Figure 9-56 shows the layer with a red color overlay to help you better understand what I'm referring to.)

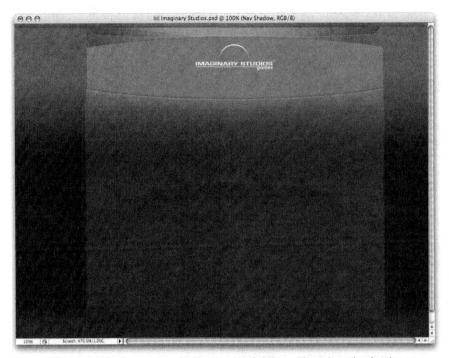

Figure 9-56. Inner Shadow settings for the Nav Shadow layer. The color value for the shadow is #004DA5.

Now flatten the layer effects by creating an empty layer below the Nav Shadow layer and merging them together. Set the layer's blend mode to Multiply (either by opening the Layer Style window or through the Layers palette) and use the Rectangular Marquee tool to select and delete the top part of the shadow (as in Figure 9-57), so that the shadow only appears on the navigation bar.

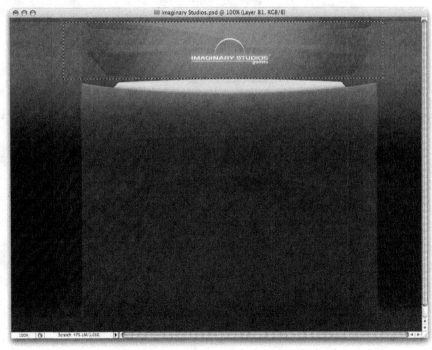

Figure 9-57. Once you've deleted the top part of the layer, the shadow is complete.

Try hiding and unhiding some of the shadows we created to see the difference in depth that these generate. Notice how much flatter the interface looks without them.

Adding details to the logo

I'll demonstrate how to add a few more details to the logo area, as it feels a little bland, and I want to draw the eye a little more towards this upper area of the site. I think the effect described in the next steps also helps emphasize the logo and make it more memorable; however, feel free to skip the next steps if you're happy with the way it currently looks. Keep in mind that I will be using the logo as an example for Flash in the next chapter, so check back here if something looks off when you're trying to follow the tutorial there.

Cloud pictures

I added some clouds and light rays to the logo, so it looks like the visor is looking out into a sky (see Figure 9-58). The clouds are just a layer above the Body Highlight layer. I took various pictures of clouds with my camera and used the Eraser tool to delete parts I didn't want. I used a few different pictures, free transformed them a little bit, and tried to get them to fade into the top part of the interface. The final cloud layer has a Hard Light blend mode. You can get pictures of clouds online on any royalty-free photography site if you don't have a camera and/or a cloudy sky handy!

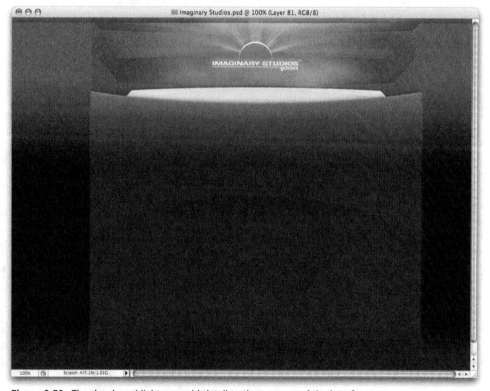

Figure 9-58. The clouds and light rays add detail to the top part of the interface.

Light rays

The light rays shown in Figure 9-59 are created using the Pen tool and a circular mask. I duplicated the layers a few times, deleted their edges to make them gradually fade out, free transformed them slightly so they don't all line up perfectly (this also helps give a 3D feel), and added a little bit of motion blur to one of the layers. I also changed the colors on a few of them just slightly and gave them a Screen blend mode. In total, there are five light ray layers.

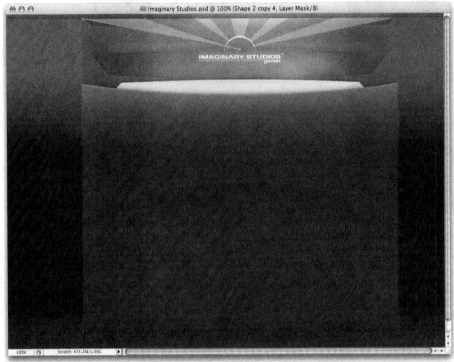

Figure 9-59. The light rays are created with the Pen tool. A mask hasn't been applied to the outer part of the rays yet, which is why they stretch across the top of the interface.

Creating the content containers

The top part of the interface is starting to come together, but the content area is pretty empty at the moment. So we're going to take care of that next and create our main content area. Remember to check your wireframe every once in a while to make sure you're staying on track.

Main content area

Now let's go ahead and create the sections that will hold our textual and graphic content, or the real message of our site. These graphics will help bring focus to the key content area of your site and will act as a guide for the viewer's eye.

Content background

Make a selection with the Rectangular Marquee tool as shown in Figure 9-60 and fill a new layer. Give this layer, which should be just above your Foundation Base layer, the name Content BG.

Figure 9-60. Starting to create the main content area

Select Filter ➤ Blur ➤ Gaussian Blur. Specify a radius of 10 pixels and click OK. Now open the Layer Style window, set Fill Opacity to 0%, and activate Color Overlay. Use a color value of #0A305F and Opacity of 40%. Click OK and return to the work-space, which should resemble Figure 9-61.

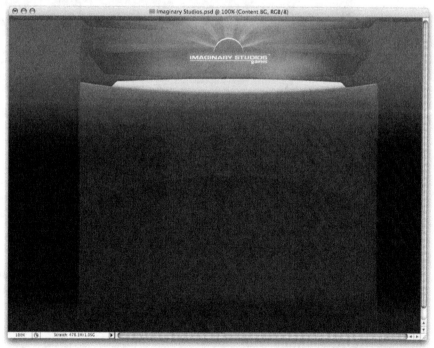

Figure 9-61. This is what the Content BG layer should look like after blurring and applying Color Overlay.

Content top

Create a new layer above the Content BG layer and name it Content BG Top. Use the Pen tool to make a shape like the one in Figure 9-62. (Notice how the top-right corner slightly curves up.)

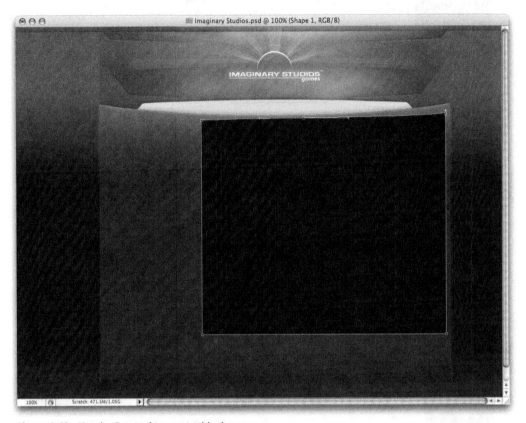

Figure 9-62. Use the Pen tool to create this shape.

Open up this layer's Layer Style window and set its Fill Opacity to 0%. Activate Drop Shadow and use the settings in Figure 9-63. For Gradient Overlay, the opacity stop values are 0% and 100%, and the color stop values are #093864 and #3474C0, as shown in Figure 9-64.

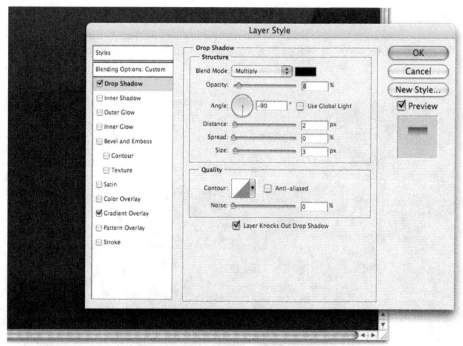

Figure 9-63. Use these settings for the Drop Shadow on the Content BG Top layer.

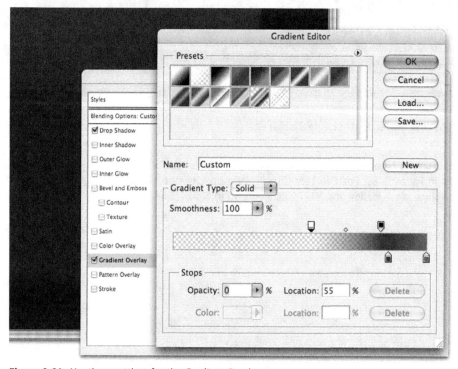

Figure 9-64. Use these settings for the Gradient Overlay.

Content borders

Duplicate the Content BG Top layer and hide the original by clicking the eye icon in the Layers palette. Rename the new layer Content Borders and drag it below the hidden Content BG Top layer. Nudge the new layer 4 pixels to the right. With the Rectangular Marquee tool, make a 1-pixel wide selection of the left side of the Content Borders layer and nudge it 8 pixels to the left. Do this while holding down the Ctrl+Alt+left arrow keys (or the Cmd+Option+left arrow keys on a Mac). This clones the selection in 1-pixel increments.

Now unhide the Content BG Top layer and open the Layer Style window for the Content Borders layer. Set Fill Opacity to 0% and activate Gradient Overlay using the settings in Figure 9-65.

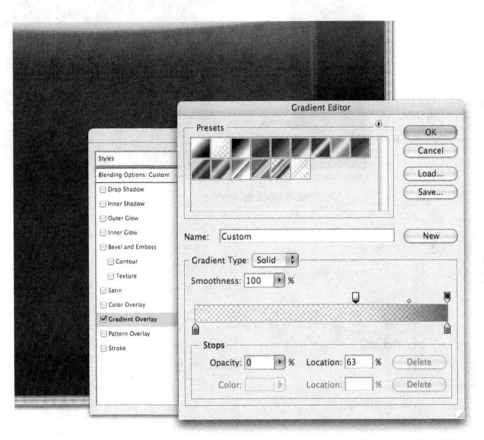

Figure 9-65. Use these settings to color the Content Borders layer and make it appear as if it's fading out.

Left column content area

Now we'll create the content area for the news on the left. Make a new layer and name it Left Content. Select the Rounded Rectangle tool (press U) and set its radius to 5 pixels (see Figure 9-66).

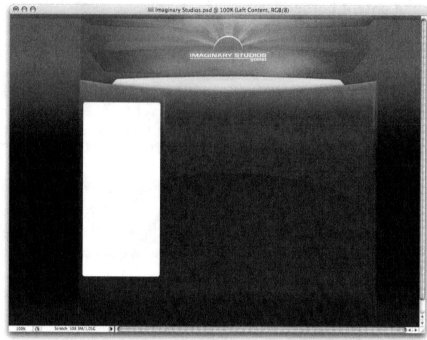

Figure 9-66. Use a 5-pixel radius for the Rounded Rectangle tool when you create the left content area.

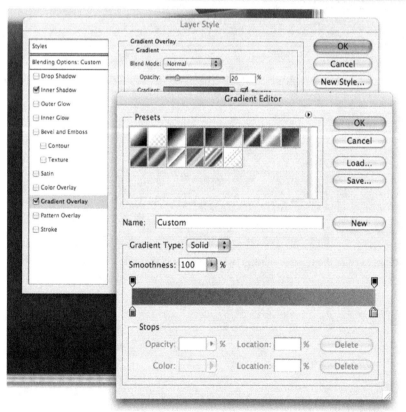

Use the wireframe layer as a general guide when you draw the Left Content layer. When you've drawn the shape, open up the Layer Style window. Set Fill Opacity to 0% and enable Inner Shadow. For Gradient Overlay, the color stop values are #0152B, #21A1F91, and #75C7FF. Notice that the last two color stops are very close, with only 1% location dividing them, as you see in Figure 9-67.

Figure 9-67. The color stop values are #0152B, #21A1F91, and, #75C7FF. Notice that the last two color stops are very close, with only 1% location dividing them.

Content and buttons

This is the final step of the tutorial. As shown in Figure 9-68, add text size buttons above the Left Content layer, dummy text, and an image placeholder. By now you should be able to do all these things yourself! The text size buttons are simply shapes rendered with the Rounded Rectangle tool that have a drop shadow and a highlight layer.

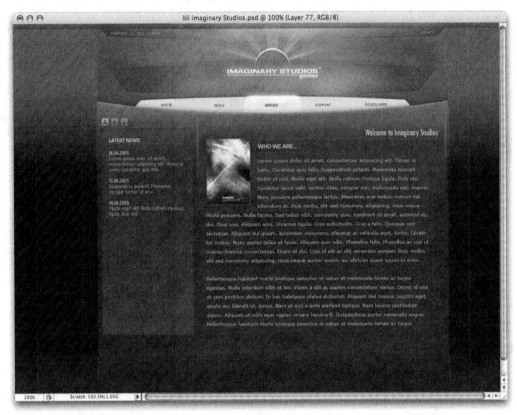

Figure 9-68. The final interface with sample states for the buttons *(A full-color version of this figure is available in the color insert.)*

Mouseover states

Notice that the first text size button and the Games button in the navigation bar look different. They represent the mouseover states of the buttons. For the text size buttons, their mouseover state is simply a slightly brighter color overlay in the Layer Style settings. The navigation bar, on the other hand, actually has another layer to represent its mouseover state. The new layer is immediately above the Nav Bar layer and has a rectangular shape. It has a 0% Fill Opacity, a 13-pixel white Outer Glow, and a 50% opacity white Color Overlay.

Moving from Photoshop to Flash

Now that the interface is complete, you should start thinking about how you're going to transfer these layers to Flash. The first thing I usually do is to save the entire interface as a PNG, with all of the content layers and button layers hidden. I import this in Flash and set the PNG as my background layer; this will serve as a guide much like the wireframe layer in Photoshop served as a guide.

I start by deciding which layers I'm going to redo entirely in vector and which ones I'll export as PNGs. As a general rule, try to use vectors with large parts of the interface that need to be animated—it will help a lot with both file size and playback speed. Sometimes, however, certain graphics aren't possible to re-create in vector. Or sometimes it's just not worth it. For example, a very complex vector object can slow down playback more than just using a single PNG for the same graphic. See Chapter 10 for much more about PNGs and moving from Photoshop to Flash.

So where would I use vectors with our Imaginary Studios interface? Pretty much the entire bottom part of the interface can be redone in vector, as can the navigation bar. Consider what we were using the most in Photoshop: gradients, the Pen tool, and shadows. We can easily re-create all of the shapes in the interface in vector and apply the same gradients in Flash. Even the top visor part would be possible to re-create in vector using a combination of "soften fill edges" for the shadows and transparent gradients to simulate the erasing we did (not to mention applying the new Glow, Blur, and Drop Shadow filters found in Flash 8, which make designing in Flash so much more powerful than before).

So the next step is to start planning the Flash file. At this point I also connect with my twin brother and complementary coding monster, Luigi. It's a good idea to start thinking ahead as to how the Flash file will have to be structured for dynamic content. You also need to consider how you're going to load the different pages and subsections of the site. Is everything going to be contained in a single FLA file? Or are you going to be loading separate SWF files based on what the user requests (as is highly recommended)? What kind of dynamic content will integrate with the interface?

Summary

After this chapter, you should have a strong understanding of how to design an interface in Photoshop from initial planning, to constructing, and final tweaking. We keep discovering more and more that gradients are a vital asset when creating depth. The previous chapter discussed simplicity in creating realistic-looking objects, and the same concept is carried over here. With just a few tools, we've been able to easily create a very convincing-looking environment, without needing dozens of filters, plug-ins, or external renders. In fact, the only Photoshop filter we used in this entire tutorial was Gaussian Blur.

Here are some of the lessons you've learned from reading this chapter:

- Photoshop is the industry-standard static raster design program and a very powerful tool for interface designers.

- There are different ways to design an interface for Flash, whether it involves starting in a raster program or designing immediately in vector. Neither approach is right nor wrong, you simply need to discover which works best for you.

- The desire to constantly better your work is an important characteristic that all designers should have. Seeing flaws and ways to improve your work constantly is what drives you as a designer to better yourself. Try to never lose this trait, but also realize when it's time to say "enough" and move on; otherwise, you risk wasting too much time.

- Designing in a nondestructive way allows you to preserve your original graphics so that you can easily make modifications at a later stage without having to start over. Examples of nondestructive tools are adjustment layers and the new Smart Objects in Photoshop CS2.

- Try to design all your sites for minimum 800×600 screen resolution users. This is the safest way to ensure all visitors will have an enjoyable and nonfrustrating experience when viewing your site.

- Keeping a layer with the wireframe of your site is an easy way to ensure your design stays on track with your initial specifications.

- Try to always name your layers and place them into logical groups. This will help you a lot when your file becomes very big.

- Using simple shape fills and the Layer Style window effects allows you to very easily and quickly create and control your shapes. This also enforces the nondestructive method, as you can always go back to the Layer Style window and make modifications.

- When moving from Photoshop to Flash, you need to consider which shapes you will convert to vector. PNG is a great raster format that allows you to easily import complex graphics into Flash while preserving their transparency. PNGs are discussed in detail in the next chapter.

In the next chapter, I'm going to carry on this tutorial a little further by demonstrating how PNGs can be of great benefit to a Flash designer.

Chapter 10

MOVING FROM PHOTOSHOP
TO FLASH AND EFFECTIVE PNGS

by Guido Rosso

In the last chapter, I mentioned that PNG images can be a great benefit to Flash designers. So what exactly are PNGs and how can you benefit from them?

PNG (pronounced "ping"), which stands for Portable Network Graphic, is a raster image format. The PNG format is similar to GIF, yet improves on its shortcomings in various ways, such as supplying a much wider range of color depths and transparency and achieving greater compression.

The thing that interests us the most as Flash designers is the full transparency support. Look at Figure 10-1 and notice the difference between the GIF (bottom left) and the PNG (bottom right) generated from a graphic in Photoshop (top) and layered over a gradient background. GIF transparency basically works on an on/off basis, whereas a PNG can store a full range of alpha transparency. Notice that the borders of the butterfly on the right blend perfectly with the background, without any hard lines or blocky corners.

When you use a PNG with a transparent background in Flash, it blends perfectly with other layers behind it. This allows you to achieve certain effects that wouldn't look as clean and smooth with a GIF, or wouldn't be possible without redesigning the graphic in vector.

From a programming point of view, PNGs are a smart choice not only for their excellent image quality, but also because PNG is an open source library. Implementing the

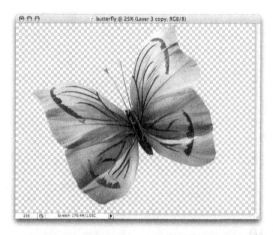

Figure 10-1. The top window demonstrates the original graphic in Photoshop, whereas the bottom images represent the butterfly saved as a GIF (left) and as a PNG (right) layered over a gradient background.

GIF format into a program requires royalties because the compression method is patented, whereas PNG is royalty free.

In this chapter, you're going to learn how to prepare graphics and specific layers in Photoshop to be saved as PNGs. From there I'll take you through a couple of examples demonstrating how you can use PNGs effectively in Flash. As a final step, you'll learn how to export a vector graphic, made in Flash, to create a raster object that you can reimport and use in Flash.

Preparing the files

In Chapter 9, we completed the design of the Imaginary Studios interface in Photoshop. Now we need to move what we've done so far to Flash. As mentioned in the previous chapter, re-creating an interface in Flash means that you'll have to redesign certain parts of it in vector.

So how do you decide which layers of the interface should be redesigned in vector and which layers should be saved as PNGs? You should start by figuring out what parts of the interface to animate. If you want a part of the interface to animate, you need to separate it from the background and place it on its own layer in Flash. As a general rule, a vector graphic will animate better in Flash than a raster graphic. However, a very complex vector graphic (made up of many shapes, groups, and separate objects) can cause a lot more slowdown than a single raster graphic. You're going to have to experiment and do a little trial and error to figure out which way works better with different objects.

The background

Before demonstrating how to redesign a part of our Photoshop interface in vector format, we need to prepare the background graphics for the Flash file. We're going to use PNGs to create two background layers in Flash. One will be our completed interface, as we left it at the end of Chapter 8, and the other will be the same interface stripped of all content.

Open up your Imaginary Studios Photoshop file from Chapter 8. Go to File ➤ Save for Web (press Alt+Shift+Ctrl+S on a PC or Option+Shift+Cmd+S on a Mac). Select PNG-24 from the Preset pull-down menu on the right, and save this file as interface_content.png.

> *Try to save your files in an organized directory structure that will make it easy for you and other team members to find them later. For example, all my projects are under a* RealitySlip Clients *directory on my local server (you should also be running a version control system, especially if multiple people are working on the same files). Under* RealitySlip Clients *I have a directory for every client, and under a specific client I create a new folder for every project. This helps if you're working on multiple projects for the same client, or if in the future you might be working on new redesigns of the site. On my system, this project would be saved under the following structure:* RealitySlip Clients ➤ Imaginary Studios ➤ 2005 Website. *Under* 2005 Website *I have the following folders:* PSD, Flash Dev, *and* Site. PSD *is where I store all my Photoshop files,* Flash Dev *is where all development Flash files are saved, and the* Site *folder contains the actual test version of the site with all HTML, CSS, and PHP code included. All my PNGs for this tutorial are saved under* RealitySlip Clients ➤ Imaginary Studios ➤ 2005 Website ➤ Flash Dev ➤ Import.

Now we need to clean up the interface to save a version of the background without any content. Hide all the layers that make up the content, the logo, and the navigation bar. We're hiding the logo and navigation bar because we'll be re-creating the navigation bar in vector and we'll be animating the logo. We're hiding the content because we're going to focus on redesigning the interface first, not the content. This means that the content won't be hiding any design elements. Your file should now look like Figure 10-2. Save this as interface_clean.png.

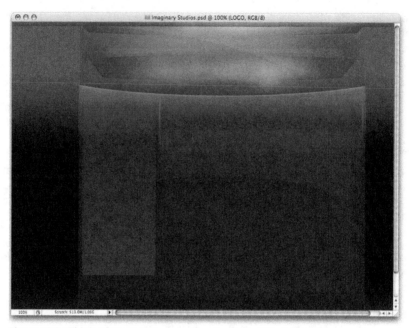

Figure 10-2. This is what your interface_clean.png should look like.

The logo

Since we're going to animate the logo in Flash later, we need to save it as a PNG in Photoshop. Let's start by unhiding it (leave the rays hidden). We need the background of the logo to be transparent, and we're going to do that by using the Knockout setting of the Layer Style window. Start by creating a new layer below your logo and name it Logo Bounding Box. Draw a rectangular selection that includes the logo and glow as shown in Figure 10-3.

Fill the selection and open its Layer Style window. Set Fill Opacity to 0% and Knockout to Deep, as shown in Figure 10-4. Notice that as a result of the new Knockout setting, this layer's Fill Opacity affects all the layers below it.

Figure 10-3. With this rectangular selection, you're going to create a shape that renders all the layers below it transparent.

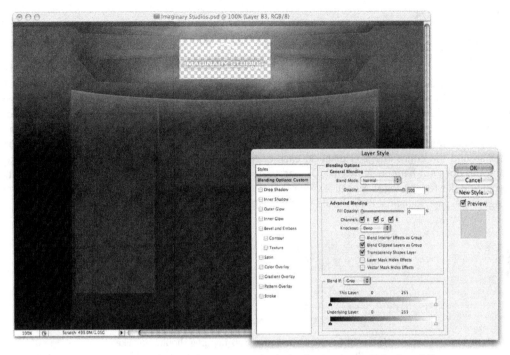

Figure 10-4. Using a Deep Knockout setting, we've made the background area of the logo fully transparent.

Knockout *is a great way to quickly render various layers invisible without having to hide them one by one. The* Deep *setting causes the layer's* Fill Opacity *to affect all the layers below it, whereas the* Shallow *setting affects only the layers in the same* Layer Set. *If the layer isn't in a* Layer Set, *both settings have the same effect. Note that if you have a* Background *layer (for example, if you didn't set a transparent background in the* New file *window), then the* Knockout *setting will reveal the background layer; the* Background *layer's opacity won't be affected.*

Now you can do a load selection on the Logo Bounding Box layer and copy merge (use Ctrl+Shift+C on a PC, Cmd+Shift+C on a Mac). Create a new file. The New window will automatically select the width and height for the new file based on the dimensions of the logo you copied. Add 2 pixels to the automatic Width and Height settings (e.g., if automatic setting for width is 200 pixels, change it to 202

Figure 10-5. This is what your logo.png file should look like in Photoshop.

pixels). This is to prevent an issue that can occur in Flash whereby the borders appear smeared. This happens when you import a PNG whose outer pixels aren't fully transparent. By adding 2 pixels to both height and width, we ensure that there will be a 1-pixel, fully transparent border to the graphic.

Paste the copied logo into the new file, as shown in Figure 10-5. Select Save for Web from the File menu and save the file with the name logo.png.

The logo rays

We also want to animate the rays behind the logo, but we want them to animate separately from the logo. To achieve this, you have to save the rays as a separate PNG.

Create a bounding box layer for the rays and give it a Knockout setting of Deep, as you did previously for the logo. Now do a load selection, copy merge, create a new file, and stop for a second at the New file window. Once again, increase the width and height (which was detected from the copy merge you did) by 2 pixels, in a similar manner to what you did on the last page. The reason for doing this is that Flash sometimes blurs pixels that are on the border of a PNG with transparency. Adding a 1-pixel border around the entire image (1 pixel on each edge, therefore 2 for height and 2 for width) ensures that this does not happen. Now click OK and paste the copied rays into the new file (which is exactly what you did for the logo). Select Save for Web from the File menu and save the file with the name logo_rays.png. Your final PNG should look like Figure 10-6.

Figure 10-6. This is what your logo_rays.png should look like in Photoshop.

The Flash file

Now we're going to switch to Flash and import all the PNGs on separate layers. Start by opening Flash and setting your document size equal to the width and height of your interface_clean.png file. Also set the frame rate of the movie to 26 frames per second. The next chapter contains more information on frame rates. Import both background PNGs into Flash.

Name your layers as in Figure 10-7. You can hide/unhide the layers as a guide while you're working on redesigning the interface in Flash. You should have the Content Guide PNG layer hidden as you work on the graphics pertaining to the interface. The Content Guide PNG should be visible as you start working on graphics and text that are part of the content of the site. Ultimately both these layers will be hidden and deleted.

Figure 10-7. Import the background PNGs on two separate background layers.

The Flash file you've just created will serve as a foundation for the rest of the project. The background PNG layers serve as a guide for the interface as you export separate raster graphics from Photoshop or re-create specific parts of the interface in Flash. A PNG works great as a background guide layer because it's lossless and remains true to the original colors.

In its current state, the file works perfectly as a demo or for a pitch. File size is probably not an issue at this point, as you'll probably be presenting the file to your client in person and not over the Internet. At a later stage, however, the PNG background layers will have to be removed.

Now import the logo and rays PNGs. Use the Content Guide layer to help you position and correctly align the logo and rays. Now place your logo and rays in a Layer folder called Logo. Notice that you can also collapse the layer set so the layers contained in it are hidden. Separating relevant layers into Layer folders will help you easily identify the layers on the timeline when you have to go back and edit the keyframes. Your file should now look like Figure 10-8.

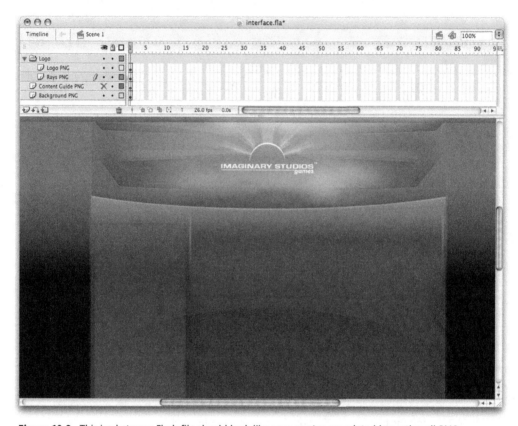

Figure 10-8. This is what your Flash file should look like once you've completed importing all PNGs.

Navigation bar tutorial

In the next sections of this chapter, we're going to start working with Flash's design tools to convert our design to vector. We'll be focusing on the navigation bar.

Re-creating in vector

Now that your file is ready, you need to take a look at your interface and decide what can easily be re-created in vector. The first thing that catches my eye is the navigation bar. We can easily redesign the shape in vector and use a few gradients to achieve a very similar look to the raster image.

Since I created my initial shape in Illustrator, I can easily just copy and paste it into Flash. However, it's very simple to create a similar looking shape in Flash using the Pen tool. Take a look at Figure 10-9 and notice how the vertex points and curve handles define the shape. Alternatively, you can download my EPS file for the shape from the book's download page at www.friendsofed.com.

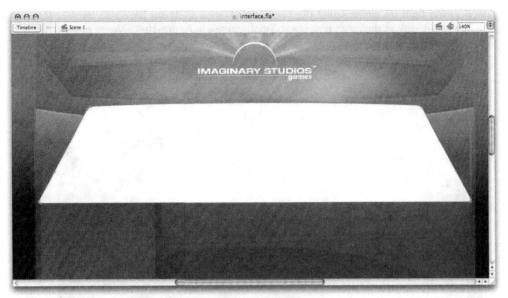

Figure 10-9. Re-create this shape in Flash using the Pen tool.

Now use these gradient settings to color the shape of the navigation bar: #B9E2FE, #CCE7FE, #DEEDFE, and #B9E2FE (see Figure 10-10). You'll also have to use the Gradient Transform tool (press G) to align the gradient vertically.

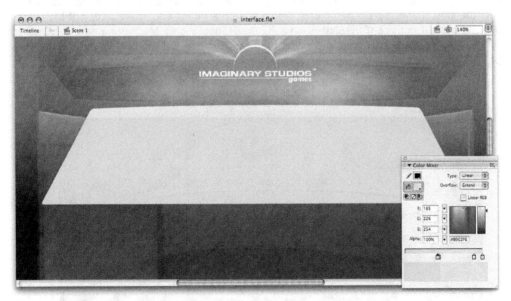

Figure 10-10. Settings for the gradient stops

The color fill is starting to look similar to our original navigation bar, but to make it identical to the Photoshop version, we need to add the subtle gloss effect. To achieve this, copy your shape and paste it in a new layer above the original. Give it a linear gradient with two white color stops, but give the color stop to the right 0% alpha. Using the Oval tool, draw a circle on the same layer as this new shape, and make it look as similar as possible to what you see in Figure 10-11. We're going to use this shape to cut out the rounded bottom part of the gloss effect.

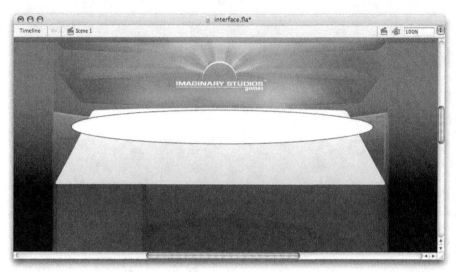

Figure 10-11. Use the Oval tool to create a circular shape.

Now your gloss shape is "cut" by the circular shape. Notice that you can select the top and bottom parts of the gloss shape as separate objects. Before you do anything else, make a copy of the circle's outline and paste it in place (Ctrl+Shift+V on a PC, Cmd+Shift+V on a Mac) into a new layer named Circle Outline. Now hide that layer and select the circular shape and the bottom part of the gloss shape, as shown in Figure 10-12, and press Delete.

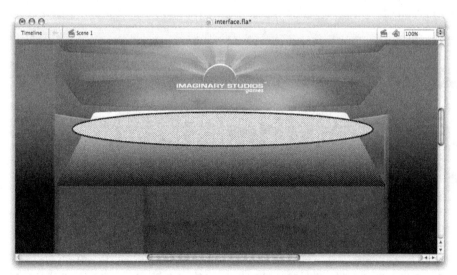

Figure 10-12. The circular shape cuts into the gloss shape, allowing you to select different parts of it.

Now use the Gradient Transform tool to align the gradient correctly, as shown in Figure 10-13. Remember to refer to your Content Guide PNG layer to see what the final gloss effect should look like.

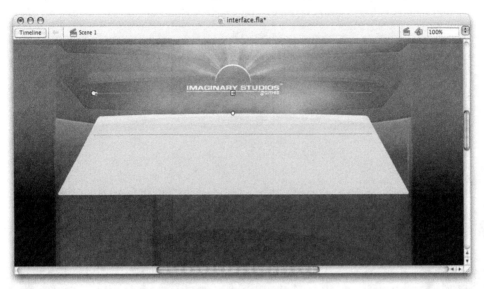

Figure 10-13. Use the Gradient Transform tool to correctly align the gloss effect.

Unhide the Circle Outline layer, copy the outline, which will help add to the realism of the gloss effect, and paste it in place on your gloss layer. You'll notice that you can now select the bottom part of the outline, as demonstrated in Figure 10-14. Go ahead and select it and press Delete, then lower its alpha to 3% from the Color Mixer palette.

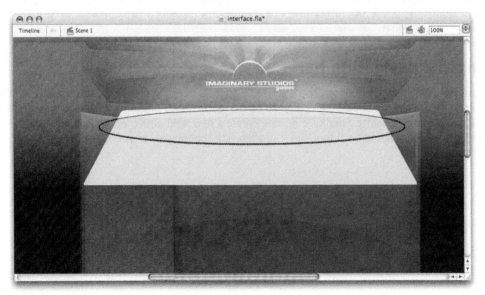

Figure 10-14. Select the bottom part of the outline and press Delete.

Now duplicate your original navigation bar shape from Figure 10-9 on a new layer and apply a vertical gradient, black to fully transparent black. Press F to use the Gradient Transform tool to correctly align this shadow effect so that it looks like the one in Figure 10-15.

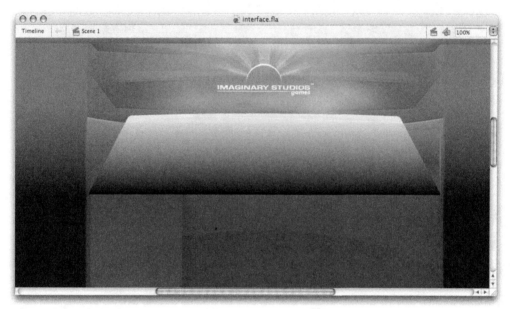

Figure 10-15. This is what your navigation bar should look like with the new shadow layer created on top of it.

Later, when we animate the navigation bar, the shadow layer will stay in place while the rest of the bar moves. It's important to notice that shadows and highlights shouldn't move in sync with the object when it's animating; this is one of the principal elements to creating a believable sense of depth in your animations.

Masking the navigation bar

The navigation bar is complete; however, it currently appears over the rest of the interface. Only the top part of the navigation should be visible. Since our background image isn't layered, we need to achieve this effect by creating a mask. To do this, create a new layer above your navigation bar layers and create a shape using the Oval tool. Get it to align with the top part of your interface, as shown in Figure 10-16.

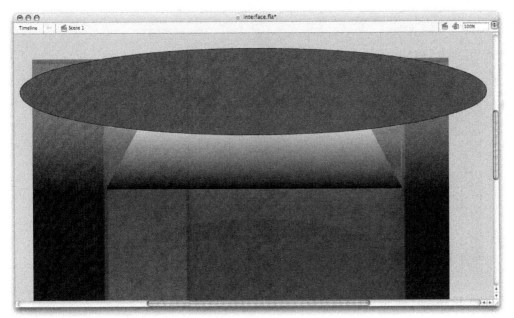

Figure 10-16. The shape you'll use to mask the navigation bar. Masking the bar will make it appear to lie behind the front interface.

Now right-click the name of this new layer in the timeline and select Mask. You can also double-click the icon next to the layer name to bring up a Layer Properties window, from which you can select Mask under the Type options.

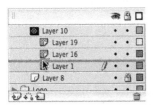

Figure 10-17. Drag a layer up to associate it with the mask layer.

To associate the navigation bar layers with the mask, drag them up, towards the mask layer, until the mask layer's icon dims, then release. Look at Figure 10-17 for an example of this. Do this for all the layers (you should have three).

To see the effects of the mask, you have to either output your movie or lock all the layers in the mask, including the top mask layer. Try locking all the layers, as shown in Figure 10-18, to see what the final mask effect is like. If your mask doesn't align correctly, you probably didn't position your oval layer mask correctly. Refer back to Figure 10-16 for the correct alignment.

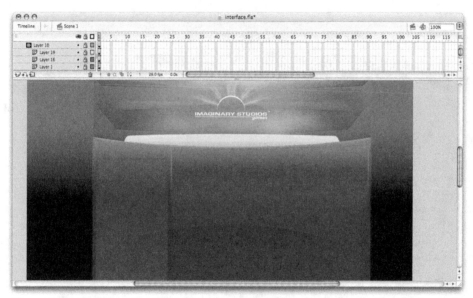

Figure 10-18. Lock the mask and the layers associated with it to preview the masking effect.

Adding details

To finish off the top part of the design, I added the text links on the top (Bookmark, Tell a Friend, Contact) and the text links in the navigation bar (Home, News, Games, Support, Downloads). I also added two black-and-white horizontal lines between each text link to define the bounding areas of the actual navigation buttons. The black-and-white lines, slightly transparent and aligned right next to each other, create an illusion of depth (where black is the shadow and white is the highlight) and make the buttons stand out a little more. This can be seen in Figure 10-19.

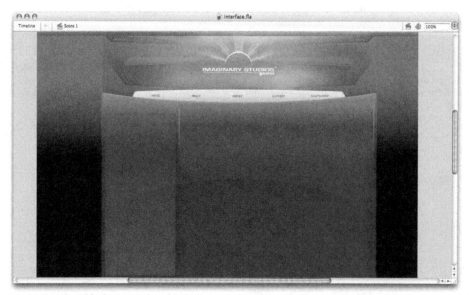

Figure 10-19. With the text links added, all the design elements of our navigation bar are now complete.

Animating the navigation bar

To animate the navigation bar, we need to convert all the layers that make up the navigation bar into a single symbol. The quickest way to do this is to select all the layers (apart for the shadow layer, which we don't want to animate) and press F8. Doing this, however, will also flatten all the layers into one layer in the new symbol, which will cause the separate fills and strokes from each layer to merge. To avoid this, select each layer one by one and press Ctrl+G or Cmd+G to group them. Every layer should now be an individual group. Now when you convert them into a symbol, the layers will retain their own shapes and arrangements.

When you press F8, select Movie clip as behavior. You'll probably have to assign some ActionScript functions to your buttons later, and you need the symbol to be a movie clip to be able to achieve this. This can always be changed later if you make a mistake or simply forget about it, but it's a good idea to think about these things ahead of time, as they'll save you from having to make tedious corrections in the future.

Now you can animate the navigation bar and apply effects such as blur or glow to it. For a clean effect, I recommend simply animating the navigation bar so it appears to slide out from below the front interface. Try to keep these build animations as swift as possible; nobody wants to wait a minute for the interface to animate before reaching your content. In fact, your entire interface shouldn't take longer than a couple of seconds to build entirely. Try adding a keyframe at the beginning and one at the end of your animation. Move the Y position of your navigation bar so that in the first keyframe it is completely invisible to the mask. In the final keyframe, keep it in the original position. Use an ease value of 100 and play back your animation.

My final navigation bar animation can be found in the code download as nav_bar.swf. For more details on animating and creating complex animations, refer to Chapter 11.

Logo tutorial

We could re-create something similar to the logo area we designed in Photoshop in vector, by replacing the motion blur effect with the new glow filter and gradients. However, this wouldn't result in much of an improvement in file size or playback speed, and thus isn't worthwhile spending time on. Instead, we'll animate the logo and the rays.

Animating the logo

To animate the logo, convert both the Logo PNG layer and the Rays PNG layer to movie clips by selecting them and pressing F8. In this case, we're using movie clips because we want to be able to use the new layer filters in Flash 8.

Start by hiding the Rays PNG layer. Now create a motion tween for the Logo PNG layer. Experiment with scaling and the blur filter. I created three keyframes for the filter. The first keyframe starts at 28% scale with a blur of 35, the second keyframe has 110% scale and no blur, and the final keyframe is at 100% scale. You can see this in Figure 10-20. Try your own animations as well. You should have a general idea and sense of style for the entire interface. We'll go more in depth on motion and animation techniques in the next chapter, but for now keep in mind that uniformity in animation is just as important as uniformity in design.

For an example of what my logo animation looks like at this point refer to `logo.swf`, found in the code download.

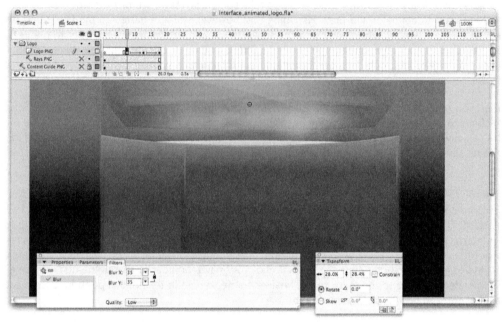

Figure 10-20. This is what my Logo PNG motion tween looks like.

Animating the rays

Go back to your Rays PNG layer and unhide it. As you did with the Logo PNG layer, create a motion tween and experiment with different keyframes. I used more scaling and the advanced color settings this time. The movie clip in my first keyframe is 186% wide and 18% tall with 0% Alpha; in my second keyframe it's scaled 127% with the advanced color settings shown in Figure 10-21; and in my final keyframe all settings are 100%. These settings boost all Red, Green, and Blue settings to the max, making the rays look as white as possible: a quick and non-CPU-intensive way to achieve an additive-like effect for the animation.

For an example of what my final logo animation looks like, refer to `logo_rays.swf` in the code download.

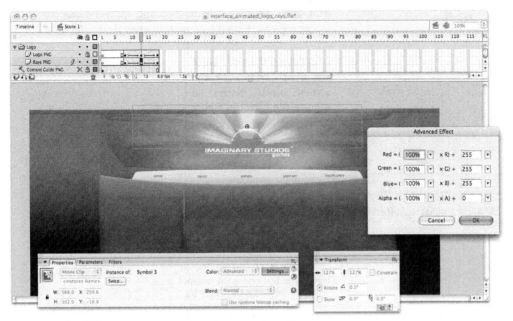

Figure 10-21. This is what my Rays PNG motion tween looks like.

Exporting vector objects to create raster assets

We can also use PNGs to help us apply effects to specific objects that we wouldn't be able to use solely in Flash. For example, take one of our icons from Chapter 7 and paste it into a new Flash file. Now go to File ➤ Export ➤ Image to convert this graphic to raster so that you can open it in Photoshop. Select PNG, and you should get the window shown in Figure 10-22.

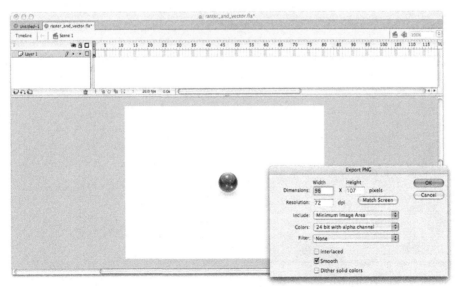

Figure 10-22. Export your icon as a PNG.

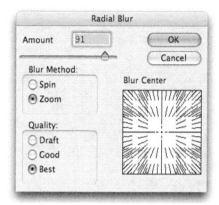

Figure 10-23. Apply a radial blur effect in Photoshop.

Now open the PNG in Photoshop and apply a radial blur to it. Make sure you select the Zoom option, as shown in Figure 10-23.

I duplicated the layer twice and used Linear Light and Screen blend modes to achieve the effect in Figure 10-24.

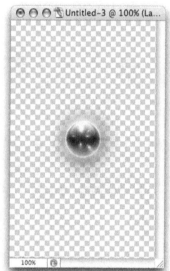

Figure 10-24. Three different layers. The first one is the original icon, the second is the radial blur with Linear Light, and the third is the radial blur with Screen.

Now save this image as a PNG and import it back into your Flash file. I imported on a new layer called Photoshop PNG. Try to animate this layer so that it coincides with your vector object (see Figure 10-25). You can achieve a lot of different effects using this technique. As an example, take a look at orb_blur.swf in the code download.

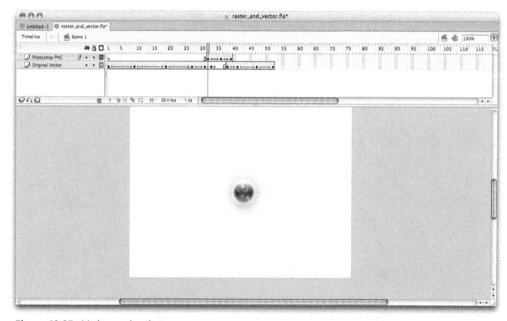

Figure 10-25. My icon animation

Summary

Aside from photo editing (the subject of Chapter 13), you've pretty much encountered all the graphical asset creation related to building an interface in Flash at this point in the book. Don't get the wrong idea though; you're far from finished. I just barely touched on animation in this chapter, and in the next few chapters you're going to learn much more on the subject.

You learned the following lessons in this chapter:

- PNGs are the best way to bring transparent raster graphics into Flash.
- Vector graphics are generally better than raster graphics for animated effects in Flash. The opposite is true when the vector object is so complex that it starts hindering playback performance. In this case, it's a good idea to convert to raster or experiment with Flash's new run-time bitmap caching.
- Combining vector and raster graphics and effects can help achieve unique and widely diverse effects.

Chapter 11

CREATING ANIMATED EFFECTS

by Michael Kemper with Guido Rosso

The Flash community, and the design community as a whole, has learned to integrate motion concepts into Flash-based experiences for enhanced learnability and usability. Hardly anyone wastes his or her time creating long and excessive intro animations with Flash anymore. Interfaces are becoming more sophisticated and intuitive because designers have become comfortable with employing motion to imply how to use them: motion design in an interface can guide users from one section to another, keep the user interested as content loads, indicate interactive elements like buttons, as well as add to the overall continuity of the experience in the form of transitions between pages. When used tastefully, animation and motion design can help make your interface one of the experiences that people remember and come back to again and again. It's also another aspect of the overall design that can make the experience more intuitive, as well.

If you're like us, animating is the most natural thing for you to do in Flash. We attribute this to the fact that we began using Flash primarily as an animation tool; however, in the past we have also often felt constrained with the animation capabilities of Flash, having also been avid users of Adobe After Effects. After Effects gives you more control over every aspect of animations and provides many more preset options for special effects. Obviously Flash needs to be limited because of the restraints of file size and online delivery, but from a purely animation perspective, having gone between the two programs, it's clear to us the limitations of Flash.

There are also many similarities between these two programs, and with some creative workarounds, similar effects can be created in both applications. As Flash continues to evolve into a more robust tool for animating, it's becoming easier to achieve After Effects–type motion treatments without importing PNG sequences or video composites—both can easily inflate the file size of Flash projects when they are imported to the stage, and it's much more efficient to be able to create such effects from scratch in Flash.

In this chapter, you'll learn about some of the handy new features built into Flash to give you more control over tweening and visual effects. You'll see some cool filter combinations in action; and we'll also cover some of Flash's built-in workflow functionality to help you create better animation effects quickly and consistently. We'll also explore animation using ActionScript and demonstrate production techniques for producing interactive animation.

Cause, effect, and timing

By now we've covered in detail all the benefits of Flash. However, as designers, we think the one feature alone that initially attracted us to Flash was the ability to animate every part of an interface. From the outer frame to every individual icon and text, everything can move, fade, and transition smoothly onto the screen.

Don't overdo it! As an interface designer, you must consider usability before artistic quality. Use Flash's advantages to quickly load your content and display it as fast as possible. Most people who hate Flash sites feel that way only because they think Flash takes forever to load. We know that this isn't the case. Flash loads very quickly when used efficiently, even faster than HTML (especially in sites with high dynamic content). So why have all this power if you're going to stick a 30-second animation of your interface building at the beginning of every page refresh?

In addition to color, contrast, and scale, use animation to emphasize important areas of your site. Your animations should guide your viewers' eyes and keep them absorbed.

Newton's Third Law of Motion states, "For every action, there is an equal and opposite reaction." This is a great rule to keep in mind when you're animating. Creating a believable and well-paced animation flow relies entirely on your timing and one action leading to another. Obviously you're not going to be creating a true physical environment; however, you can learn from nature and use these concepts to make your animations intuitive and purposeful. Remember to keep your animations central to your concept or theme.

For example, a site for kids would most likely be fit for exaggerated and elastic physical movements, as you often see in cartoons. A sports car site, on the other hand, would require quick accelerations, yet very smooth movements, implying a sense of speed and control. You can easily achieve these effects in Flash by using simple keyframes.

Realistic car

Let's take the realistic car example and break it down. Place an image of a car on your stage and create two keyframes. Create a motion tween and make your car move from the left side of the stage to the right side of the stage. Change your file to a decent frame rate (25 to 30 is good) and press Ctrl+Enter (Cmd+Enter on a Mac) to watch your car move. It works, but it doesn't look very realistic, right?

This is because in reality cars, and everything else in our world, have to overcome friction before they can start moving (this force is called *inertia*, and it's the exact force required to set an object in motion). They also have to apply a counterforce (or braking action) to slow down and come to a stop.

So how can you simulate these forces in Flash? Since a car needs to apply a certain force before it can begin moving, you want it to start moving very slowly and gradually accelerate. To achieve this, you need to take a look at your first keyframe. Select it and look at your Property inspector. Notice that it has 0 easing right now. *Easing* controls how Flash interpolates the frames between one keyframe and another. Try changing the setting to -100 (or full Ease In) and watch your movie. See how it now starts very slowly and gradually moves faster until it reaches its fastest movement at the final frame?

This is looking better, but it's still not believable enough. That's because you need to apply the same concept to the end of your animation. A car slows down in reality by applying a braking force, causing it to gradually come to a halt. To achieve this effect, you need to add another keyframe to your animation. Select one of the frames in between your two initial frames and press F6 to automatically create a new keyframe. Now set the easing to 100 (full Ease Out) and hit Ctrl+Enter (Cmd+Enter) to watch your animation. Notice how the car starts out slowly, reaches its peak velocity, and gradually slows down until it stops. You now have a much more believable car animation, and all it took were two settings and an extra keyframe.

To improve even more on this effect, you could animate the wheels of the car and shift the body of the car slightly as it accelerates. When a car starts moving forward, you generally feel like you're being pulled back into the seat, and when it starts slowing down, you feel like you're being pushed forward. This is exactly what Newton's Third Law of Motion is about, and what you're actually feeling is the opposite reaction to the forces that are causing the car to move forward and to stop. You can simulate this effect by making the body of your car tilt back a little when it starts moving (rotate the body of the car slightly counterclockwise, but leave the wheels in place) and tilt a little forward when it stops moving. This is a slight exaggeration, as you'd only really see this in a car that's accelerating a lot; however, it looks believable because the viewer will (consciously or unconsciously) relate to the feeling of being in that car.

Cartoon car

In cartoons, you generally see animators apply the same effects and concepts that we considered in the previous realistic car example, but they're massively exaggerated and break the laws of physics in just about every movement. When they break the laws of physics, however, they do it in a way that seems believable, which is what makes it entertaining to watch.

Let's take the car animation from before and transform it into a cartoon-like animation. Add an extra keyframe at the beginning of your animation and make the car move slightly backwards (to the left) before it starts moving forward. Try using an Ease Out value of 100 for this. Now add a keyframe to the very end of your animation and make the car move back to the left a little after it's moved all the way to the right. Try an Ease Out value of 100 here as well.

Now move your keyframes, if necessary, so that your initial and final motion tweens are the longest (5 to 10 frames) and so that your middle motion tween is actually very short, like 1 to 3 frames (this is the tween where the car actually moves from left to right and covers the most distance). Watch your car animation and notice how the car bounces from the left side of the screen to the right. This has lost realism; however, it still looks believable because you've applied the basic cause-and-effect principles.

Depth

You can practice this effect also with scaling to help achieve a realistic illusion of depth and 3D. For example, if you take an image of a car from the back, you can scale it from 100% to a very small 10%.

Make it slightly fade out on its final keyframe (using alpha or tint effects). Now add a middle keyframe and make your car first ease in and then ease out. This will make the car start slowly, reach full speed, and gradually come to a stop, as you did in the realistic car example, only this time it will appear to shoot off to the horizon.

Implying speed

Remember that you want to keep most of your interface animations very brief. For the most part, these will be animations that react to the user's input (such as a mouse hover), so you want your transitions to be quick so that users can immediately achieve what they need to without feeling like the speed of the animations is hampering their research. So how can you make your animations short, yet imply speed without making them jerky?

Use the concepts discussed in the car examples. Start with three keyframes instead of two, so that you can make the first movement very quick (1 to 3 frames) and the final movement very smooth (5 to 10 frames). Easing values for the first keyframe is up to you, depending on the style you want to achieve; however, it's safe to say that all final tweens should have an Ease Out value of 100; otherwise your animations will appear to pop at the very end, because they will achieve maximum velocity and then simply come to a halt. This makes the animation unrealistic and awkward, so try to avoid it.

Motion blur

Motion blur is an effect that occurs in film. When an object moves too fast for the shutter speed of a camera, it actually registers on different portions of the image, creating the effect of a blur. To achieve a clean picture, the shutter would have to open and close before the object moves enough to impress its shape on multiple locations on the 2D plane of the photograph. Movies like *The Matrix* use cameras with incredibly high shutter speed to capture minute details of a fast movement that would otherwise just be a blur with a regular camera.

Although we don't see motion blur quite like this in real life, we've come to expect it because we see it so much in movies and TV. Adding it to your animations isn't absolutely necessary and will vary depending on the style you want to achieve. However, if you do choose to add motion blur, it will make your animations look more convincing.

In Flash 8 you now have a Blur filter as part of the new layer effects. The great part of this new feature is that it will animate from one keyframe to another, so you can add some blur to the keyframe where your object is moving the fastest (which is the keyframe after the -100 easing), and it will automatically increase and decrease throughout the tween.

As great as this effect looks, it can seriously slow down playback performance. Even if it doesn't right now, chances are that once you've got your full interface, dynamic content, and other animations happening, the playback performance will start to suffer. This will also depend on the amount of blur you apply and the size of your graphic, so experiment and test as much as possible.

Faking motion blur

There are three alternatives to creating a motion blur in Flash without using the filter effects. The benefit to generating such an effect without utilizing the Blur filter is that your file can be backwards compatible with earlier versions of the Flash Player plug-in.

The first way would be to open your graphic in Photoshop, apply a Motion Blur filter, and export it as a PNG file. Then swap your standard graphic with the blurred graphic while it's animating. Experiment also with placing your blurred graphic on another layer and making its alpha value fade in and out so that the blur appears only when your graphic is moving very quickly.

The second way to create a motion blur is to duplicate your graphic and slightly offset it by one or two frames from your original animation. Try to also lower its alpha value in respect to the original graphic. Duplicate it more than once to create a more convincing effect. This technique can be just as processor intensive as the layer effects, if not more so, and for that reason it's the least recommended. However, it can be used to achieve some interesting psychedelic effects.

The final way to fake a motion blur is by using a gradient. Create a box and make give it a gradient with three color stops from left to right: 0% alpha, 100% alpha, and 0% alpha. This gradient should be the same color as your object (or whatever color is most evident). Make it about the same size as your object, and use it to replace your object when it reaches its maximum speed. It should only be visible for 1 to 3 frames. This technique works very well and is the least processor intensive of all. If you don't have objects in the background, you can increase efficiency by replacing the 0% alpha color stops with the color of your background so that no transparency calculations need to be made.

Animation style

Before we cover some of the principles for creating advanced interactive animation, we'll deconstruct variations on animation style to reveal best practices and tips for achieving desirable motion effects. By now, you've probably seen many digital implementations of animated speed, cause and effect, and perspective in films, on TV, and in Flash. Regardless of the medium, the best examples to reference for creating immersive animations like these are derived from real life. Observing the physics of stretching and releasing a rubber band, dropping a ball, or pouring maple syrup can provide a lot of inspiration for motion/animation junkies. This section will cover how to achieve motion effects using the timeline, and later in this chapter, "ActionScript animation techniques" shows you how to achieve the same effects using classes and ActionScript.

Frame rate

The default frame rate in Flash is 12 frames per second (fps). We're sure there's a reason for this, but to this day we haven't discovered it. 12 fps typically makes for a jerky animation that appears to be sucking your processor of its last ounce of life. On the opposite end of the fps spectrum is the maximum limit—120 fps. It's common knowledge that using an excessive frame rate doesn't necessarily enhance an animation's performance (usually only in extremely special circumstances). One thing excessive frame rates will do is use unnecessary additional processor resources, which we all know is bad.

It's important to establish your frame rate at the onset of your project, especially if you're planning on syncing your animation with streaming video content. Modifying your frame rate after completing your production process in circumstances such as video syncing will leave you rekeying all of your motion design. A handy trick to use for syncing up video with timeline animations is to place a blank sound file set to a continuous looping stream on the same timeline as your animation. Simply export a 1-second WAV or AIFF file from a sound editing application and import that small, blank sound file into Flash. Then create a keyframe where you anticipate sync issues and use the Property inspector to insert the imported sound file as a looping stream into the new keyframe. This will make the animation skip frames as necessary to keep up with the audio stream, which will run parallel to the video stream.

Over years of experimenting with fps for different types of projects, from animated cartoons to upbeat Flash commercials, we've found that we get the most flexibility and best performance at 32 fps. It's within the recommended 30-to-40 fps range, and allows us to create very quick animations or very slow, smooth tweens.

Animation effects

Aside from your basic ease in and ease out animation controls, Flash provides several different ways to achieve more detailed tween effects, each with their own benefits and production requirements. Many different styles of animation are used pretty consistently by Flash designers. Generally, it's a good idea to select a style on a project-by-project basis and stick with it throughout that project. This will maintain continuity between all the animations in the interface and keep the production method consistent. Not only will this benefit the user by keeping the feeling of the interface familiar, but it will save production time and effort as well. To get inspired for your own unique styles of animation, it's good to take in as much as possible the physics of the natural world. The kind of physical effects you will notice usually fall into three categories:

1. **Elasticity:** Think rubber band. This is the motion of something reacting to the mass of its own weight shifting.

2. **Bouncing:** An obvious example is a ball dropping onto the ground. A basketball bounces lower and lower each time it hits the ground until finally it rests in one place.

3. **Overflow:** A good example of overflow is sea waves lapping against the shore. In observing these, you can see how they rush with tremendous power towards land and break suddenly, only to creep with slowing motion up the remainder of the shoreline until dissipating into the sand. So this type of movement is fast, then it breaks, and finally it creeps to a standstill.

These three effects in particular are good examples to deconstruct from many different perspectives because they can each be consistently achieved using keyframing, custom easing, or ActionScript.

Elasticity

Springy tweening is pretty common in Flash interfaces, and it can be the most complex effect to work with. This is motion that makes an object appear stretched, flexible, and rebounding. Elastic motion involves an object traveling along a path to exceed its destination incrementally over time until it settles on its intended spot. There are many ways to pull this off using keyframes and tweening.

Basic keyframing and tweening
One way to show elasticity is to keyframe it. To do so, place the object you wish to tween on the stage in Flash, then choose the length of your animation by selecting a point on the timeline and pressing F6 to create a new keyframe.

At the end of the soon-to-be animation, select the object on the stage that you wish to animate and move it to the spot it will animate to, as shown in Figure 11-1.

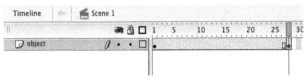

Figure 11-1. Timeline with movie clip placed on the first keyframe and the last keyframe

Next, duplicate that keyframe several times on the timeline, starting with the last one and working backward. To do this, simply copy the last keyframe and paste it at different previous points in the timeline, as in Figure 11-2. Each replica of the keyframe will be the apex of the elastic motion.

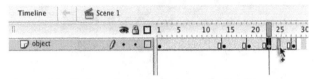

Figure 11-2. Keyframe being duplicated on the timeline

Starting with the second keyframe from the beginning of the timeline, select and nudge the movie clip on stage away from its end position. Next, do the same thing to the third keyframe in the sequence, except nudge the movie clip on stage in the opposite direction. Continue to repeat this for each following keyframe in the sequence—each time, nudge it a little less (see Figure 11-3). This is the foundation for creating an illusion of elasticity.

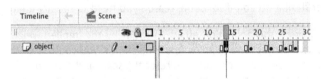

Figure 11-3. Selecting every other keyframe and nudging the movie clip on the stage

Once the animation is keyframed, click and drag along the timeline and create an "in" motion tween for the entire sequence in the Property inspector (see Figures 11-4 and 11-5). You can achieve different variations on this animation effect by alternating the ease in and ease out motion between each keyframed segment, or experiment with an all "out" ease for the duration of the sequence. Figure 11-6 shows a snapshot of the Find Furniture logo animated with an elastic motion.

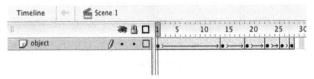

Figure 11-4. Selecting the timeline to create a tween

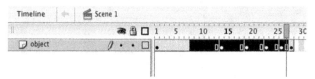

Figure 11-5. Keyframes tweened on timeline

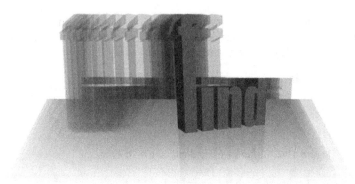

Figure 11-6. Onion skin preview of the Find Furniture logo animated horizontally with an elastic motion

This technique will give your animation the motion of something "snapping" to a point with elastic motion. It's the least flexible to edit if for some reason you need to modify it later.

When you are polishing off this animation effect, introducing the implied weight of the object being animated can enhance the effect you're going for. For instance, you could scale the object horizontally as it reaches the end of each approach and then reset the scale as it rebounds. This technique implies weight being thrown along with the motion, and makes the idea of the animation more believable. (You can see this in the download example file elasticScale.fla.)

Custom easing

To achieve an elastic animation using the tween editor, make two keyframes as you did in the previous example: one for the starting point and one for the end point of your object's path.

Create a motion tween between the keyframes, as shown in Figure 11-7, and click the Edit button next to the in/out lever in the Property inspector to open the Custom Ease In / Ease Out dialog box.

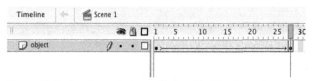

Figure 11-7. One tween between first and last keyframe in animation

As discussed in the previous chapter, this dialog box displays a graph showing percentage of easing along the amount of frames you are tweening. To achieve the elastic effect, create many points along the path of your object in the editor window, and stagger each point (or node) so they form a wiggly line like the one in Figure 11-8. The lines high points should get less squiggly and closer together as the path approaches the length of the tween. (You can see this in the download example file elasticCustom.fla.)

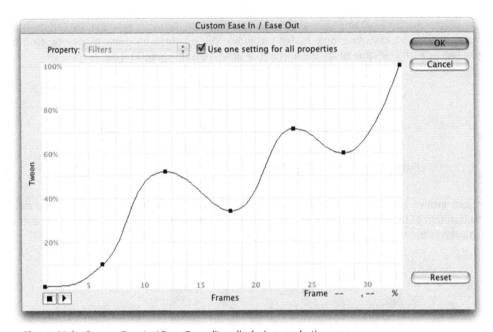

Figure 11-8. Custom Ease In / Ease Out editor displaying an elastic curve

Using the Custom Ease In / Ease Out editor may give you slightly less control over your elastic tween motion because it does not include the ability to scrub the timeline as you are plotting points, but it still makes the effect possible while requiring fewer keyframes on the timeline, which saves file size. Depending on how you like to use Flash, using this editor may even make it easier for you to edit your animation later on if need be.

Bounce

A bounce tween should give the impression of an object gravitating in a direction and then hitting a barrier it cannot pass. Once it hits the barrier, the object reacts by retreating and then falling toward the barrier, getting incrementally closer to the barrier until the object is at rest.

Basic keyframing and tweening

Creating a bounce tween effect on the timeline is very similar to creating an elastic animation. You start by creating the keyframes from the starting point to the ending point of the object's path, as shown in Figure 11-9.

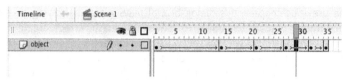

Figure 11-9. First and last keyframe of the bounce animation

Next, duplicate the last keyframe several times as you did in the previous example. On the keyframes leading up to the last keyframe, only nudge the movie clip on stage on every other key, each time nudging less as each keyframe nears the end of the timeline (see Figure 11-10).

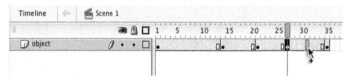

Figure 11-10. Duplicating keyframes for bounce tween

Begin your motion tween, shown in Figure 11-11, with an ease in, and alternate ease out and ease in for the duration of the motion. This gives the impression of the object having weight as it retreats and then gravitates towards the barrier.

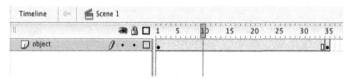

Figure 11-11. Selecting between keyframes and tweening motion

To polish this animation off and provide perspective, you can scale the object in the animation down as it approaches the destination of the tween. Scale it down, then slightly back up, down again and slightly up, and then down at the last keyframe. This technique implies distance away from the user, which might breathe some extra life into the animation. (You can see this in the download example file bounceKey.fla.)

Custom easing

To create this type of tween using the Custom Ease In / Ease Out editor requires creating a "wave" pattern with the nodes like the one you see in Figure 11-12. To successfully achieve this, you need to grab the handles of each node and drag them so they form a hard edge along one side, and then a smooth even curve along the other side. The wave gets smaller and tighter as the curve in the graph progresses along the tween's duration. (You can see this in the download example file bounceCustom.fla.)

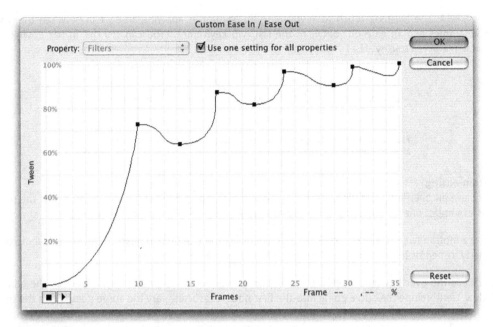

Figure 11-12. Custom Ease In / Ease Out editor displaying a bounce curve

Overflow

The overflow tween effect is quick in the center and slow at the beginning and end of its duration. The object being tweened should appear to extend slightly beyond its destination at the end of the motion.

Basic keyframing and tweening

The most basic way to set up this motion requires at least four keyframes on the timeline. Just like in the previous examples, place your object on the stage and then create a keyframe several frames later on the timeline that contains the object moved to its destination.

Next, create a regular motion tween between the keyframes, as illustrated in Figure 11-13. Now you should have the object moving from one point on your stage to another.

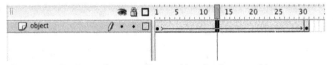

Figure 11-13. Tween between first and last keyframes of bounce animation

Now, create a new keyframe at either end of the animation, relatively close to the two original keyframes. Click and drag the two new keyframes towards the center of the animation, as shown in

Figure 11-14. The finishing touch to keyframing this motion is applying an ease in between the first two keyframes and an ease out between the last two keyframes. (You can see this in the download example file overflowKey.fla.)

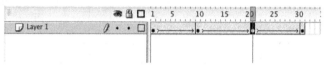

Figure 11-14. Creating keyframes on selected points of the timeline after the tween is applied

Custom easing

To achieve an overflow animation using the tween editor, make two keyframes as you did in the previous examples: one for the starting point and one for the end point of your object's path.

Create a motion tween between the keyframes and click the Edit button next to the in/out lever in the Property inspector to bring up the Custom Ease In / Ease Out dialog box.

To achieve the overflow motion effect, create two points along the path of your object in the editor window. Gently slope the curve going into the first node, drastically vary the curve going from the second to the third node, and then gently slope the curve between the third and final node, as shown in Figure 11-15. This will slowly ease the object towards the middle of the motion, and speed it up for a short distance during the middle and slow it back down at the end. (You can see this in the download example file overflowCustom.fla.)

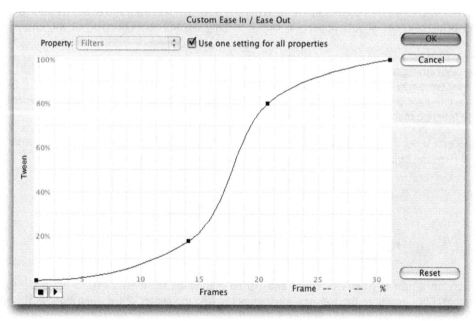

Figure 11-15. Custom Ease In / Ease Out editor displaying an overflow curve

At this point, you now know several different techniques for creating motion effects on the timeline in Flash. There are endless motion styles to use on any given project, but an important guideline to follow is to stay consistent and stick with one main style per project. You can create a library of motion styles by observing motion in the real world and implementing your own interpretations in Flash. Iterating on these styles and perfecting them will give you an endless pool of motion concepts to pull from when beginning new projects.

Sometimes a particular idea requires that you forego animation using the timeline and program the movement using ActionScript. This is often the case if the images or other content in the project is dynamic or loaded from external sources. Implementing motion using ActionScript has gotten a lot easier with this last version thanks to some prewritten class files that install with Flash.

ActionScript animation techniques

So far in the chapter, we've gone through a few motion techniques by using keyframes and tweening. In this section, we'll cover some similar animation effects, but create them using ActionScript.

Using class files has many benefits for Flash development in general, the main reason being that they are very easy to reuse on all of your projects. So once you get the hang of it, using class files for animation, among other things, can exponentially increase your productivity over several projects. And it's easy getting up and running for animation using class files because all the code you need is already written for you! That's right, Flash ships with a library of class files for animating components, and they work on movie clips, as well.

Setting up the movie

Before setting up ActionScript-based animations, it's a good practice to write all the ActionScript in an .as file or into a single keyframe on its own layer on your timeline. This will localize all of the code in one spot and allow you to make changes during testing quickly instead of clicking through nested movie clips or using the Movie Explorer to search for snippets of code.

To animate movie clips using the class files that come with Flash, the first step is to include the class files using an import statement. This grabs the necessary class file from your Flash install and includes it when you compile SWFs during the publishing process. The two classes you'll be using are the Tween and easing classes, which you'll import by adding the following statements to a keyframe on the timeline:

```
import mx.transitions.Tween;
import mx.transitions.easing.*;
```

Scripting animation

For this animation example, we'll demonstrate by using a movie clip of a logo to animate. It's placed on the stage and the instance name for the movie clip is logotype.

The basic format for utilizing the class files imported previously is as follows:

```
Tween(object, property, function, begin, finish, duration, seconds)
```

The best way to create an ActionScript mechanism for tweening movie clips is to wrap the preceding tweening code inside a function and activate the function based on user interaction. This is the ideal technique because it makes it possible to reuse the tweening code for any movie clip placed on the stage by passing variables to that function for an instance name or any other property you can think of to customize the motion. Following is an example of a function that will work for this method:

```
function tweenPlacement(object, finish, duration) {
    //the following grabs the variables sent to the function and uses
    //them to define the tween
    var motionTween:Tween = new Tween(object, "_x",➡
    mx.transitions.easing.Elastic.easeOut, object._x, (finish), duration, true);
}
```

As you can see, this function uses the Elastic class. Here's a description of this and other classes you can use:

- Elastic: Generates a reaction effect where the object exceeds and contracts beyond its destination point until it settles on its intended destination
- Back: Creates an overflow effect by appearing to extend the object being tweened beyond its intended destination point
- Regular: Allows you to create basic easing
- Strong: Similar to Regular, but will add speed towards the beginning or end of the tween
- Bounce: Creates a bouncing effect with the object tween
- None: Generates a linear transition that is even and smooth

You can use the following methods to vary the effect of the preceding classes:

- easeIn: Creates the easing effect at the beginning of the transition
- easeOut: Creates the easing effect at the end of the transition
- easeInOut: Creates the easing effect at the beginning and end of the transition

To activate the function, for this example use an onPress function like so:

```
logoType.onPress = function() {
    // the following calls a function and sends it the instance name
    //of the item being pressed as well as the finish and duration for the class to
utilize
    tweenPlacement(this, 400, 1);
};
```

It's also possible to utilize this method to tween filter effects. The following function could be called in a way similar to the tweenPlacement function by passing the instance name and using it to blur the movie clip on the stage:

```
function tweenFilter(object) {
    var blurTween:Tween = new Tween(object, "blur", Regular.easeOut,➡
    0, 5, 1, true);
    blurTween.onMotionChanged = function() {
        object.filters = [new BlurFilter(object.blur, object.blur, 100)];
    };
}
```

Remember: to utilize this or any other filter class, you'll need to import the appropriate class files. In the previous example this would be

```
import flash.filters.BlurFilter;
```

Depending on how complex your Flash systems get, you can load the variables used to manipulate these movie clip properties dynamically, or even let the user interaction define them. Another great argument for using code-based tweening is that it will automatically apply consistent motion to your design work—which is especially important for animating interactive elements like menu systems.

Deconstructing interactive animation

Now that you've seen some basic animation techniques, we'll move on to more advanced topics. While other animation applications might be able to create better standalone motion sequences, what makes Flash such a sexy platform is that Flash animations can be interactive. This capability adds a whole new level of experience to motion graphics, and creates greater opportunities for expression of an idea or feeling. Now we'll deconstruct some techniques to help you communicate your next big idea and cover some tips and tricks for baking animation into your interactions.

Figure 11-16. Carousel menu system that displays blog entries

This particular navigation example is going to be for a photo blog we're building, which you see in Figure 11-16, but the actual navigation system can be used for just about anything. Here is how it works: each "page" icon represents a month page in a calendar. The user can click the left or right toggle arrows to rotate through all of the months and, eventually, years. As the user clicks one of the arrows, all of the pages shift in the desired direction. Each icon has a nested dynamic text box that displays the icon title, in this case month and year.

Setting up the animation

It's generally a good idea that when you're creating an animated interaction, the entire thing be modular and contained within a single movie clip. This is the best way to build your animated interfaces for a few key reasons:

- It keeps your root timeline organized.
- It will allow you to activate different states of the interaction independently of what is happening on the root timeline.
- If you need to move the interaction to a new location in the design for any reason, you just move the movie clip on the root instead of once more keyframing the motion to fit the new spot.
- You can reuse that work in other designs simply by pasting the movie clip into a new FLA.

We've gotten into the habit of designing and building/animating interactions as prototype concepts that we save for the right project. This way we have a library of animated menu systems or concepts ready for code to plug into. These prototypes, or "sketches," are also nice to have in our back pocket when we're trying to sell a client on a concept. Building animated interactions as nested movie clips makes it easy for you to drop these prototypes right into your new designs and tweak them to fit visually. Doing this also saves development time by reusing existing code and animation.

For this example, start by drawing or importing the artwork for your interactions to the Flash stage. Once you have the interface you're going to be working on all together on the stage, select all of the graphics and press F8 to make it a movie clip, as shown in Figure 11-17. This is a good way to start your workflow because you assign a registration point within the movie clip that best suits your needs—typically top left if you'll need to get its position on the stage using ActionScript during your development process.

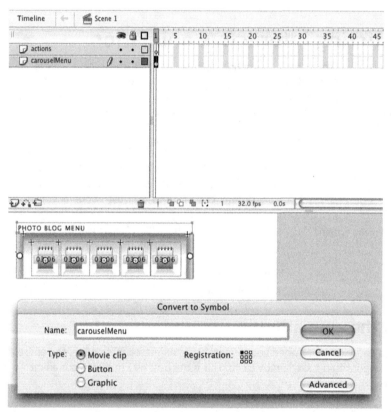

Figure 11-17. Creating a movie clip symbol out of the many items in the example

Generally it's a good idea to make each primary element of your animation an individual movie clip, and place those movie clips on layers named after them (see Figure 11-18). An easy way to do this is to utilize the Distribute To Layers option after creating all of your movie clips: select the symbols by clicking them on the stage or clicking the layer on which they reside in the timeline and press Ctrl+Shift+D (Cmd+Shift+D). We recommend creating movie clip symbols over graphic symbols so you retain the flexibility to apply filters and blend modes to the symbols. This also gives provides you with the ability to use the extensive ActionScript functionality of a movie clip, which a graphic doesn't have. When you have multiple items that are exactly alike, like the page icons in this example, then only create one symbol for that object and duplicate it for every instance you want it for on the stage. This saves file size on your final output and keeps all of your symbols consistent if you need to modify them in any way, since you'll only need to change your symbol in one place for changes to happen globally. This is an object-oriented method for doing your design production and will translate well to an application programming workflow.

Next, distribute your movie clips to layers (something we always do) and then create an actions layer and a labels layer, as shown in Figure 11-19. Click and drag from the top to the bottom of your timeline and press F5 to generate blank frames in preparation for animating. To keep your timelines organized, also create folders to contain layer sets—or layers that contain similar items. In this case, put all of the page icons on separate layers in a layer folder. To create a layer folder, click the folder icon along the bottom left of the timeline. Then click and drag layers into the folder that you wish to group together.

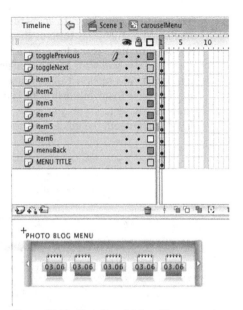

Figure 11-18. Each item is placed in a separate movie clip on a separate layer.

Next you create the animation states, which are keyframes that are labeled using the Property inspector. These labels will provide a specific reference point for ActionScript to tell the playhead to jump when the user rolls over, clicks, or tinkers with the menu at all. For a button, the states would be something like Up, Over, Down, Out, or Clicked. This particular animation will require In, Out, Next, and Previous, as illustrated in Figure 11-20.

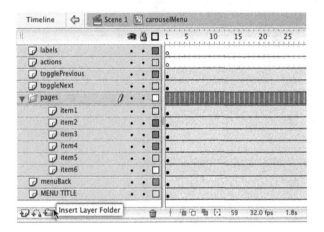

Figure 11-19. Organizing graphics on the timeline inside a folder

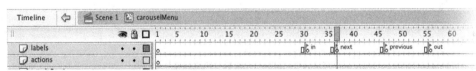

Figure 11-20. Animation states on the timeline

You want the page icons to animate on a slight arch, so they appear to get closer in the center of the menu and further away towards the edges. To do this properly, animate the icons along a curved path so that they move along the same arch consistently. This requires creating a guide layer: right-click the topmost layer you want to animate along the path, in this case the topmost layer containing an icon, and select Add Motion Guide. Guide layers are similar to mask layers in that they affect the layers placed below them, but only if the layers below are associated with the guide layer. On the guide layer, draw an ellipse to use as your path, as you see in Figure 11-21. Then select and drag all of your icon layers underneath the guide layer to associate them all with the same guide.

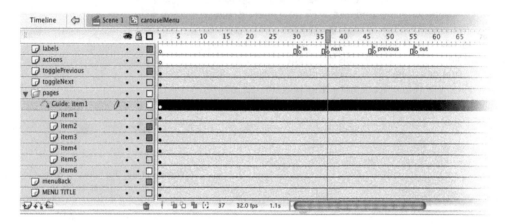

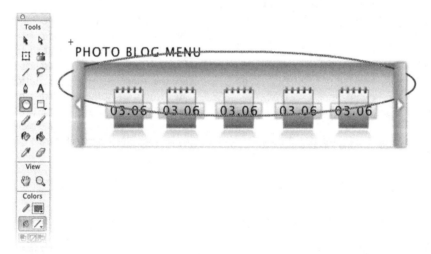

Figure 11-21. An oval shape is created on a guide layer to determine the path to animate the icons along

Before continuing, we want to show you how to further enhance the illusion of perspective with the placement of the icons. To achieve this, simply scale the icons in greater increments as they move out from the center. Keep the middle icon at 100%, the next ones out at 90%, and the icons on each end at 80% (see Figure 11-22). Since you'll be showing five icons at once, your animation will require a sixth icon to remain in limbo and fill the void of the end icons as they shift position during the animation. Scale the limbo icon to 50% to increase the perspective effect you're looking for.

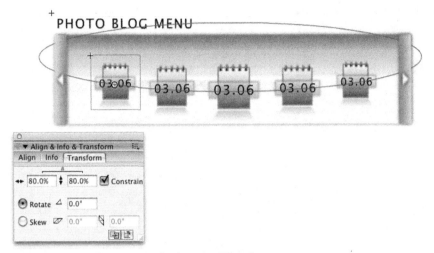

Figure 11-22. Scaling a movie clip along a guide path

Now you need to snap all of the icons on layers associated with the guide layer to the ellipse on the guide layer. To do this, just click and drag the page icons on your stage so that they snap to the ellipse on your guide layer, as Figure 11-23 demonstrates. Once they are snapped to the ellipse, they will tween along its arch.

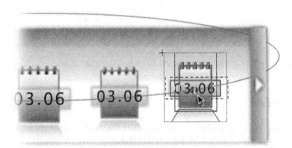

Figure 11-23. Attaching/snapping a movie clip to a guide path

That last step to setting up your animation is to prepare instance names for the icons in the Property inspector so that each icon can be referenced using ActionScript (see Figure 11-24). Each icon title will eventually be populated dynamically, so giving each icon a unique instance name now will also apply it to each instance of that symbol on keyframes you create next in your animation process. Otherwise, you risk having to go through every keyframe after the interaction is animated and apply the instance names individually, which is a real hassle. If you anticipate radically varying your instance names from the symbol name, you might want to give your movie clips instance names before distributing everything to layers. This way the layer title will retain the instance name instead of the symbol name and provide better insight at first glance which movie clip is on which layer.

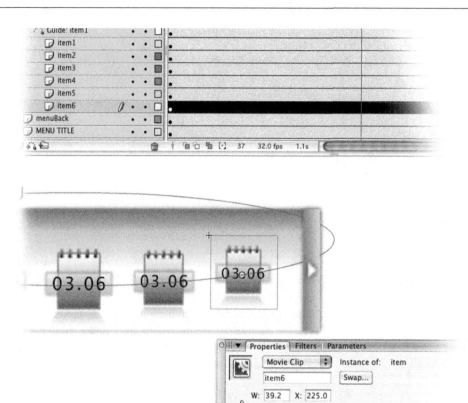

Figure 11-24. Applying instance names to movie clips before animation

Animating the menu

Once again, click and drag from the top to the bottom of your timeline, but this time select a single column of frames and press F6 instead of F5 on your keyboard to generate keyframes, as shown in Figure 11-25.

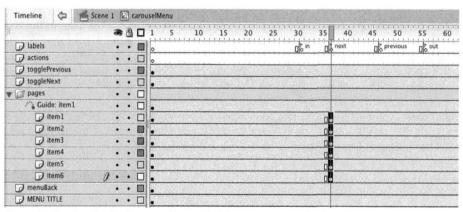

Figure 11-25. Creating keyframes across multiple layers to set up an animation state

Next, click and drag down on the timeline to select all of the new keyframes, hold down the Option key on your keyboard, and click and drag the entire column of keyframes over 12 frames. This will duplicate all of the dragged keyframes to the new location on the timeline, as Figure 11-26 illustrates. This will be the length of your Next animation. Depending on the frame rate of your movie, you'll want to vary the length of these types of transitions. Try not to make your transitions too long—just long enough so that the interaction is clear in its purpose. The frame rate of this movie is 32 fps.

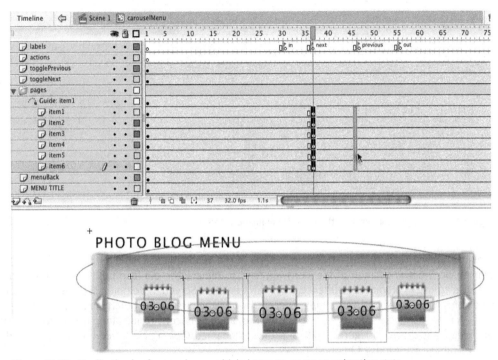

Figure 11-26. Duplicating keyframes along multiple layers to create an animation state

Since the Next animation will move all of the page icons to the left, you need to click and drag each icon on the stage to the left of its current position. As you drag each icon, be careful to make sure they remain snapped to the ellipse on the guide layer as you place them. After they are all placed, scale them appropriately to continue the illusion of perspective—as if the center icon is closer to the user and the outlying icons are further away (see Figure 11-27).

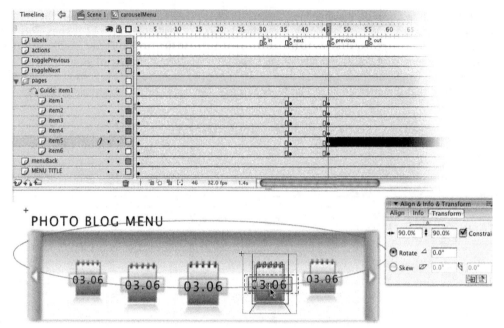

Figure 11-27. Positioning items on the stage for animation states

This animation will need to loop—meaning the end of the animation will need to look exactly like the beginning. So the new position of the icons will have to replace the old icon positions. You have the guide layer to use as a point of reference, but it isn't enough. So you'll use onion skins. If you haven't used onion skins before, it's a very simple concept that will help make your animation style more consistent—not to mention improve your workflow. The onion skin icons reside along the bottom left of your timeline, as shown in Figure 11-28, and they are named Onion Skin, Onion Skin Outline, Edit Multiple Frames, and Modify Onion Markers.

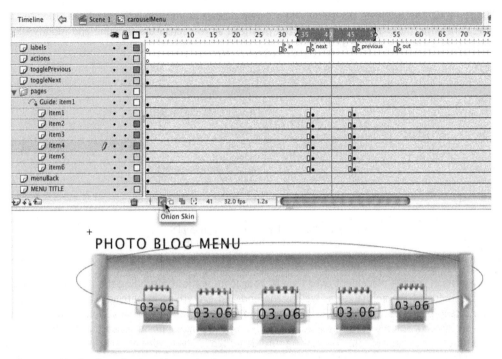

Figure 11-28. Preview of onion skin on the stage

- Onion Skin: This shows incremental changes between keyframes.

- Onion Skin Outline: This also shows the same incremental changes, but as outlines.

- Edit Multiple Frames: This enables you to edit content in several frames at the same time.

- Modify Onion Markers: This lets you access preferences for the timeline markers used for onion skins.

> *It's important to note here that an onion skin doesn't modify your file at all—it's just a preview mode to provide an additional perspective of your animations.*

Next, click the Onion Skin icon to reveal the changes that occur from one set of keyframes to another. When you use the Onion Skin option, markers appear along the top of the timeline, as shown in Figure 11-29. These indicate the beginning and the end of the onion skin preview. They are relative to the playhead—and the playhead is in the center. Click and drag each marker to the beginning and end of the animation you want the onion skin preview for.

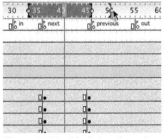

Figure 11-29. Displaying the onion skin tolerance on the timeline

Once you have the appropriate preview, select Anchor Onion from the Modify Onion Markers drop-down menu (which appears when you click the appropriate icon along the bottom of the timeline), as you see in

Figure 11-30. This will keep the onion skin preview in place as you scrub the playhead along the timeline. Otherwise, the markers move with the playhead as you scrub the timeline and modify the preview, as they may encompass additional keyframes.

Figure 11-30. Locking the onion skin in place so clicking the timeline won't move it during the workflow

Now you can see the placement over time of your icons without scrubbing the timeline. You can see the beginning of the animation as well as the end and everything in between, all in one preview. If your screen resembles Figure 11-31, as it now should, it should be clear that you need to adjust the new positions of some of your icons to match that of the original positions so that the animation will loop. After adjusting the icons and making sure they snap to the guide layer, click the Onion Skin icon to return to your normal stage preview mode.

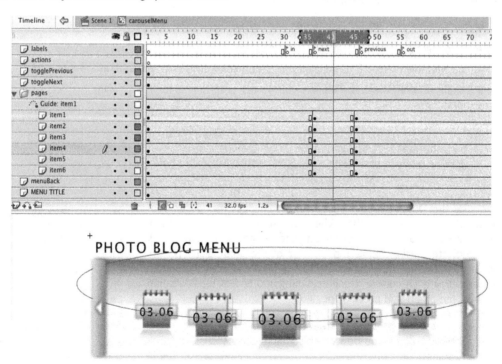

Figure 11-31. Adjusting items on the stage based on the onion skin preview

Now select the frames between your two columns of keyframes and create a motion tween so that you can scrub the timeline and see the movement of each icon from one position to the other.

For the Previous animation, you want the icons to animate exactly the same, only in the opposite direction. To achieve this, start by selecting all of the frames of the icon's animation on the timeline and duplicate them by holding down the Option key on your keyboard and dragging them to a new location on the timeline; you do this so the first keyframe of the animation is directly under the previous label, as you see in Figure 11-32. Next, remove the tween between your copied frames, and once again click and drag to select them all on the timeline, then select Modify ➤ Timeline ➤ Reverse Frames. Now create a tween between the reversed frames to get the exact same animation as before, but in reverse.

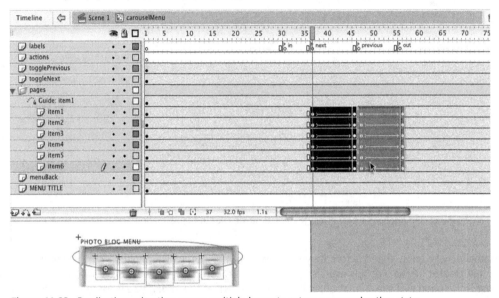

Figure 11-32. Duplicating animation across multiple layers to set up a new animation state

> Note that reversing your keyframes with a tween applied will sometimes cause "popping" of graphics in the final animation and other inconsistent results, so always remove tweens before reversing frames.

Now that you have your basic animation created, you're going to apply a subtle Blur filter to all of the page icons at the beginning of the next and previous labels to enhance the illusion of speed and movement. To do this, select all of the objects on the stage that you want to blur, and in the Property inspector click the Filters tab and choose Blur from the + icon (see Figure 11-33). For quick, small animations, we suggest you use the default Low quality setting to conserve processor resources for the end user—this way the animation is guaranteed to react smoothly when the menu system is used. In general, we also recommend that you only apply a blur to either the X or Y of an instance but not both for the same reason. This is a good rule to employ across all filter effects in Flash that have similar options.

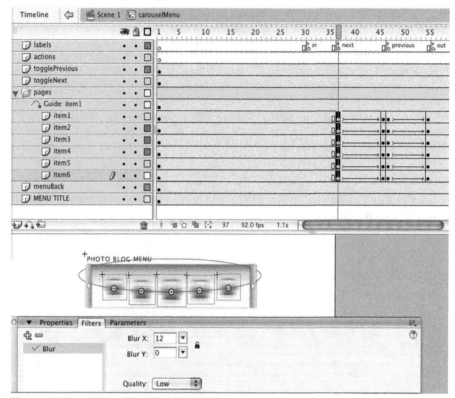

Figure 11-33. Applying a blur effect to several movie clips in the animation across many layers

Another way to imply speed is to ease your tweening in or out, which applies a curve to your tweening that creates inertia. For this exercise, you want your icons to start tweening slowly, then speed up towards the middle of the animation, and slow back down at the end. If you were to use conventional in-and-out easing on the tween, you would have to create lots of keyframes to accommodate this technique. In previous versions of Flash, the only options you had for tween easing was the percentage of in easing and out easing, but now you can utilize curve-based easing similar to the curve-based layer tweening in After Effects.

So to apply your tween variation, select the tween on the timeline. In the Property inspector, click the Edit button next to the easing percentage. The Custom Ease In / Ease Out dialog box will appear, as Figure 11-34 shows. This is basically a graph that displays the amount of easing over the span of keyframes in the tween, and here you can apply your tween modifications to all of your tween properties, or select individual properties like position, rotation, scale, color, and filters, or apply individual tweens to each property.

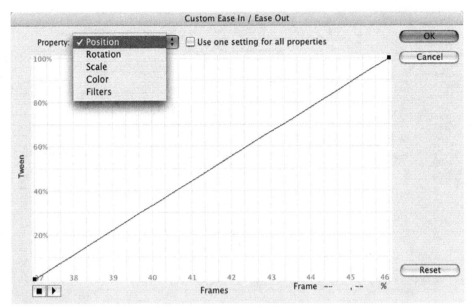

Figure 11-34. Creating a custom ease for the menu animation

You don't need a very complex tween for every property of your object, so keep the Use one setting for all properties check box selected. To add nodes as shown in Figure 11-35, just click the graph where you want to modify the tween. Then stretch the handles that appear on either side of the node to affect the curve of the tween by percentage over the tween's lifetime. To apply the tween modification, click OK.

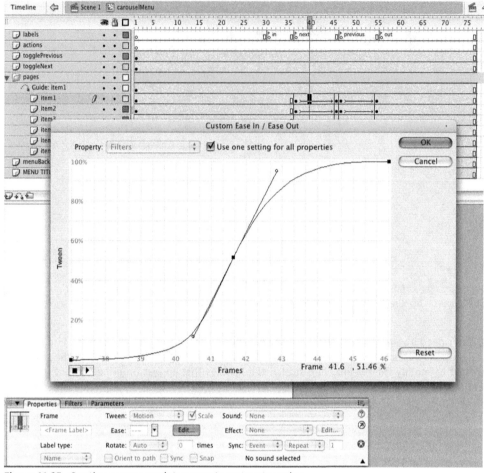

Figure 11-35. Creating a curve graph to generate custom tweening

At the end of the Next and Previous animations, place a keyframe on the actions layer. At the end of each animation, put a gotoAndStop("in"); action in each new keyframe, as shown in Figure 11-36, so that the animation resets after each toggle.

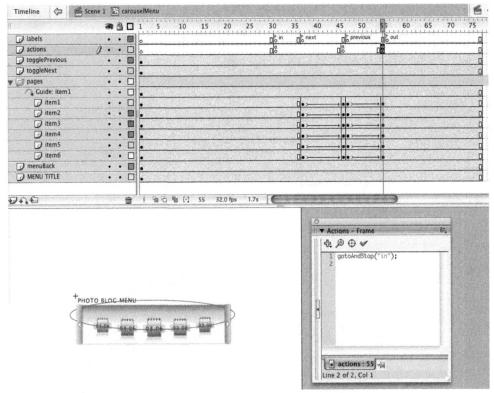

Figure 11-36. Applying basic timeline scripting to control the animation states

To finish off the animation for the menu of the photo blog, create the In and Out animations so that the interaction transitions in before the user views the menu, and transitions out once the user selects a month. On the actions layer, place a keyframe under the in label and put a stop(); action inside it. Also place a keyframe on the actions layer at the end of the Out animation and put a gotoAndStop(1); action inside of it (see Figure 11-37). It's important to note here that if you're telling the playhead to jump around an animation based on the user's mouse movements/actions, it's a good idea to always use labels instead of numbers unless you're certain the frame number of that state will not change in the future. In this case, you know that you'll always want the playhead to go to the first frame after it completes the Out animation.

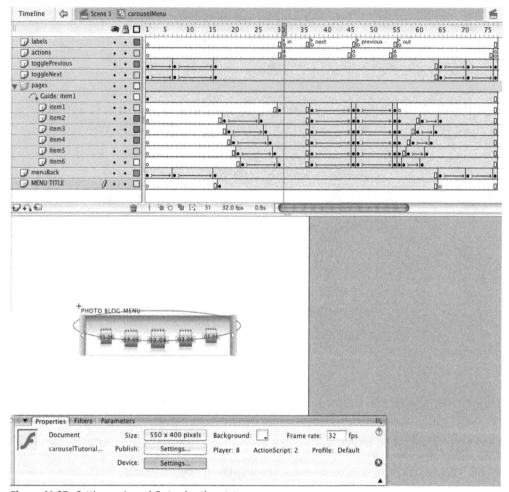

Figure 11-37. Setting up In and Out animation states

Setting up the icon

Now that the menu is animated, it's time to animate the states of the page icon. When you set up your movie clip, you used the same icon movie clip for all of your different months, but gave them different instance names in the Property inspector so that Flash would treat them as individual symbols on the stage. This means that you can assign unique properties to each one using ActionScript. So when you change the timeline of one of the instances of the page icon on the stage, that change will reflect in all other instances where you use that same symbol.

To begin, double-click into the page icon timeline. The way you organize this timeline is similar to the menu timeline in that there is an actions layer and a labels layer, and each symbol is on its own layer named after it. Since this page icon symbol has a label that will have text dynamically assigned to it, have the dynamic text box on its own layer called LABEL. Also include a btn layer with a transparent movie clip called btn and assign the instance name btn in the Property inspector. This will act as a "hot spot" to reference in ActionScript to activate the movie clip's states, which is a little trick you can use to keep the hot spot of the movie clip from changing shape based on the animation state. Otherwise, the hot spot changes and the animation might pop to and from states as the user interacts with it. We usually only use this trick for movie clips that act as buttons. The states you'll be using for this time-line are Over and Out. So you'll create an animation to play when the user mouses over the icon, and an animation to play when the user mouses out or away from the icon. The first keyframe on the actions layer just has a stop(); action in it, and the same action is applied to a keyframe at the end of the implied Over animation.

Animating the icon

You want the icons to lift slightly and glow when users roll their mouse over it, and then return to its original position once they roll their mouse off of it. Just like in the menu movie clip, you duplicate all the layers you'll animate by using the Option key shortcut so that you have a column of keyframes at the end of the (soon to be) Over animation state.

On the keyframe that holds the paper symbol, select the paper symbol on the stage and bump it up a few pixels. Next, apply some filter effects to the symbol of the paper so that it appears to glow. Although this is a subtle effect, we can say from our own experience that you'll need to apply multi-ple effects to the symbol to make it believable. Apply a Glow, Inner Glow, and Adjust Color filter, as shown in Figure 11-38. Just like before when you applied the Blur filter, these filter settings are acces-sible using the Filters tab in the Property inspector.

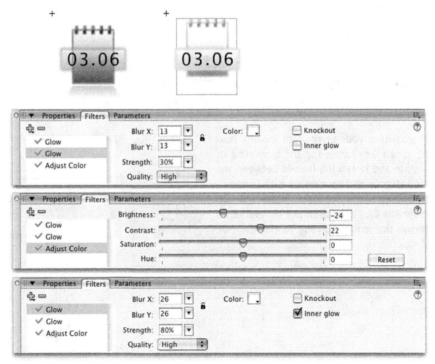

Figure 11-38. Displaying all of the filter settings applied to the movie clip

In case you might want to apply these same filters with the same settings to another movie clip some-where else in your FLA, select the + icon as if you were going to add a new filter, except this time select Presets ➤ Save As. The Save Preset As dialog box appears, as shown in Figure 11-39. Enter the name you want to save your filter effects as (in this case itemEffect), and click OK. Now if you want to apply the same combination of filters to another movie clip in your movie, you just have to click the + icon in the Property inspector and choose Presets ➤ itemEffect to automatically apply them to your selected movie clip symbol.

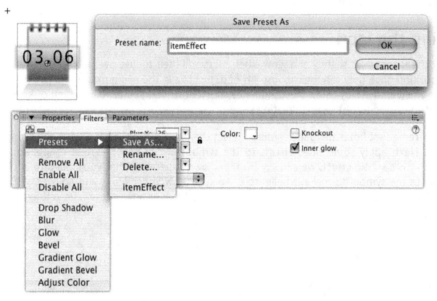

Figure 11-39. Saving filter presets in the Property inspector

Now that you have your Over state looking how you want, create keyframes for the beginning of the Over state and tween the frames between the original appearance and your new treated appearance as shown earlier in the menu interaction. Do the same for the Out animation but in reverse, so that it shows the icon returning to normal (see Figure 11-40).

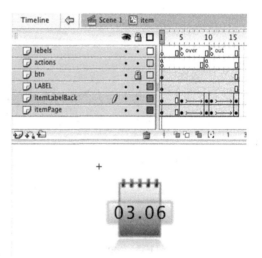

Figure 11-40. This shows how the timeline is organized to create the mouse over and mouse out interaction for the icon.

Scripting the interaction

The last steps before integrating this menu to work with dynamic data is to script the interactions that make it function for the user. We generally try to keep all of our ActionScript on one keyframe on the root timeline. Or better yet, in an ActionScript file that is imported into the SWF during publishing. For this example, nest the actions inside the menu movie clip and use relative paths to assign properties so that you'll be able to paste the entire menu into different scenarios without recoding it. Later you might localize the code to work from the root timeline or a class file if it's helpful or necessary. The following script makes the next and previous toggle arrows work:

```
// tells the clip to play previous label when the user clicks the
// previous arrow
togglePrevious.onPress = function() {
  gotoAndPlay("previous");
};
// tells the clip to play next label when the user clicks the
// next arrow
toggleNext.onPress = function() {
  gotoAndPlay("next");
};
```

Here is an example of how you might begin to handle the clicking scenario for the icon interaction:

```
// Holds actions for transitioning out and loading dynamic content
function loadSection() {
  gotoAndPlay("out");
  // place content scripting here
}
// Over action for icon
item1.btn.onRollOver = function() {
  item1.gotoAndPlay("over");
};
// Out action for icon
item1.btn.onRollOut = function() {
  item1.gotoAndPlay("out");
};
// Click action for icon
item1.btn.onPress = function() {
  loadSection();
};
```

Depending on what you're using to load in dynamic content, (XML, PHP, Flash Remoting, etc.), you would handle that code in the loadSection() function. You could also put the ActionScript that handles the icon animation in a class file and load it into each page icon externally. Either way you choose, this production method is universal with respect to many different programming styles.

Summary

Flash is becoming a much more robust animation tool, and designers have additional flexibility to integrate After Effects–type motion graphics into their interactions. Using a standard workflow to bake animations into interactions can minimize ActionScripting and keep the FLA structure consistent—so designers don't need to relearn how a movie was originally built in order to tweak the animation.

We've presented the following lessons in this chapter:

- Motion design can make interactions more intuitive and help direct the user.
- Setting up animations with states in a modular and consistent fashion makes it easy to quickly and efficiently animate interactions.
- 32 fps is a good frame rate standard for Flash.
- Use a streaming blank audio clip on your timeline to sync animation with video content.
- There are many animation styles you can create using Flash; some of the most enduring styles are achievable on the timeline and in the Custom Ease In / Ease Out editor.
- Using the Custom Ease In / Ease Out editor minimizes keyframes and simplifies the timeline.
- Using ActionScript to animate results in files that are easy to reuse on all of your projects.
- Nesting movie clips makes it possible to activate animations independently of what is happening on the root timeline.
- Onion skins can help you create looping animations and give you a broader perspective of your motion design.
- Designers can achieve sophisticated effects in their interfaces by combining multiple filters on movie clips.
- Filter presets save time and help maintain consistency across your FLA.
- Designers can combine labels and basic localized ActionScript to control animation.

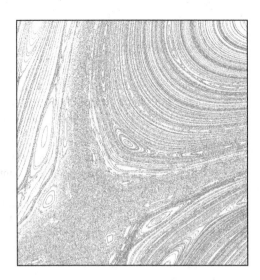

Chapter 12

FLASH TEXTURES

by Michael Kemper

Designers not only have the flexibility to treat static images and motion graphics with Flash filters and blend modes right on the timeline, they can also apply them dynamically using ActionScript. This feature makes it possible to achieve design treatments unlike anything ever seen in Flash before. The benefits of treating graphics in this way by using ActionScript are twofold:

1. These effects can be modified dynamically without re-keyframing the timeline.

2. Certain techniques, such as using displacement maps, achieve effects that could only otherwise be generated in a video application like After Effects and then imported at a heavy download cost to the viewer.

In this chapter, you'll get familiar with applying filters and setting properties using ActionScript to create truly unique texture effects for static symbols and motion graphics.

Creating texture with displacement maps

As I touched on earlier, displacement maps are one of the most innovative techniques for creating texture in Flash. This exciting new functionality is not overly complicated to achieve and is very accessible to designers with basic ActionScripting skills. First I'll cover one technique for applying displacement maps to still images, then I'll cover some techniques for applying them to motion graphics.

Still images

First I'll start by showing you how to set up the bitmaps you will be using to displace your graphics within Flash in this example. It's good to start with a texture in mind like water, sand, fire, bumpy, smeared, etc., and create a bitmap that emulates that texture in Photoshop. I typically consult online photo banks, like Getty Images (www. gettyimages.com), and use a photo from there to get started.

Treat your image to embody the character of the texture you would like to imply and then save it as a JPG. If you want an extreme ripple effect, then it would serve you well to apply a Ripple filter to your image in Photoshop. Likewise, if you want a rough and scratchy texture, you could apply a Dust and Scratches filter in Photoshop. For this walkthrough, I'm going to use an image I found using Google of a relief map of the USA, shown in Figure 12-1. Before exporting the image from Photoshop, I tweaked the brightness and contrast so that the texture would seem more extreme. I size and crop my images to be a reasonable file and screen size that will be manageable in Flash. Remember: the image you use for displacement mapping is still in the FLA and exported to the SWF when you are finished, so be conscious of file size and CPU strain, just as you would be for any other project in Flash that uses bitmaps.

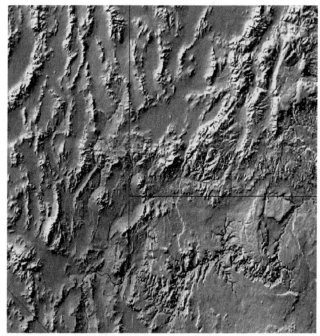

Figure 12-1. The image that I'll use for this example was found on Google.

Once you have an image optimized and exported as a JPG from Photoshop, open up a new Flash document and import the image to the stage.

Select the image and press F8 on your keyboard to turn it into a movie clip. Name it mainTexture. To keep your file organized, select the layer and on your keyboard hold down Ctrl+Shift+D (Cmd+Shift+D on a Mac) to distribute this new symbol to its own named layer, as I've demonstrated in Figure 12-2.

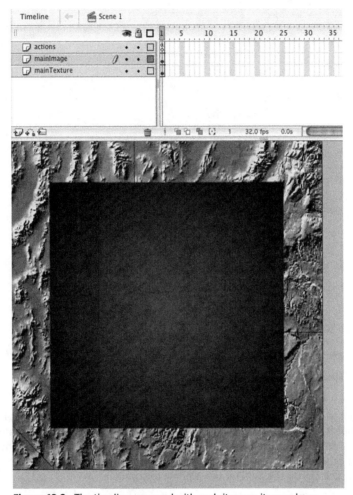

Figure 12-2. The timeline prepared with each item on its own layer

Now select the leftover layer and draw a gradated shape. Select the new shape and press F8 on your keyboard to make this a movie clip, also. Name this movie clip mainImage. Later, you can make this a bitmap instead of a gradation-colored shape to add depth to an actual photo if you'd like. Distribute this to its own layer as before.

Since you'll be using Flash's own native class files, you need to make sure the path to those class files is set correctly in the ActionScript 2.0 settings in the application preferences. To access the preferences in Flash, select Flash Professional ➤ Preferences from the top menubar. The Preferences dialogue box will pop up, as shown in Figure 12-3.

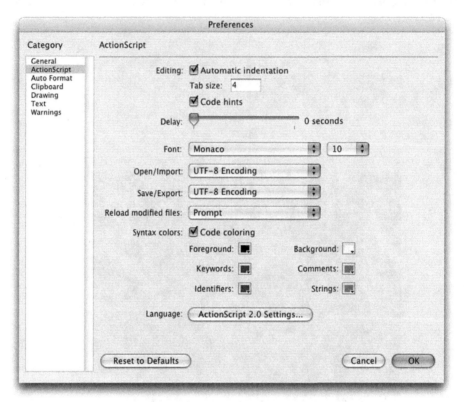

Figure 12-3. Flash Preferences dialog window

Select ActionScript from the menu on the left, then click the ActionScript 2.0 Settings button. Another dialog box will appear with a list box containing class file paths (see Figure 12-4). Create a new path by clicking the + icon along the top and type in $(UserConfig)/Classes. This tells Flash where to find class files when referencing them in the ActionScript window. Click OK in the ActionScript 2.0 Settings dialog box and then click OK on the Preferences window to continue.

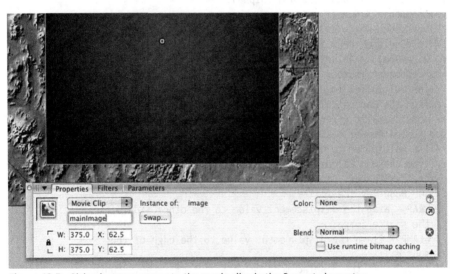

Figure 12-4. The ActionScript 2.0 Settings dialog box

Make sure you give mainImage and mainTexture corresponding instance names in the Property inspector so you can reference them using ActionScript (see Figure 12-5).

Figure 12-5. Giving instance names to the movie clips in the Property inspector

Now, on the leftover blank layer, double-click the name of the layer and rename it actions. Select the blank keyframe on the actions layer and type the following code:

295

```
// Import the proper class files for the displacement map effect
// (these install with flash)
import flash.display.BitmapData;
import flash.geom.*;
import flash.filters.*;
// Create a bitmap object that contains the size of your imported
// texture image
var mapBitmap:BitmapData = new BitmapData(mainTexture._width,➥
mainTexture._height);
// map your imported texture image to the bitmap object created above
mapBitmap.draw(mainTexture);
// set up variables to define the properties of the displacement
// map filter
//
// A flash.geom.Point value that contains the offset of the upper-left
// corner of the target movie clip from the upper-left
// corner of the map image.
var mapPoint:Point = new Point(0, 0);
// Describes which color channel to use in the map image
// to displace the x result. Possible values are 1 (red),
// 2 (green), 4 (blue), and 8 (alpha).
var componentX:Number = 1;
// Describes which color channel to use in the map image
// to displace the x result. Possible values are 1 (red),
// 2 (green), 4 (blue), and 8 (alpha).
var componentY:Number = 1;
// The multiplier to use to scale the x displacement result
// from the map calculation. Higher numbers will achieve a
// more dramatic effect.
var scaleX:Number = 100;
// The multiplier to use to scale the x displacement result
// from the map calculation. Higher numbers will achieve a more dramatic effect.
var scaleY:Number = 100;
// The mode for the filter.
// WRAP - Wrap the displacement value to the other side of
// the source image.
// CLAMP - Clamp the displacement value to the edge of the
// source image.
// IGNORE - If the displacement value is out of range, ignore
// the displacement and use the source pixel.
// COLOR - If the displacement value is outside the image,
// substitute (defaultColor, defaultValue) value.
var mode:String = "wrap";
// Specifies what color to use for out-of-bounds displacements.
var color:Number = 0;
// Specifies the alpha transparency value to use for out-of-bounds
// displacements.
```

```
var alpha:Number = 0;
// Create a holder for the filter and grab all of the variables
// created above to define the displacement map
var filter:DisplacementMapFilter = new DisplacementMapFilter➡
(mapBitmap, mapPoint, componentX, componentY, scaleX, scaleY,➡
mode, color, alpha);
// Apply the filter created above to your graphic on the stage
mainImage.filters = new Array(filter);
// hide the bitmap texture
mainTexture._visible = false;
```

Now when you preview the FLA, you will see the bitmap image applied as a displacement map to the gradated image, as Figure 12-6 illustrates. Whatever texture you want to use for the bitmap image will work; you can even apply this to another bitmap.

Figure 12-6. Showing the bitmap, graphic, and the bitmap applied to the graphic

Animated images

It is possible to apply displacement maps to many different kinds of objects, from video components to animated movie clips. Using displacement maps can have a dramatic effect on animated images. It can give the impression of watery fluid, rippling fabric, or a raging fire. One very cool application of displacement maps is to apply them to animated text transitions. In this next example, I'll explore more bitmap textures to modify the application of DisplacementMapFilter to affect animated symbols.

When creating a bitmap to use with an animated displacement map, it's best to keep it simple for a couple of reasons:

1. You want to minimize CPU strain as the viewer's computer will still have to process the bitmap you will be animating.

2. You can achieve dramatic results with very simple bitmaps—practice restraint when creating your bitmap texture for animated effects.

Following are some examples of bitmaps I've applied in the past using the Displace Bitmap filter. Figure 12-7 shows a bitmap created by painting lines across a white canvas in Photoshop and then applying a Ripple filter. I'll use this bitmap a little later to show you how to create water ripples.

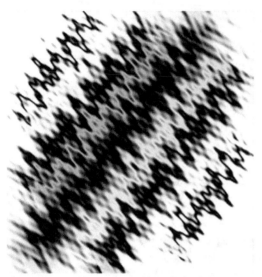

Figure 12-7. A bitmap created by painting lines across a white canvas in Photoshop and then applying a Ripple filter

Figure 12-8. A bitmap created by painting lines across a white canvas and varying the brush stroke in size

Figure 12-8 presents a bitmap created by painting lines across a white canvas and varying the brush stroke in size. This would be ideal for using as a fabric blowing in a breeze like a flag.

The bitmap in Figure 12-9 was created by painting lines across a white canvas in Photoshop and then applying a Twirl filter. Again, this could be used for a water effect, but instead of a rippling wave, it could produce the motion of a drop falling into a larger body of fluid.

Figure 12-9. A bitmap created by painting lines across a white canvas in Photoshop and then applying a Twirl filter

Figure 12-10. A bitmap created by painting a dot using a very large brush size on a white canvas in Photoshop

The bitmap in Figure 12-10 was created by painting a dot using a very large brush size on a white canvas in Photoshop. Applying this as a displacement map would cause a fish-eye effect—giving, say, a flat image of a globe a 3D appearance.

Notice they are all very simple and are all in black and white. I focus on creating the basic texture I want to work with. Nothing more is really necessary—using a photorealistic image for this technique will most likely result in an overcomplicated displacement as well as the viewer's processor chugging to view the effect.

For this example, I'm going to show you how to create a rippling water effect using an image of water in a pool, shown in Figure 12-11, being displaced by a very simple bitmap I created in Photoshop, with black lines and a white background.

Figure 12-11. The graphic I'll displace with my texture bitmap

Start by setting up the Flash file. As you did before with the static image displacement map, open a new Flash document and import your bitmap. Figure 12-12 shows the optimized image of the water I imported to illustrate this walkthrough.

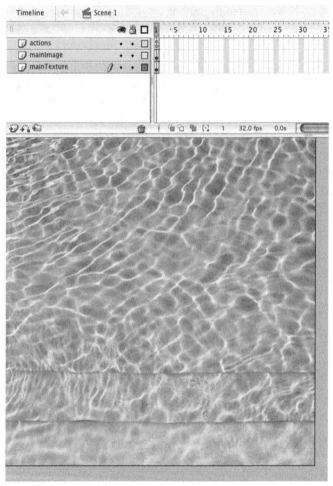

Figure 12-12. Again, the FLA is set up in the same basic way with movie clips distributed to individual layers and actions and labels layers.

Make both your files movie clips, naming the bitmap for the displacement mainTexture and the image you want to displace mainImage. Distribute the movie clips to layers and rename the leftover layer actions to keep your file organized.

Now double-click into the mainTexture movie clip, and select the texture bitmap. Again, make it a movie clip symbol by pressing F8 on your keyboard so you can animate it on the timeline.

You want the water effect to loop, so you'll create a looping animation in the mainTexture movie clip. To do this, first tween the bitmap texture so that it appears the same on stage with the playhead at the beginning and end of the timeline. It is important to note that tweening the alpha channel will fade the bitmap's texture effect and give the final product a smoothing look. This will add strain to the viewer's processor, but if it's done appropriately, this can be minimized and it's worth it—especially if you're trying to achieve a looping animation as in this example (see Figure 12-13).

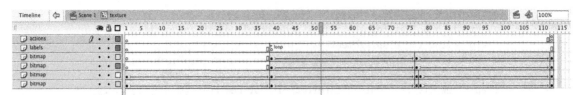

Figure 12-13. The timeline with the looping functionality implemented

Then create two new layers. Name one of them labels and the other actions. What you want to do is set a point in the timeline where the playhead can jump to when it has completed the animation, which will be a seamless visual continuation of the animation on stage, also known as the *loop*. So, on the labels layer select the loop point in the timeline and create a keyframe by pressing F6 on your keyboard. Label it loop by using the labels input text field in the Property inspector. At the end of the animation, create a new keyframe and open the Actions palette. In the Actions palette, type the following:

```
gotoAndPlay("loop");
```

This will tell the playhead to jump to your label loop once it hits the end of the timeline in the nested movie clip mainTexture. Now that the animated bitmap is complete, it's time to add the ActionScript to the _root timeline.

The best method for applying the displacement map to an animated movie clip is different because you need the filter to change based on the animation in mainTexture's timeline. To do this, utilize the onEnterFrame function and apply it to the mainTexture movie clip. Using onEnterFrame can be processor intensive because it's constantly running so long as the clip it's applied to remains on the stage. In the previous example with the still image, you created variables to define the properties of the displacement map. In order to optimize this technique's performance, you are going to forego defining all of the Displacement filter's properties as variables beforehand so the viewer's CPU has less to evaluate during the onEnterFrame. That is, having the properties for the filter right in the statement saves Flash from having to grab the variables and place them in the statement, and the result is quicker performance.

Select the keyframe on the actions layer on the _root timeline. Open the ActionScript window and type the following code:

```
// Import the proper class files for the displacement map effect
// (these install with Flash)
import flash.display.BitmapData;
import flash.geom.*;
import flash.filters.*;
// create the onEnterFrame function and attach it to mainTexture
mainTexture.onEnterFrame = function() {
// Create a bitmap object that contains the size of your imported texture image
   var mapBitmap:BitmapData = new BitmapData(mainTexture._width,➥
mainTexture._height);
   // map your imported texture image to the bitmap object created above
   mapBitmap.draw(mainTexture);
   // hide the bitmap texture
```

```
    mainTexture._visible = false;
    // Create a holder for the filter and set all of the properties
    // to define the displacement map
    // Here are the properties being set: (the bitmap, mapPoint,
    // componentX, componentY, scaleX,    scaleY, color, alpha, mode);
    dMap = new DisplacementMapFilter(mapBitmap, new Point(0, 0), 1, 1, 25, 25,
"clamp");
    // Draw a new bitmap using the size properties of the texture
    // movie clip above
    this._parent.mapBitmap.draw(new Rectangle(mainTexture._width,➥
     mainTexture._height));
    // Apply the filter to your graphic on the stage
    this._parent.mainImage.filters = [this._parent.dMap];
};
```

Now when the FLA is published or previewed, the animated mainTexture movie clip will displace the mainImage movie clip (see Figure 12-14).

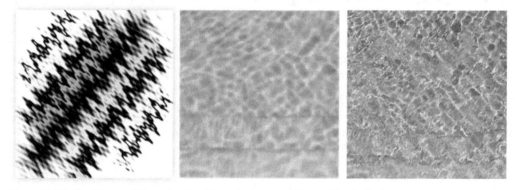

Figure 12-14. The bitmap of the water, the bitmap texture, and the combined effect

It is easy to apply this effect to just about anything in Flash, including text and video, as you can see in Figure 12-15. The object and texture can even be loaded externally as long as they are loaded inside the proper movie clips.

This is a line of dynamic text for animation
This is a line of dynamic text for animation purpose

Figure 12-15. Showing an example of text being animated using the displacement map

Summary

Using the new `DisplacementMapFilter` can drastically enhance static and animated designs. With this feature it is possible to create professional-looking motion graphics almost completely in Flash—effects that would otherwise have to be created in programs like After Effects and then imported. And better yet, these effects can be applied to image files loaded externally for even greater flexibility.

Now that you've completed this chapter, you've learned the following lessons:

- Designers can easily program visual effects into their motion designs using the new filter effects in Flash.
- Applying filter effects for displacement maps have a very encouraging Return On Effort.
- Displacement maps can be applied to still images as well as animated images.
- Bitmaps for displacement maps should be as optimized as possible to keep down file size and CPU strain for the viewer.
- Using less complex bitmaps for displacement textures will minimize strain on the viewer's CPU.
- Designers can create looping animations using alpha channel tweens to smooth the transitions into the loop effect.

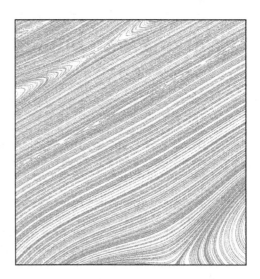

Chapter 13

PHOTO EDITING IN PHOTOSHOP AND FLASH

by Brian Monnone

Flash is a superb application in itself for vector content creation—we know this. By itself, Flash can import nonvector or bitmapped images and apply all kinds of effects or styles to them; however, in general, advanced techniques must begin in a photo editing program. You will learn the reasons why in this chapter.

Numerous photo editing tools are available today, but the one that I will focus on in this chapter is the industry standard, Adobe Photoshop, currently in version CS2. As you might already know, Photoshop is an extremely powerful program for bitmap image manipulation and creation. This book only grazes the surface of it. The subject of Photoshop has filled entire books, so here I will only focus on the necessary tools and techniques that you may need for your Flash applications. The purpose of this chapter is to make you familiar with some of the Photoshop editing techniques for preparing a bitmapped image for use in Flash to create the maximum level of professionalism in your final work.

You will also explore the new capabilities of Flash 8 that allow you to produce image effects natively, and compare creating the effects in Flash and creating them in Photoshop.

Last, you will see techniques to get the best image quality at the lowest possible file size for your final Flash application using Photoshop and Flash.

Working with bitmapped images

Importing bitmap images like JPGs, GIFs, or PNGs into Flash is common. As a matter of fact, Flash can import many different file formats like Photoshop 3 PSDs, TIFs, BMPs, and PCTs, among others. This makes Flash extremely flexible. I've found that importing PNGs (Portable Network Graphics—a patent-free alternative to the GIF) gives the most flexibility, because PNGs support lossless compression and background transparency without jagged edges. This gives the images imported into Flash a much cleaner look. During export, PNGs provide better control over the level of compression because they are a lossless format to begin with, allowing the developer to ultimately choose the level of compression wanted on the exported image.

So jumping right in, let's explore PNGs using a high-resolution JPG edited in Photoshop, then exported as a PNG, and finally imported into Flash. Our goal here is to "clip" or "knock out" our subject in the JPG in Photoshop so we can have a transparent background. This allows us to change the background in Flash as needed or apply certain effects to produce a clean image. At the same time, together we will explore some of the tools in Photoshop and what they do.

To help understand this technique, take a look at the JPG in Figure 13-1.

Figure 13-1. Original, unaltered image from Hawaii

This is an image I took, while vacationing in Kauai, of a lighthouse called Kilauea. To prepare this image for our Flash application, we will want the lighthouse to be lined up straight and removed from the background. Take note of some of the issues with this image:

- The image size and resolution is too high to use effectively in Flash. It needs to be scaled down.
- The lighthouse is tilted to the left. We need it to be vertical.

- We want to remove or clip out the background so we are only left with the lighthouse.
- We want to color-correct the image.

I chose this image because it will allow us to use several different techniques in Photoshop to get it ready for Flash. It's always helpful to think about what kind of editing needs to be done to an image before importing it into Flash.

Scaling down our image size

Open the image in Photoshop. The first thing we need to do is resize the image so that it is a more manageable size. Right now the image is 1600×1200 pixels and 180 dpi, far too large for our Flash application.

In the top menu, select Image ➤ Image Size (Ctrl+Alt+I on a PC, or Cmd+Option+I on a Mac). As shown in Figure 13-2, you need to reduce the dpi to 72 or 96, depending on whether you work on PC or Mac, respectively (these are the native ppi values for PC and Mac computer monitors).

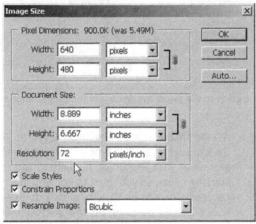

Figure 13-2. Image Size dialog box

Straightening up our lighthouse

Next we want to make sure the image is lined up straight. Make sure you have rulers showing—if not, in the top menu select View ➤ Rulers (Ctrl+R on PC, or Cmd+R on Mac). Drag out a guide from the ruler area around the image, as shown in Figure 13-3. You can drag a guide out from anywhere inside the ruler area.

Drag the guide out to match the top ball of the lighthouse. Basically, you want to pick a registration point and then line the guide up to that point (see Figure 13-4).

Figure 13-3. Drag a new guide from the rulers.

307

Figure 13-4. Match the guide to the top of the lighthouse for a registration point.

Figure 13-5. Convert the default Background layer to a normal layer for modification.

As the image stands, the main layer in Photoshop is called the Background layer. This type of layer is reserved for the main background of your Photoshop document. You cannot edit or change its stacking order, so you need to convert to a regular layer in order to proceed. This can be done by simply double-clicking the layer in the Layers palette to bring up the context menu and choosing Layer From Background, as you see in Figure 13-5. Rename the layer lighthouse.

Now that the Background layer is converted to a layer type, we can edit it. Let's rotate the lighthouse image. To do so, select Edit ➤ Transform ➤ Scale (or press Ctrl+T on a PC or Cmd+T on a Mac). The image will now have a box around it with handles to grab and a registration point in the center of the image. Move the registration point over the ball of the lighthouse at the top of the image, as shown in Figure 13-6.

Now move the mouse over one of the corners from the outside box. You will see the cursor change to a ¼ circle with arrows indicating that you can manually rotate the image, as shown in Figure 13-7.

Figure 13-6. Create the registration point on the top of the lighthouse to rotate around.

Figure 13-7. This icon indicates that the image can be rotated.

Click and hold down the mouse button, then move the mouse slightly to the left and adjust the lighthouse position until it is aligned with the guide we drew earlier (see Figure 13-8).

Figure 13-8. Line the lighthouse up vertically with the guide.

You should notice that the image rotates "around" the registration mark that we moved to the top of the lighthouse. This makes lining up the lighthouse to the guide much easier.

309

This is a good time to point out that, as in Flash, you have many ways to accomplish the same task in Photoshop. In this case, we could have entered a specific value into the Rotate box in the Options palette at the top of the screen. You'll notice that once you select a tool or perform a command in Photoshop, the top bar will change to accommodate settings specific for that tool or mode. Since we are in Transform mode, the top Option toolbar looks like what you see in Figure 13-9.

Figure 13-9. Option toolbar for the Transform tool

The fifth box from the left is the properties box in which you manually input an amount instead of dragging the image on the canvas as we did earlier. This setting is simply called Rotate. I personally prefer to use the draggable handles on the canvas because I can see the results immediately rather than having to input a number in the box and then hit Enter to see the results until I get it right. If you use the draggable handles method on the canvas, keep in mind that if you want to tweak your rotation slightly before committing to it, you can adjust the 10th increment in the Rotate properties box to help set the value closer to what you want. It's completely up to you.

Moving on, let's remove the guide, because we don't need it anymore, and it might get in the way at this point. Select the Move tool from the Tools palette or simply press V on your keyboard. Next, move the tool over the guide, and you'll see that the cursor changes, indicating that you can drag the guide. Simply drag the guide all the way into the ruler area at the left or right of the canvas to remove it.

So what have we done so far that we could not have done in Flash? Well, not much, but Photoshop is a tool specifically made for bitmap image manipulation—Photoshop will do a much *cleaner* job of rotating the image than Flash.

Removing our image background

Now we need to remove the background from the lighthouse image. Again, this can be accomplished in many different ways; I'll show you my way. Essentially, what I like to do is create a new layer under the image layer. Then, with the Eraser tool, I methodically erase the portions of the background I don't need. I think this way is the best because you have complete control over what is erased and what is not. Keep in mind that patience is a virtue. Take your time, and remember that you can always use Undo if you have gone too far and erased something you wanted to keep by accident.

Figure 13-10. Create a new layer.

First create a new layer in the Layers palette as shown in Figure 13-10, and move it underneath the lighthouse layer. Call this new layer orange bckgrnd.

Next we need to fill the layer with an orange color. I like to use orange for my backgrounds when I know I will be cropping out the background for an image. That way I can see the background easily through the cropped out section of the image and determine where I am at and what I've erased. Double-click Set Foreground color to open the Color Picker dialog box. For simplicity, make sure the Only Web Colors check box is checked, and choose the color #cc6633, as shown in Figure 13-11.

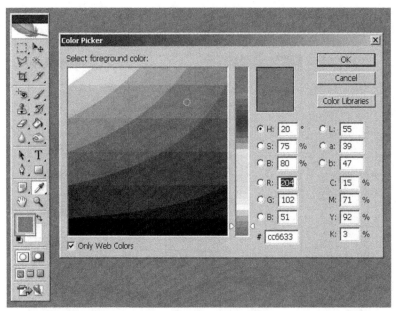

Figure 13-11. Color Picker with Only Web Colors turned on

Now select the Paint Bucket tool (click the paint bucket icon or press G on your keyboard) and fill the new layer.

Keep in mind that some tools are grouped together on the toolbar. For example, the Paint Bucket tool also shares the same button location as the Gradient tool, as you see in Figure 13-12, so simply pressing the keyboard shortcut may not activate the tool you need. Once a tool is selected from a group, it will remain as the selectable tool on that group until you select the option for a different tool in that group.

Our layers are now set up for us to start cropping the background out. Choose the Eraser tool, which is exactly to the left of the Paint Bucket tool (or press E on your keyboard).

Before you start chopping away at the background with the Eraser tool, you need to know that behind this tool is a vast array of brushes and options. Let's take a moment to look at a small sampling of the stock brushes and options available. Again, there are multiple ways to get to and set these tools. With the Eraser tool selected, the Brushes palette (located at the top right in Photoshop by default) appears as shown in Figure 13-13.

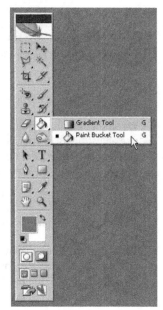

Figure 13-12. Paint Bucket tool

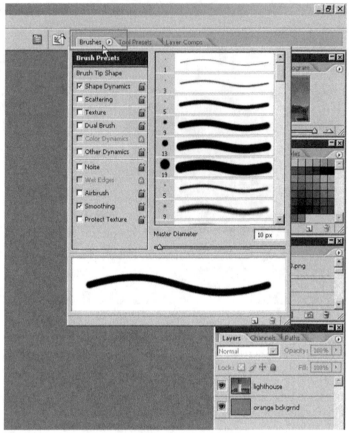

Figure 13-13. Brushes tab located near the top of Photoshop.

For the purposes of this exercise, let's leave the default settings as they are to start with, using the round brush about 10 pixels in size.

We won't be using the Brushes panel—I've just highlighted it so you know it's there for specifying precise adjustments to your brushes. Another area for adjusting the Eraser tool is again located in the top Options toolbar. Again, notice how the Options toolbar changes to adjust attributes of the selected tool, in our case, the Eraser tool (see Figure 13-14).

Figure 13-14. Options toolbar for the Eraser tool

These options include another area to change the brush type, diameter and hardness, mode, opacity, and flow. The Mode setting determines how the brush acts on the canvas. The options are Brush, Pencil, and Block. The Brush mode will mimic a paint brush with many strands to produce very clean aliased edges. The Pencil mode is very rough and will produce very jagged or pixilated edges. The Block mode is similar to the Pencil mode, but is limited to a block shape. You'll notice if you choose the Pencil or Block modes, the Flow setting becomes inactive. Only the Brush mode allows this setting. Keep in mind it is not uncommon to adjust these settings for various projects in Photoshop. But because we want to completely eliminate the background from our image, we will use the Brush mode setting with Opacity and Flow set to 100%. The Opacity setting adjusts the strength of the Eraser tool. Erasing at 100% removes the pixels completely. A lower amount erases the pixel partially, giving the erased area some transparency. The Flow setting determines how quickly the brush will erase. A lower flow rate will take numerous passes to erase the pixels completely.

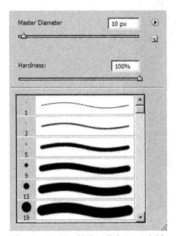

Figure 13-15. Right-click to quickly change the brush properties for the Eraser tool.

For this exercise, we will mainly be using the quick adjustment menu to make changes on-the-fly as needed. With the Eraser tool selected you can right-click (or Ctrl-click on a Mac) to get to the quick menu, as shown in Figure 13-15.

This will be our most important menu right now because, while erasing the background, you will need to adjust your brush size often to get into the different nooks and crannies in the image.

This menu has two important features you will want to adjust often: Master Diameter and Hardness. Master Diameter adjusts the actual diameter of the brush—2500 is the maximum and 1 is the minimum. The other setting, Hardness, determines what percentage of the edge of the brush will *not* be feathered, and can be set from 0 to 100%. The closer this is set to 0%, the more the brush is feathered, and the more the eraser marks will feather the edges so that you can attempt to blend the eraser marks better or aid in aliasing. As shown in Figure 13-15, set Hardness to 100% so that there is *no* feathering; specifying a Master Diameter setting of 10 pixels is a good starting point.

Before attempting to erase anything, it's essential for you to zoom in on the different areas of the image as you go, so you can be more accurate with your deletions. Click the magnifying glass icon in the Tools palette (or press Z) to open the Zoom tool. Choose a section of the lighthouse you want to start working on and then click and drag a small box over the image with the Zoom tool to zoom in on that section. I like to start around the more complicated areas of any image. In this case, the top section of glass and rails fit the bill.

With the Eraser tool selected, use small strokes and clicks to carefully remove the background from the lighthouse. You will see the orange layer below the lighthouse start to show through as well, as demonstrated in Figure 13-16. This will allow you to easily spot any areas of background that have been left behind when you are cleaning up your work.

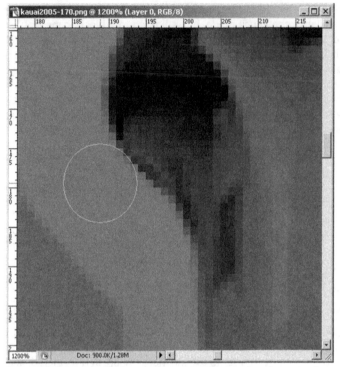

Figure 13-16. Orange background layer showing up after the parts of the lighthouse image have been erased

After finishing up your zoomed section, you can easily move around the image by holding down the spacebar and then clicking and dragging the image to where you want to go next—you will see the cursor turn into an open hand cursor. This is a much faster way to move the image around than trying to use the scrollbars. Once you get the image in place to start erasing again, simply let go of the space-bar, and the last tool you used will become available again.

You will find that increasing or reducing the size of the eraser will aid in this task. There are times when you will even have to reduce the eraser to 1 pixel to get into the really tight corners. You may also have to set the hardness of the eraser to 0%; that way you can lightly erase some pixels around a difficult area. For example, around the railing and windows you may want to set your brush up with a master diameter of 3 pixels and a hardness of 0%. This way the brush just slightly erases the edges while the middle portion of the brush is erasing at 100%. This aids in keeping some of the image so it maintains the aliasing, and the image doesn't look pixilated around the edges (see Figure 13-17).

Figure 13-17. Change the brush size to get into the tight spots in the lighthouse.

One thing to note is that if you change the hardness of the brush to 0%, it will appear that the brush gets smaller. This is because Photoshop is telling you that the area that will be erased fully, or 100%, is within the circle cursor. Anything just outside of that circle cursor will only be erased slightly or less than 100%, depending on the amount of hardness you chose.

This may sound complicated, but once you get the hang of the technique, it will become second nature. Remember to zoom in and out to check your progress along the way. Things may not appear the same way zoomed in when you zoom out to the actual pixels. After awhile, you will begin to develop a work flow, something like the following:

1. Select the Zoom tool to zoom in on your image.

2. Select the Eraser tool to erase.

3. Change the size of the brush and hardness.

4. Zoom back out to check work.

5. Repeat the preceding steps until your work is done.

Again, this process may seem monotonous, but the results are typically better than trying to use automated tools like the Magic Wand tool. Once you finish erasing the background, your image might look something like what appears in Figure 13-18—I hid the orange layer so you can see the transparency showing through the railing.

Figure 13-18. Entire lighthouse with the edges of the background erased

Finally, to make sure you erase *all* the background, in the top menu select Image ➤ Reveal All. This will increase the canvas to reveal the entire image, so you can check that you've completed the job, and unexpected pieces of the image don't show up later.

With all the fiddly bits now done, again, you have a choice when deciding how to remove the rest of the image—you can set up a larger brush for the eraser with 100% hardness, 100% opacity, and 100% flow, and scribble out large portions; you can select the Rectangular Marquee tool from the toolbar (or hit M on the keyboard), select a large portion of the image to the left and right of the lighthouse, and then hit Delete on the keyboard; or you can do a combination of both.

You get the idea. The thing to keep in mind is to make sure you don't leave any unnecessary background behind, as it could affect your work later in Flash. You can test to see whether you missed some areas by using the Transform tool to display the outlined box around your lighthouse. If the box is not tight around the lighthouse, then you have some background leftover somewhere. Press the Esc key and find the extra material. Do this over and over until your Transform box is tight around the lighthouse, as shown in Figure 13-19.

Figure 13-19. Lighthouse with the rest of the background removed

Color-correcting our image

By now you should have the background knocked out completely and be confident that the lighthouse is the only thing left on the canvas. However, several problems still exist, so the image is not ready for Flash just yet:

- The glass at the top of the lighthouse is still a bluish color because of the blue sky from the photo.
- The rails are still very blue because they are so thin they picked up a lot of the blue from the sky behind them.
- The body of the lighthouse has also picked up the blue from the sky and must be color-corrected too.
- Last, if we really want to be particular, the red bulb at the top has also picked up a little of this blue and is really dull.

We have to get the blue hue out of our image, but we don't want to use a single technique because we will not get the best results. Let's start with the main body.

First we will remove the light blue tint on the lower half of the lighthouse. With the Rectangular Marquee tool, draw a box around the lower half of the lighthouse only. Next, in the top menu, select Image ➤ Adjustments ➤ Replace Color. Now sample a portion of the blue on the left side of the lighthouse, about where my eyedropper is in Figure 13-20.

Figure 13-20. Replacing the blue hue shadow on the body of the lighthouse to be a more neutral gray

Next, adjust the Fuzziness setting to 100, then set the Saturation level to −100. The blue areas of the selection will basically get replaced with gray. When you are happy with the result, click OK. Now make sure the selection you created with the Rectangular Marquee tool is deselected. You can easily do this by pressing Ctrl+D (or Cmd+D on a Mac).

Now we need to work on the rails. Using the Zoom tool, zoom in on the top half of the lighthouse where the rails are. Since we can tell that the rails are a darker gray color if we look at the center railing, we can simply remove the color from the bluish portions of the rails. To do this, choose the Sponge tool (select the Sponge Tool menu option or press O) as shown in Figure 13-21.

Figure 13-21. Selecting the Sponge tool

In the preferences box at the top, make sure that Mode is set to Desaturate and Flow is set to 100%. Now, right-click (Ctrl-click on a Mac) to bring up the brush options and set Master Diameter to 10 pixels and Hardness to 100%.

Again using short strokes only, "paint" over the rail areas that had the background removed from them. Continue doing so until the rails appear gray or dark gray. With the same tool, paint over the small antennae on top of the lighthouse too. Once finished, your rails and the antennae should no longer contain any blue tint; they should be gray or dark gray, but not black.

Next, let's address the blue behind the windows. Removing the blue in this area with the Eraser tool would be really difficult, especially since the windows are not totally transparent anyway—you'll notice that the windows actually have a slight green tint to them. Let's use this to our advantage. Instead of knocking that color out, we will work off the green tint to make the blue behind the other windows match it. This will give the windows a fuller green tint than they already have, making the color in the windows appear to be green on purpose, thus solving our problem. Keep in mind that there are probably a dozen different ways you can do this. Which method is better really depends on the image you are working with. My approach is really just color correcting.

Figure 13-22. Selecting the Lasso tool

The first thing we need to do is isolate the glass section of the lighthouse. To do so, select the Lasso tool (or press L), as shown in Figure 13-22.

Now carefully draw around the group of lighthouse windows, as shown in Figure 13-23. Don't worry about the railings; they will not be affected.

Figure 13-23. Using the Lasso tool to select the windows of the lighthouse

It doesn't have to be perfect in this case because the background is transparent. Now with the section of windows in the image selected, select Image ➤ Adjustments ➤ Selective Color to bring up the Selective Color dialog box. Inside that box, choose the category Blues from the drop-down menu. Set the color sliders as follows: Cyan, –80%; Magenta, –71%; Yellow, +32%; and Black, +85%; and make sure the method is set to Absolute, as shown in Figure 13-24. All windows should now really start to match that greenish tint in the windows on the far right of the lighthouse. Click OK.

Figure 13-24. Use Selective Color to adjust the hue of the windows.

Now we need to bring back a little of the trim around the windows for believability. The trim around the windows should not be green, but maybe a bit more brown or grayish. To do so, we need to amp up those colors a bit.

Select Image ➤ Adjustments ➤ Match Color. In the dialog box that appears, set Luminance to 160, Color Intensity to 100, Fade to 30, and check the Neutralize box, as shown in Figure 13-25. A couple of things should happen to the glass and trim. The trim should look great. There is a good amount of separation from the glass and trim to add to the effect. The glass should now look a little less green, and to my surprise I like it that way. The more faded green adds to the realism of faded green tinted glass. I like it, so let's move on!

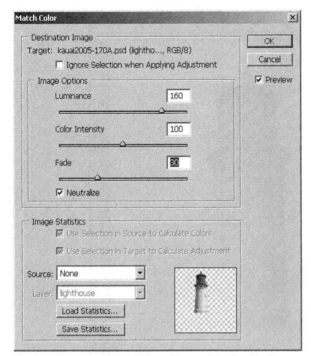

Figure 13-25. Tweak the window trim area by adjusting the color using Color Match.

The last part of the lighthouse we need to correct is the red bulb at the top. This is easy. It has a just a slight bit of blue on the left side and is a bit dull, even for an old lighthouse. Repeat the process for removing the blue from the body of the lighthouse, making sure you select only the red bulb.

Now we need to brighten up the red a bit. With the bulb still selected, select Image ➤ Adjustments ➤ Hue Saturation and adjust the Saturation levels to +30, as shown in Figure 13-26. Click OK.

The lighthouse is done! Let's take a look at a side-by-side comparison of the before and after images in relation to the color correction, shown in Figure 13-27.

Our changes do not jump out at us. What is important is that we have tweaked the image just enough to remove it from its captor, the blue sky background, which planted the lighthouse in the original scene. Now that the blue hues are gone from the lighthouse, we can place it just about anywhere with the maximum level of professionalism.

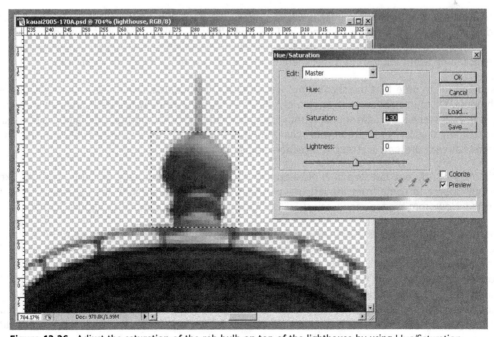

Figure 13-26. Adjust the saturation of the reb bulb on top of the lighthouse by using Hue/Saturation.

Figure 13-27. Before and after color correction comparison

Your adjustments with different images will vary, obviously, but the thing to keep in mind is that trial and error is necessary. Try something out, and if it doesn't work, make some adjustments or try something different altogether. Maybe try the Channel Mixer command or the Replace Color command. The nice thing about Photoshop is that there is no one set way to do things for most tasks.

It's important to note that the shadow has anchored the light source coming from the right of the lighthouse. Of course, if you need to, you can flip the image horizontally to match other shadows or lights in your scene if the light source is not coming from the right. An important design tip is to make sure that any shadows you have in your scene, whether they are on text or another object, match the shadows already present, in strength, direction, and so forth.

With that, let's do one last step in Photoshop and flip the image horizontally, because I typically like my light source to come from the left (my personal preference). Make sure the lighthouse layer is selected. Now from the top menu, select Edit ➤ Transform ➤ Flip Horizontal to flip the lighthouse.

The last step in this process is to finally decide how large we think we need the image to be in Flash. We want to size the image down in Photoshop, not Flash. Again, Photoshop is made to do this and does it very well. For the purposes of this exercise, let's size it down to 75% of its current size. From the top menu, select Image ➤ Image Size. At the bottom of the Image Size dialog box, make sure that Scale Styles, Constrain Proportions, and Resample Image are all checked. At the top of the box in the Width area, click the drop-down button and choose Percent. Next, enter 75 in the Width field, as you see in Figure 13-28. You'll notice the Height field will do the best it can to match the Width field because we made sure that Constrain Proportions was checked.

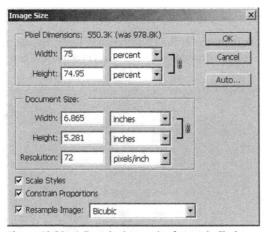

Figure 13-28. Adjust the image size for use in Flash.

The entire image is now 75% of its original size. Now, for the sake of keeping the image file size in Flash as small as possible, we need to crop out most of the transparent space around the lighthouse. To do this, use the Rectangular Marquee tool again and draw a box around the lighthouse, making sure that the box is not intersecting the lighthouse image at all (see Figure 13-29).

Next, select Image ➤ Crop. We have optimized the image space as much as we can for now. Finally, let's export the image as a PNG so we can take full advantage of the work we did removing the background. Again from the top menu, choose File ➤ Save As. In the Save As dialog box, specify the appropriate location to save the PNG. In the Format drop-down box, choose PNG and give the image a file name. Click Save.

It's a good idea to save the Photoshop file as a *new* file after the resizing (I'm a file-saving freak—it's never bad to have too many versions of a file floating around in case you realize that you need to go back a few versions).

Now, let's move into Flash.

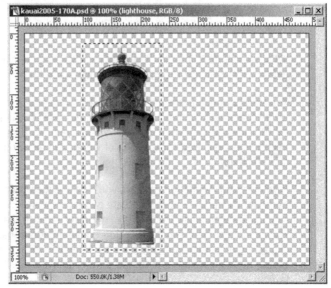

Figure 13-29. Crop the image.

Images in Flash

I've created a starter mini website for the Kilauea Lighthouse in Kauai, Hawaii, as shown in Figure 13-30, for the sake of this exercise. You can download it from www.friendsofed.com.

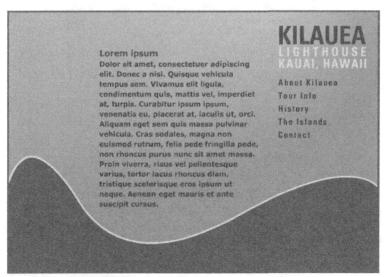

Figure 13-30. Basic layout of the website

What we will do is import the image into the Flash movie and create a soft shadow coming from the lighthouse. We'll also explore the new filters and blend modes in Flash 8.

You should notice there are a total of 16 layers and 2 folders. Inside the Body Assets folder are the layers containing the intro animation of the page. You'll also see a Top Assets folder, which contains the Border and surrounding Large Mask layers. As discussed in previous chapters, it's important to keep things organized for the sake of working in an optimized environment. This helps maximize time and efficiency.

If you play the animation in Flash, you'll notice it contains no lighthouse. It's our job to add the lighthouse in. To start, we need to create two layers, which will be the main lighthouse layer and the layer to hold the lighthouse shadow. It's important to note that if I wanted to use the new Shadow filter in Flash 8 in a standard way, I really don't need an additional layer. I could just use the lighthouse movie clip as my object to apply the filter to. However, for the sake of taking things a bit further for exploration, I will show you how to add a more convincing shadow to the lighthouse, which requires two layers.

Click the Body Assets folder to highlight it. Then in the top menu select Insert ➤ Timeline ➤ Layer (or click the Insert Layer icon in the timeline window) to add a new layer above the Body Assets folder. Repeat this process one more time. Name the topmost new layer LH and the bottom layer LH Shadow, as shown in Figure 13-31.

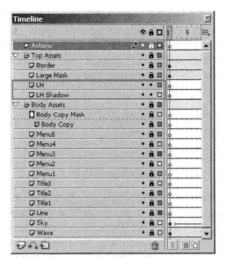

Figure 13-31. Insert new layers and name them.

Now move the timeline marker to frame 320 and insert a blank keyframe to both layers there.

We are now set up to import the lighthouse into layer LH on keyframe 320. With frame 320 selected in the LH layer, choose File ➤ Import ➤ Import to Stage (or press Ctrl+R on a PC or Cmd+R on a Mac). This is a shortcut that you will use all the time, so you might want to get used to using this one! The Import dialog box appears. Navigate to your lighthouse_cropped.png and select it. Click Open. You'll see the lighthouse is now on the stage positioned at 0,0 (x,y).

You can select multiple frames in a layer to add keyframes, delete them, or add effects at one time.

Now we need to convert the PNG into a movie clip. With the lighthouse selected, from the top menu again select Modify ➤ Convert to Symbol or simply hit F8 on the keyboard to bring up the Convert to Symbol dialog box. Again, get used to using this shortcut, as you will use it a lot. Rename the symbol to lighthouseMC and make sure the type is Movie Clip.

The Convert to Symbol dialog box has an Advanced button at the bottom to access some advanced features. I like to have it open in case I need to quickly apply some setting to the movie clip while I'm creating it. This may save a few clicks down the road. For example, an additional setting included here is the Linkage property section, as shown in Figure 13-32. This section allows you to assign an identifier name to the symbol so Flash can access the symbol dynamically with ActionScript or make the symbol accessible for linking to destination documents.

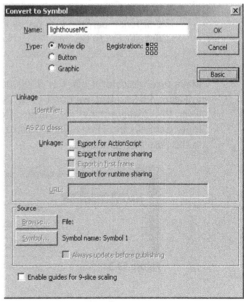

Figure 13-32. Convert PNG to a movie clip.

Next, let's reposition lighthouseMC where we want it. After trial and error I found the best spot for it is located at the x- and y-coordinates of 0, 75. You can position lighthouseMC in that exact position by entering the values at the bottom of the Flash interface in the panel called Properties. If the x- and y-coordinates are not visible, then click the little arrow on the bottom right of the panel, which you can see in Figure 13-33, to expand it to show the information area.

Figure 13-33. Expand the Properties box to see all options.

Now that lighthouseMC is in position, we need to make a copy of it on the layer below it. You can easily copy the frame with lighthouseMC on it by making sure that the frame with lighthouseMC is highlighted and then using Ctrl+Alt+C (PC) or Cmd+Option+C (Mac). Then in layer LH Shadow select frame 320 and use Ctrl+Alt+V to paste the copied frame. Now we have two instances of lighthouseMC on both layers at the same frame number. Note that we have two instances of lighthouseMC on the stage at this point.

OK, now the fun part. We will create a shadow from the lighthouse using the new native filters in Flash 8. At this point, go ahead and lock and hide the LH layer so it's not modified by accident. In the LH Shadow layer, select the lighthouseMC on the stage.

Now, in the bottom panel again you will see the Filters tab. Click that, click the + sign, and choose Drop Shadow. Let's adjust some of those settings. Set Blur X and Blur Y to 10 and make sure the lock icon is locked. This will make sure that the x and y blur amounts are equal. Set the Strength to 15% and the Quality to High.

> With the Quality setting set to High, animation performance is decreased. To improve animation performance on symbols using a drop shadow or any other filter effect, set the Quality to Low.

Make sure the color is black or #000000. Angle should be set to 45 and Distance set to 0, as you see in Figure 13-34. Now, we don't need the lighthouse to actually be visible since we have it in the LH layer; this is where things get a little different. The three check box options on the right are Knockout, Inner shadow, and Hide object. Check the Hide object option to hide the "source" of the movie clip, in this case the lighthouse.

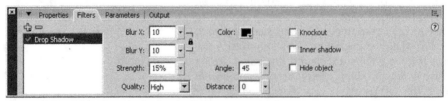

Figure 13-34. Add a drop shadow to the lighthouse movie clip.

What we want to do is skew the shadow to the right to make it look as if it is working correctly with the light source, the sun in the lighthouse PNG. Again, after trial and error, I found the settings that work the best. If you don't have the Transform panel open, do it now by clicking Window ➤ Transform or pressing Ctrl+T (PC) or Cmd+T (Mac). In the Transform panel, make sure Constrain is not selected. We want independent control over width and height. Leave the Width set to 100%. Set the Height to 70%, as shown in Figure 13-35. Next, click Skew and set it to 45 degrees. You should notice that the shadow's x- and y-coordinates are way off now. Under the Properties panel set the x-coordinate to 16 and the y-coordinate to 275.

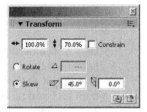

Figure 13-35. Transform the shadow to look like it's being cast on the ground.

To check your work so far, unhide the LH layer. As you can see in Figure 13-36, this is a much better shadow for the lighthouse, and it was created natively in Flash. We'll explore some of the other filters in Flash 8 in a bit.

Figure 13-36. Preview of our work so far

In the spirit of keeping things animated like the page build-in, let's add a slight build-in animation to our lighthouse and shadow. I left the lighthouse and the shadow separate so I can animate them differently.

Unlock the LH layer. In frame 340, add a keyframe in both layers. Back on frame 320, create a tween between frames 320 and 340. Now select the lighthouseMC on the stage in layer LH and in the Properties panel under the Color setting choose Advanced. Now click the Settings button next to Advanced. In the Advanced dialog box, set Alpha to 0% and the Red, Green, and Blue settings to 255, as shown in Figure 13-37. Click OK.

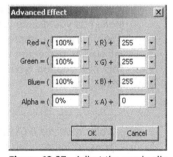

Figure 13-37. Adjust the movie clip at the start of the tween.

What this does is make the lighthouse completely transparent and pure white. When you play the animation back, it looks as if the lighthouse appears on the stage from nothing to a really bright "overexposed" effect. This is much more interesting than the standard fade-in. The shadow, on the other hand, can use the standard fade-in because, after all, it's just a shadow. Lock the LH layer and select the lighthouseMC movie clip in the LH Shadow layer. In the Color drop-down list on the Properties panel, choose Alpha and set it to 0%.

Let's add some slight motion to the clips. To me, less is more. In this case, I only want to move the lighthouse by about 25 pixels up from the bottom. So when the animation builds, the clips will have some slight motion fading up from the bottom. So with both layers unlocked, on frame 320 select both clips and move them down 25 pixels. The new coordinates for the lighthouse should be (0, 100) and the shadow should be (–16, 250). To polish the animation a little, let's add some easing as well. Select the keyframes on frame 320 for both clips. In the Properties panel at the bottom, move the ease slider to 100. This type of easing is generally called "easing out" because the animation begins by moving fast and then slows down once it gets to the end of the tween.

If you play the animation back, you'll notice the lighthouse comes in from the bottom of the stage and fades at the same time. Nice, subtle, clean.

The last thing to consider is compression on the images for the final Flash movie. You typically have the option of a blanket approach to compress all the images at one time by choosing a compression setting for the images during export in the Export Flash Player dialog box. This, however, is not good practice, because one setting may not work well with all the images in your Flash movie. If you get too conservative with your JPEG compression, the images will look great, but at the expense of file size. If your setting is too aggressive, you will have a lower file size, but the image quality will suffer. So the "shotgun" approach is just bad. The best way to optimize your bitmapped images is to adjust the compression setting individually for each image.

You can do this in the Library. Simply right-click (Ctrl-click on a Mac) and choose Properties or highlight the image in the Library and click the little blue "I" icon at the bottom of the Library. This will bring up the Bitmap Properties dialog box, as shown in Figure 13-38.

From here you can change the settings to optimize that one image. The setting called Allow smoothing has been greatly improved and will attempt to smooth out any image artifacts on bitmaps that have been greatly scaled larger or much smaller. The Compression drop-down menu lets you decide whether you want to use JPEG or lossless compression. In most cases, you will want to make sure this is set to Photo (JPEG). The next option you see is Use document default quality.

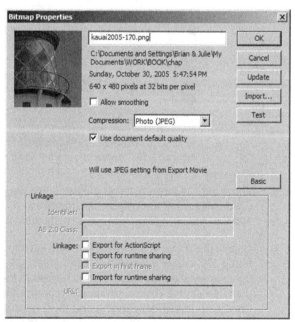

Figure 13-38. Adjust the compression quality of the PNG for final export.

Note: Imported JPGs carry with them compression information while importing into Flash, so when using JPGs this option will read Use imported JPEG data.

Uncheck this option to reveal the Quality setting. Here is where you can increase or decrease the level of compression on the image. A lower number actually increases the amount of compression you apply, making the image lower in quality and lower in file size. This is most definitely a trial-and-error situation.

You must try a number, click the Test button, and then view the results in the preview window. You can move and scale the image around inside the preview window to view the results. There is one rule of thumb that can be applied here: you know you want to optimize for the lowest possible file size and greatest image quality.

That said, start with a high compression, say 30. Then slowly bring that number up until you are happy with the quality and file size of the image. Click OK and move on to the next image if need be. This approach maximizes bitmap quality and file size, producing the best possible Flash movie.

> Tip: Never use 100 in the JPEG Quality box. This means that the image has little or no compression. No image will ever need JPEG Quality set to 100. If high quality is needed, even a setting of 90 will do great, and the file size will be significantly less.

Exploring blend modes

Blend modes combine the colors of one movie clip or image (the base image) with the colors of another image (the blend image) to produce a third image. The first image has to be a movie clip, but the second image does not. You can only apply one blend mode to a movie clip at a time. Here are the descriptions according to Flash 8's help features:

- **Add:** Creates an animated lightening dissolve effect between two images
- **Alpha:** Applies the transparency of the foreground on the background
- **Darken:** Superimposes type
- **Difference:** Creates more vibrant colors
- **Erase:** Cuts out (erases) part of the background using the foreground alpha
- **Hardlight:** Creates shading effects
- **Invert:** Inverts the background
- **Layer:** Forces the creation of a temporary buffer for precomposition for a particular movie clip
- **Lighten:** Superimposes type
- **Multiply:** Creates shadows and depth effects
- **Normal:** Specifies that the pixel values of the blend image override those of the base image
- **Overlay:** Creates shading effects
- **Screen:** Creates highlights and lens flares
- **Subtract:** Creates an animated darkening dissolve effect between two images

Figures 13-39 through 13-50 show how the different modes will affect our lighthouse.

Figure 13-39. Normal and Layer modes

Figure 13-40. Darken mode

Figure 13-41. Multiply mode

Figure 13-42. Lighten mode

Figure 13-43. Screen mode

Figure 13-44. Overlay mode

Figure 13-45. Hardlight mode

Figure 13-46. Add mode

Figure 13-47. Subtract mode

Figure 13-48. Difference mode

Figure 13-49. Invert mode

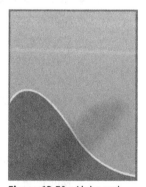

Figure 13-50. Alpha and Erase modes

Blend modes can dramatically change the appearance of the object. Keep in mind that the underlying image or object will affect the results of the blend mode. Because of this, the results could be dramatically different. For example, when we use the Lighten blend mode with our standard background, it looks like what you see in Figure 13-51.

If you change the background by adding a large black "X" behind the lighthouse but in front of the original background, you can see the lighthouse show though the black better, as you see in Figure 13-52, whereas it did not with the original background.

The blend feature in Flash 8 allows it more flexibility with images mirroring what Photoshop can do. This makes Flash 8 even more of a stand-alone tool, requiring less work than Photoshop. Another new feature really makes Flash even more appealing for the designer: filters.

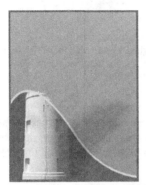

Figure 13-51. Lighten mode

Figure 13-52. Effects of Lighten mode with other objects

Filters

Filters allow us to natively add a drop shadow, glow, blur, bevel, gradient bevel, and gradient glow, and make color adjustments all on the fly without leaving Flash at all. Even though only seven filters are available, each one can be customized for a new set of results. Once you've customized a filter in a way you like, you can even save it as a preset for use again later. Filters can be applied to movie clips, text objects, and buttons. Note that filters do not work on symbols. We used the Shadow filter prior to this point, so let's explore the others. With the lighthouse selected, click the Filters tab at the bottom of the Flash window, normally grouped with the Properties tab. Click the + sign in the upper left of the Filters tab and choose Blur filter.

The Blur filter does just that: it blurs the image according to the Blur amount set for the x-axis and y-axis. The higher the number, the blurrier the object gets. Keep in mind that you don't have to keep the x-axis and y-axis locked. If you unlock them and set the y-axis to 0 and the x-axis to 50, it will look like the object is moving very fast across the page horizontally (see Figure 13-53). Again, this eliminates the use of Photoshop for blurring an image to imply speed while animating in Flash.

The Quality setting can affect the look of the blur as well. There are three settings; and for the most part all the filters have this option. For the Blur filter, you can achieve a couple of different types of blurs. I look at it like this: if the Quality setting is set to Low, the blur looks like a lens blur in Photoshop, as demonstrated in Figure 13-54. This seems to mimic the background blur from a camera's depth of field.

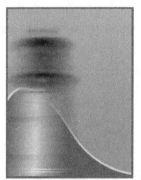

Figure 13-53. A horizontal Blur filter effect

Figure 13-54. Lens Blur filter set to low quality to mimic a lens blur in Photoshop.

> Note: The Quality *setting will greatly influence the playback smoothness when animating the object. The* Low *setting will play back significantly better on slower computers than if the* Quality *setting were set to* High. *This holds true across all the filters that use the* Quality *setting.*

The other two Quality settings, Medium and High, are more like a Gaussian blur in Photoshop (see Figure 13-55). These are typical blurs.

The Glow filter also can serve multiple functions besides just adding a glow. You have to explore the settings and discover what options are available to you. In this case, when we add the filter to our object, we see we have the same settings as Blur and also a few more: Strength, Knockout, Inner glow, and the ability to change the color. The standard use of the glow is again straightforward. It adds a halo around the object, and you can adjust the Quality from Low to High.

Figure 13-56 shows an example of white glow with X and Y set to 20, Strength set to 50%, and the Quality set to Low.

Figure 13-55. Lens Blur filter set to medium–high quality to mimic a Gaussian blur in Photoshop

Figure 13-56. Glow filter

Standard stuff. What is different, though, is that you can also add a stroke or line to the outside edge of an object as well. This is unique because Flash did not have the ability to add a stroke to images with alpha channels before. To get a stroke using the Glow filter, set the X and Y blur amount to 5, Strength to 1000% (not 100%), and Quality to Low. Voilá, a stroke has been added to a bitmapped image with an alpha channel (see Figure 13-57). It's not a perfect stroke, meaning that it does have a slight blurriness to it, but it's very minor and can pass as a stroke any day.

The other features of Glow include Knockout and Inner glow. Knockout removes the object from the stage while maintaining the glow areas. Inner glow simply moves the glow from outside the object to the inside of the object. These can create some really nice effects when used properly.

Understand that these are only tools. Your imagination is where these simple tools can become powerful.

> Note: When the Quality setting in Glow is set to Low, the glow wraps tightly around the object's alpha channel. When Quality is set to High, the glow is much looser around the object.

The next filter is Bevel. I know what you're thinking . . . Bevel? No thanks! Wait a second, take a look at Figure 13-58, which shows you something the Bevel can do.

Again, don't think of these filters in the literal sense. Just because this filter is called Bevel doesn't mean you have to end up with an image that looks like what you see in Figure 13-59.

After tweaking the setting some, you'll find that you can create all kinds of effects with these filters. Also, you can stack the filters on top of each other or use more than one at a time per object. Really, the sky is the limit for what you can do with these new filters.

For the Bevel filter, you have a couple of settings different from the last few: Shadow, Highlight, Angle, Distance, and Type. Shadow and Highlight allow you to pick what colors you want for the shadow and highlight, which seems obvious enough. Angle is what degree the bevel will be. Distance is how far away from the edge of the object the bevel will build itself. As for Type, this determines whether the bevel will draw itself on the outside, inside, or both.

Figure 13-57. Glow filter set to mimic a stroke

Figure 13-58. Bevel filter used to add copies of the movie clip

Figure 13-59. Standard lame Bevel filter example

333

For the bevel for the lighthouse that looks like it has copies of it in the background (the nice looking one), I used the following settings: Blur, 0,0; Strength, 75%; Quality, Low; Shadow color, #996600; Highlight color, #C28A06; Angle, 8; Distance, −24; Knockout, not checked; Type, Outer.

Any number of combinations will create any number of effects. Let's move on to the next filter, Gradient Glow.

The Gradient Glow filter is different from the Glow filter due to a few very important settings. The Gradient Glow filter also contains Angle, Distance, and Type settings, and a color bar. The color bar allows you to change the color of the glow to create bands of color round an object. This can help make the glow seem more realistic or even alien perhaps, as you can see in Figure 13-60.

Figure 13-60. Gradient Glow filter tweaked out

A cool thing to experiment with is to try animating the Gradient Glow across the timeline. Make sure your start keyframe and end keyframe filters match first. Then adjust the ending keyframe and scrub the timeline to see the results. To that end, all the filters can be animated to create some really great looking animations. Again, you can create as many different animations as possible to get totally different results. Experiment, and try things out.

The next filter is the Gradient Bevel and is very similar in functionality as the Gradient Glow. The major difference is the ability to add as many colors to the bevel as you wish. Using the same technique as with the Bevel filter, Figure 13-61 shows what multiple colors can do.

It is important to note, however, that the Strength options in Bevel and in Gradient Bevel are not the same. Where Bevel essentially makes the effect more or less transparent, in Gradient Bevel the Strength slider makes the bevel use more or less of the colors defined on the color bar.

The last filter is the Adjust Color filter. This is where you can make some final tweaks to your imported PNG from Photoshop or make major changes to the image color. This filter has four sliders: Brightness, Contrast, Saturation, and Hue. Each slider can adjust values from −100 to 100.

Figure 13-61. Gradient Bevel filter tweaked

Brightness will adjust the brightness of the object. Contrast will adjust the contrast in the object or how bright or dark the colors are. Saturation adjusts the amount of color the object has. A −100 saturation will essentially make the image grayscaled. Setting this slider to 100 will amplify the colors to an extreme. If your image needs a slight boost in color, you can slightly adjust the Saturation levels.

> Note: Watch the reds and blues while adjusting this slider. Where the other colors may look great, the reds and blues may blow out, giving undesirable results.

Hue will adjust the color range of the object. This slider can change the actual colors in the image. Figure 13-62 shows the same lighthouse with the following settings applied: Brightness, 17; Contrast, 21; Saturation, 75; Hue, 180.

Figure 13-62. Adjust Color filter tweak

Quite a different lighthouse indeed. Again, the possibilities are limitless.

Once you find you like a certain setting, you can always save those settings as a preset. To do so, click the + sign again under the Filters tab and choose Presets ➤ Save As. Give the setting a name. To use that preset again, choose the setting under Presets.

> Tip: Be sure to give the preset a proper name so you know what to expect. For example, don't use Grad Glow 1. Instead, save it as something like Grad Glow Red Blue Green Blur 10. This way you know what you are getting when you select it. After all, once you create several presets, you may not remember what one might look like without trying it first. Giving each preset a proper name will save you a few steps in the creation process.

You can also turn any filters applied to the object on and off without removing them completely by clicking the green checkmark next to the filter name, as shown in Figure 13-63.

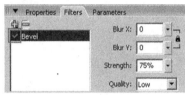

This allows you to see the exported movie with or without the filter active.

Figure 13-63. You can toggle a filter on and off by unchecking it.

Summary

With Photoshop, you are able to effectively modify images and prepare them for use in Flash. Photoshop allows you to edit bitmapped images in ways Flash cannot. Flash 8, however, has added a great new set of features. Blend modes and filters further modify your image or object until it's just right. Using the native tools given to you in Flash 8 also greatly speeds up workflow and enhances the end users' experience.

Chapter 14

FINISHING OFF YOUR SITE

by Guido Rosso

You've planned out your site, designed a prototype, built your interface and assets, and added animation and interactivity. Everything is finally coming together; however, you still have a few things to do before you launch. These include optimizing your Flash files, publishing, and embedding in HTML.

In the latter part of this chapter, I'll also discuss quality assurance, how to handle the launch of your site, and usability testing.

Optimization

It is our goal to develop websites that are as efficient as possible. This means that files should be as light and as streamlined as we can make them. Fortunately, Flash gives us the functionality to help us achieve this.

The first thing to consider is your Library. Are you reusing your symbols effectively? That is, if you're using a circle shape as a motion tween for one effect, are you reusing that same symbol for your other circle shapes? Remember that you can scale these shapes (for example, to reuse for a mask effect) and apply color tint and layer effects to achieve a specific look. All of this creates a smaller file size than actually redesigning the same shape and coloring it differently.

Another very effective way to reduce file size is Library sharing, particularly with large projects that contain multiple SWF files. Shared Library items are only downloaded once, regardless of how many SWF files reference them. This means that if you're using the same graphic in SWF B as in SWF A, the graphic will only download when you first view SWF A. When you go to download SWF B, you won't have to download the graphic again; SWF B will simply call it from the locally cached SWF A. This applies to any item that is reused in multiple SWF files, whether it's an image, an audio clip, or a font. For a detailed explanation on Library sharing and for a number of tutorials and examples, visit www.macromedia.com or read the TechNote at www.macromedia.com/cfusion/knowledgebase/index.cfm?id=tn_14767.

The Bandwidth Profiler

You can test your SWF's download performance using the Bandwidth Profiler, included in Flash. To access the Bandwidth Profiler, press Ctrl+Enter (Cmd+Enter on a Mac) to test your movie. Now press Ctrl+B (Cmd+B on a Mac) to access the Bandwidth Profiler, or go to View ➤ Bandwidth Profiler. You can also do this by directly opening a SWF in Flash.

The Bandwidth Profiler shows you how much data a user has to download at each specific frame. This obviously varies from user to user based on his or her connection speed. You can simulate a specific connection speed under the View ➤ Download Settings menu. Changing this setting will update the Bandwidth Profiler.

Each bar on the right side of the Bandwidth Profiler represents a frame in your SWF (note that you won't see any bars if your file is empty). The height of the bar represents its size. The horizontal red line represents how much data can be streamed in real time, based on the connection speed you've set. This means that frames below the red bar will play back normally, whereas frames that go above the red line will cause the movie to pause and wait until the data has finished downloading. Ideally you want everything to be below the red line; however, this isn't always going to be possible, especially for a very large and complex interface.

If this is the case, use a preloading animation before displaying your content, but be sure to do so in an intelligent way. Don't simply block access to your site until all the content has loaded. Use the pre-loader to load enough frames so that your users don't see any jumps in the animation, keeping in mind that the rest of your site can load as these initial animations are playing. Use the Simulate Download function (accessible by going to the View menu or by pressing Ctrl+Enter, or Cmd+Enter on a Mac) to watch a simulation of how your file would stream on a user's computer with the Internet connection you selected previously (under the View ➤ Download Settings menu).

Compressing assets

You can also use your Bandwidth Profiler to find which portions of your site could be compressed better. Look for frames that stick out significantly above the red line on the Bandwidth Profiler. The majority of these frames will generally contain audio or bitmap assets. It's important to test different compression settings for each of these files to achieve the highest compression possible without too much loss in quality. As a quick test, you can set global compression settings under the publish settings of your movie for all your audio and JPEG files (File ➤ Publish Settings). The better way to do this, however, is to go into your Library and customize the compression settings for each image and audio file individually. Different files will compress more with less perceivable quality loss, while other files will immediately lose a lot of quality when compressed. So you need to do a little trial-and-error work at this point to achieve the best compression setting for each file.

Unless you're compressing a PNG file, which needs to preserve transparency, it's a good idea to do most of your JPEG optimization in Photoshop's Save for Web. I find that Photoshop does a better job of optimizing file size while retaining a slightly higher quality than the JPEG compression in Flash.

Remember also to go back and swap out any placeholder graphics, such as the guide layers used in Chapter 9, with their final files. I tend to use PNGs initially; however, these should be converted to JPEGs before final publishing.

Publishing

Once your file is ready for final production, you need to publish it. To customize your publish settings, go to File ➤ Publish Settings (or press Ctrl+Shift+F12 on a PC, Cmd+Shift+F12 on a Mac). Once you've set your custom publish settings, they will be automatically applied to your test file when you press Ctrl/Cmd+Enter.

Under the Publish Settings window you have three tabs: Formats, Flash, and HTML. The Formats tab specifies what kind of files the publisher should output. You probably want to stick to Flash and HTML for your interface.

The Flash tab is the one you're most interested in. Here you can specify a number of options, such as what version of Flash you want output for (very useful if you're working in the latest version of Flash but need to ensure that your file will be viewable by users with older players, or if you're developing a file for mobile devices and need to output Flash Lite files). Other options that are interesting to interface designers are Load Order, Protect from import, and Compress movie.

Load Order is an important option to consider, even though it is often overlooked. It specifies in which order your layers should be loaded. When Flash hits a frame that hasn't been preloaded, its layers will display as they are loaded, which can be either bottom-up or top-down. Customizing this setting will help your file look right as it's being streamed.

Any SWF you put on the web should have the Protect From Import option checked. If you don't have this option checked, anybody can download your file and import it into their movies. Although this won't give them access to your code, they will still be able to copy and use your graphical assets as they wish. Checking this option also lets you set a password, so that if someone tries to import your SWF file, it will request the password. I generally leave this empty since anyone who actually needs to access this file would have access to the FLA in the first place.

The final setting I want to talk about is Compress movie. This is a setting that should always be enabled, as it reduces the overall file size of the movie by compressing your entire file (not just the individual assets). A compressed file will only play in Flash Player 6 and above, which shouldn't be a problem nowadays; however, keep this in mind in case you run into incompatibilities.

Embedding in HTML

Under the Publish Settings window you'll also find an HTML tab, as mentioned in the previous section. Here you can specify a number of options that will generate custom embedding code for you, which will be output to an HTML file. This is useful, as you can quickly copy and paste the Embed and Object tag code from this HTML file to your custom HTML file.

Pay special attention to the Flash alignment options, particularly if you're setting your dimensions to a different size from your SWF, or if you're making the movie stretch to 100% of your screen.

Window Mode is a useful setting that you can employ to make the background of your SWF transparent. Aside from the annoying advertising applications this has created, it can help you to achieve interesting effects or functionality in HTML by placing a Flash movie in an HTML layer above the rest of your site. For example, you could make a contact form in Flash and place it in an invisible layer above your interface. When someone clicks the Contact link in your navigation bar, you can unhide the layer, allowing the user to send a message and instantly return to the interface, without loading any additional HTML content or refreshing the page.

Detecting Flash

The Detect Flash Version option (on the HTML tab) will add JavaScript version detection code to your HTML. This is a very good quick way to implement Flash detection on your site, and it supports most platforms. An even better way to do this, however, is the new player-based express install.

QA testing

Quality assurance, or *quality testing*, is a concept that originally comes from engineering and manufacturing. You've probably heard of or read about the ISO 9000 series, which is simply a set of standards created by the International Organization for Standardization. It would be overkill for us, as web designers, to consider seeking ISO certification. As I'll discuss later in this section, it's already hard enough to plan and conform to a specific testing schedule due to launch dates being set in stone and the inevitable delays that afflict all projects (e.g., content delivery). However, QA in web design is just as vital a process as any other phase of development. It should never be overlooked.

Now that development of your site is complete, you need to make sure that everything works as intended. Don't assume everything is fine just because it worked when you first built it. Numerous things might have happened, from server changes to adding new features to your site, that may have broken what was working before.

The extent of QA testing you undertake relies heavily on budget and time. Some companies have dedicated QA testers that handle everything from server-load testing for a large amount of concurrent connections to expert security testing and usability testing (which sometimes is an entirely different phase of testing on its own).

Generally, however, it's enough to use your common sense. Test on multiple platforms, specifically the ones you know your users will be using. These tend to include slower and older machines. Test with major browsers and operating systems. It's a good idea to keep an older computer purely for testing purposes. Install different versions of the browsers you'll be testing, then make copies of those browsers and install different versions of Flash. Also ensure that this computer only has the most basic set of fonts installed, as this will help you detect any font embedding issues. This is a crucial part of QA testing for Flash interfaces. Not everyone who will visit your site for the first time will have the newest software.

If your site will be used as a marketing tool in presentations, be sure to test that everything looks right on a projector. Other things to check for are browser crashes, mistakes, and anything that could harm the functionality and professionalism of your work. I can't stress enough how important it is to ensure you set aside a specific amount of time dedicated only to testing. This should be an entirely unique phase of the web design process. Include it in your proposal and plan ahead for it. You should be aware of exactly how much time you'll have for testing long before you begin any kind of development. It's important to know this all ahead of time because regardless of how hard you plan, delays will happen. As the launch date gets closer, you will have to focus on finding and fixing major bugs and issues with the site that aren't up to specification first. Come up with a method of prioritizing these bugs, as it won't always be possible to fix all of the bugs before launch. Keep in mind that you need to schedule time to test your fixes as well; fixing one issue can sometimes break another part of your site.

The final part of QA testing I want to talk about is content. The major issues we generally associate with QA are obviously the more technical and complex ones; however, content checking is very important as well. Typos and mistakes can completely ruin whatever level of professionalism you may be trying to achieve. If you had a copywriter, or a specific team, work on the content, be sure to have them look over the entire site, preferably multiple times. Check for spelling and grammatical errors. It's a good idea to also get someone else to look over the content and read through all of it, preferably someone who hasn't read any of it before. Chances are you and your team have been looking at this content for quite some time now, and a fresh pair of eyes will catch things that you may have overlooked.

Launching and post launch

Site launches aren't always a defined moment in time. Ideally, you would conduct all your testing on a separate server with an identical setup to your live server, or at least on a separate directory of your live server. In this case, the moment you launch would be the moment when you take down your old site from the test server and put up the new one.

Many other times, however, a site launch happens very gradually. You might slowly transition from the old site to the new one, updating only certain parts of the site. This process can get very tedious and creates problems for you and your client as you stay in a constant state of "coming soon." Not only does this reflect badly on your client's business, but it also complicates billing matters. You obviously can't send your final invoice if the site isn't up and running as detailed in the original specifications. This situation often tends to be the case with very large and complex sites. For this reason, it's very important to have as detailed a proposal and a specification of the site's features as possible. In these cases, it's a very good idea to identify which features and specific requests pertain to "development" and which pertain to "maintenance." You would then identify the "launch" phase as the moment when development of the site shifts to maintenance.

You should also make a launch announcement to your users and to the general public. At the very least, tell your users what's going on, directly on the site, and let them know to whom they should report any bugs they may find. Consider making an offline announcement through corporate newsletters and the press.

Maintenance

Maintenance begins when the launch ends. After the launch, you should have a handoff packet ready for your client and for the team that will be conducting maintenance of the site (if you aren't handling it yourself). Your handoff packet should include all the project deliverables that were listed in your proposal, including a style guide. Project deliverables should include all your HTML files, CSS files, script files, images, Flash SWF files, and any database files (if applicable). Include all your documents, spreadsheets, flowcharts, and e-mails documenting completion of milestones. These should all be printed out and put together in a clean binding. Included should be a CD containing the other deliverables. Your style guide should list and illustrate the specific colors used on the site, with their hex values. Define typefaces and styling for headlines, body text, links, sidebars, quotes, and any other applicable styles. Include your wireframes of the site interface, with specific details on margins, padding, and line height as it applies to different parts of the interface. It's also a good idea to include examples of how to properly compress images so they don't look blocky or grainy, give examples of the images you used and show the proper compression settings next to the incorrect compression settings. Be sure to include the sizes (width by height in pixels) of every image that may need to be updated.

Source files

Source files can be a touchy subject. Some companies believe in handing everything off to the client on completion of the project, including all Photoshop PSD files, Illustrator AI files, Flash FLA files, and any compiled code. This is something I disagree with, unless the client has a valid reason for requesting them and is willing to pay for them.

The metaphor has been done to death, but when you buy a car, you don't get the blueprints for it.

It's perfectly acceptable for your client to request the source files, and if they do, simply quote them an additional price for them. However, it's always in your interest to protect your source files and know-how. You also want to be sure your client comes back to you for future updates and maintenance. Chances are you probably want to keep a certain standard of quality associated with your work. This would be difficult to maintain if everybody in your client's company who considers themselves webmasters has the ability to make changes to the core of the interface. This often ends up with the site losing the style uniformity you have established.

Handing over source files is also a risk because it gives your client or whomever may be performing updates the ability to break something. Therefore, it's a good idea to include in your contract a predetermined rate for support involved with fixing issues caused by a third party.

Continue analyzing

Handing off your deliverables and launching the site shouldn't be the end of your project. You should monitor and analyze your site's progress for at least a month. Take a look at your statistics. You should be interested in seeing where your users are coming from, who's linking to your site, and how your traffic has changed. Keep track of everything and use this data to measure how successful the launch was. If custom analytics tools aren't feasible with the budget you are working with, keep in mind that you can get a good idea of the kind of traffic your domain is getting at Alexa Internet (www.alexa.com). Simply type your domain name in the Search field and press Enter. Next, click Traffic Details for specific information. You can also do a search on Google to see which sites and specific pages are linking to you by typing in link:mydomain..com.

Usability testing

Usability testing warrants an entire book on its own. Unfortunately, it would be impossible to cover all the aspects of usability testing in even an entire chapter, and frankly that would be outside the scope of this book. If you're interested in knowing all the details, possible workflows, and real-world examples, I strongly recommend buying a book on the subject. I'll provide a broad introduction to usability testing here, which should be enough to point you in the right direction.

Usability testing can be conducted in several different phases of your web development. It's also typical to conduct usability testing before a redesign or shortly after a new launch.

The first thing to do is make sure that your content is accessible to everyone. Verify that screen readers can read your text. Also test that people of all ages (or at the bare minimum the ones pertaining to your target market) find the font size and contrast legible. Giving different text size options, which can be styled dynamically with CSS in both Flash and HTML, along with different contrast options, is a no-brainer. It's very easy to set up, greatly improves usability, and shows your users that you really are thinking about their needs.

Another principle part of usability testing is analyzing the paths that your users are taking on your site. This is done to ensure that people are actually finding the critical parts of your site, and can help you restructure or reorganize your navigation if a specific section of your site is not getting the attention it requires. A test like this can be conducted in a number of ways. One very simple and inexpensive way is simply to observe someone as he or she browses your site. Note which links that user clicks first. Ask him or her to find something specific and see how long it takes to get there, or if that user even gets there at all. This can be done with an entire group of people or even by placing a survey on your site. The best solution is to keep track of the paths your users are taking in your database. Keep track of which pages are viewed the most, which pages get the most internal or external links, and store what page they came from (this helps plot the user's path; for example, landed on home page, clicked to contact page, clicked to investor relations page, clicked e-mail info link). Something like this is easy to set up manually, or can be achieved with a number of different analytics packages that already exist. You'll have to judge whether they're worth the investment.

At its heart, usability testing is about identifying problems with the ease of use of your site, and finding ways to resolve them. For this reason, it's a good idea to conduct a usability test before redesigning, during development of the redesign, and shortly after launch. This is a great measure of the effectiveness of your redesign.

Summary

In this chapter, we looked at optimization techniques to employ to streamline your movies, tips for publishing your movies, project aftercare, and testing.

So that concludes our look at finishing off your fantastic project, and supplying aftercare, and the entire book! You should now have everything you need to plan, design, and create fantastic, professional-looking Flash sites, as well as look after the needs of your clients when the site has gone live. We hope you've enjoyed your journey—good luck with your future projects!

INDEX

XML for Flash

1-59059-543-2 $39.99 [US]

Actionscript Animation
Making Things Move!

1-59059-518-1 $49.99 [US]

Flash 8

1-59059-542-4 $36.99 [US]

ASP.NET 2.0
for Flash

1-59059-517-3 $39.99 [US]

DOM Scripting

1-59059-533-5 $34.99 [US]

EXPERIENCE THE
DESIGNER TO DESIGNER™
DIFFERENCE

Fireworks MX 2004
ZERO TO HERO

1-59059-306-5 $34.99 [US]

Paint Shop Pro 8
ZERO TO HERO

1-59059-238-7 $24.99 [US]

Windows
Movie Maker 2
ZERO TO HERO

1-59059-149-6 $24.99 [US]

PHOTOSHOP MOST WANTED
MORE EFFECTS AND DESIGN TIPS

1-59059-262-X $49.99 [US]

FLASH MX
MOST WANTED
EFFECTS & MOVIES

1-59059-224-7 $39.99 [US]

FLASH 3D CHEATS
MOST WANTED

1-59059-221-2 $39.99 [US]

FLASH MX 2004
GAMES MOST WANTED

1-59059-236-0 $39.99 [US]

ILLUSTRATOR CS
MOST WANTED
TECHNIQUES AND EFFECTS

MATT KLOSKOWSKI

1-59059-372-3 $39.99 [US]

Extending
Flash MX 2004

1-59059-304-9 $49.99 [US]

Apache Essentials
Install, Configure, Maintain

1-59059-355-3 $39.99 [US]

Dreamweaver MX 2004
Design Projects

1-59059-409-6 $39.99 [US]

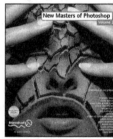

New Masters of Flash

1-59059-314-6 $59.99 [US]

New Masters of Photoshop
Volume 2

1-59059-315-4 $59.99 [US]

Cascading
Style Sheets
SEPARATING CONTENT FROM PRESENTATION

Second Edition

1-59059-231-X $39.99 [US]

Constructing
Usable Shopping Carts
DESIGNING AND BUILDING GREAT E-COMMERCE APPLICATIONS

1-59059-408-8 $34.99 [US]

EXTREME
PHOTOSHOP CS
PROFESSIONAL DESIGN AND ADVANCED ILLUSTRATION TECHNIQUES
By Matt Kloskowski

1-59059-428-2 $39.99 [US]

WEB STANDARDS SOLUTIONS
The Markup and Style Handbook

1-59059-381-2 $29.99 [US]

PODCAST
SOLUTIONS
The Complete Guide to Podcasting

BY MICHAEL W. GEOGHEGAN
and DAN KLASS

1-59059-554-8 $24.99 [US]